Developing Capital Markets in Eastern Europe

A Business Reference

Developing Capital Markets in Eastern Europe

A Business Reference

Margie Lindsay

New York University Press
New York

First published in the U.S.A. in 1992 by
New York University Press
Washington Square
New York, New York 10003

Library of Congress Cataloguing-in-Publication Data
Lindsay, Margie.
Developing capital markets in Eastern Europe : a business reference / by Margie Lindsay.
p. cm.
Includes bibliographical references and index.
ISBN 0-8147-5067-2
1. Capital market--Europe, Eastern-Handbooks, manuals, etc.
2. Capital market--Law and legislation--Europe, Eastern. I. Title.
HG5430.7.A3L56 1992 91-47686
322'.0414'0947--dc20 CIP

Printed in Great Britain

Contents

Acknowledgements

The author wishes to thank the following for their help, support and understanding in the writing of this book:

The Wilson Centre, East European Programme, Washington, DC, which kindly offered a three-month guest scholarship which the author used to research the book, as well as providing general background, ideas and information from a conference held in Sofia in September 1991 organised in part by the Wilson Centre;

Elizabeth Sellers, my able and efficient research assistant at the Wilson Centre in Washington;

the Washington, Warsaw and Prague offices of PlanEcon;

my colleagues Sally Marie Finn and Patricia Ogden.

Ten steps to creating 'Wall Street'

1 clarify the role of government agencies
2 reform tax policy
3 eliminate undue incentives and barriers to commerical banking system
4 revitalise or promote the establishment of contractual savings institutions (pension funds and insurance companies)
5 develop effective unit trust, mutual fund and investment company regulations
6 impose strict accounting and auditing standards
7 reform corporate law
8 establish the support of institutions needed for primary and secondary markets: institutions necessary for an efficient capital market include:
stock exchange and over-the-counter markets
securities brokers and dealers
underwriters and market makers
securities custodians
depository and clearing institutions
asset or fund managers
securities analysts and financial information companies
credit rating agencies
venture capital firms (later)
9 reform securities regulation
10 watch out for the most common obstacles to healthy growth

Developing capital markets is what the reform process is all about. At the end of the day, these countries want to be mirror images of London, Frankfurt, Paris, Tokyo and New York.
Source: Teresa Barger, 'How to set up a stock exchange', *International Economy*, April/May 1990

Introduction

> In a nutshell, an economy cannot mimic something that does not exist. (Issues in the Introduction of Market Forces in Eastern European Socialist Economies, Manuel Hinds, March 1990)

> A capital market may appear as an essential first ingredient in a recipe for economic success. In fact, it is almost always the natural product of a rational, market-based economy rather than the prerequisite. Capital markets rarely thrive until a country completes its macro-economic and policy house cleaning. (Teresa Barger: How to set up a stock exchange, *International Economy*, April/May 1990)

More than just the Berlin Wall crashed in 1989. The economies of Eastern Europe, carefully built on the premise of central planning, began caving in as communist control gave out. In trying to fill the black hole left by the failure of the socialist market experiment, all the countries in the region — from Albania to the once united Soviet Union — found the road to market economies anything but easy.

Embracing market economics appears deceptively straightforward on paper. In reality it is a long, hard struggle. There is little comparison between the rebuilding of Eastern Europe and the rehabilitation of Europe after World War II. At the end of the 1940s, the European countries were relatively all in the same boat. Industrial infrastructures had suffered badly, but could be rebuilt. Democratic institutions were able to be set up relatively quickly. Within a decade, the Western countries had found their feet again.

Eastern Europe, after over 40 years of communism, has a much more difficult task ahead of it. Trying to catch up with the rest of developed Europe is a daunting task. Not only do these countries need to develop the political institutions to support the emerging democracies, but they have physically to establish links with the rest of the world. Telecommunications and transport need vast improvements.

International business lives by the telephone, and in Eastern Europe making a simple call across a city can be difficult, let alone trying to contact someone in another town. Roads, rail and air transport have been neglected in most places and need significant improvement. Rebuilding is going to take years.

Trying to put into place the institutional structures needed to support both political and economic change must move quickly in order to stabilise the countries of the region. Privatisation is the latest buzz-word, but all too often the population and international business expectations are disappointed because of the slow pace. There is no easy — or fast — way to privatise Eastern Europe. Those who claimed it could be done in five years now think it may be 20 years before the majority of enterprises are safely out of state control.

Against enormous odds, however, the countries of Eastern Europe are forging ahead, some faster than others, but all with gritted determination. If nothing else, communist and central planning has taught the region that almost any other system must be better. Opting for democracy and capitalism is a popular move with Western governments and financial institutions, but is often misunderstood by the populations of Eastern Europe. At first many equated market economies with more goods, more money, less work and no risk. They have learned quickly that the transition is not without struggle. Many have lost jobs, more will face unemployment as the restructuring of outdated industries continues.

The region is facing the harsh wind of capitalism. Some are faring better than others, but all are struggling. The perceived economic leaders — Hungary, Czechoslovakia and Poland — thought they would be well on the road to recovery by the end of 1991. By the end of 1991 all three economies were still in deep recession. Needed legislative changes were either being hastily cobbled together or muddling through recalcitrant parliaments. Political stability remained elusive. Elections in Poland proved that people were disillusioned not just with the poor rewards gained so far from the market, but also with the democratic process which did not seem to respond to their needs any better than the one-party state. Czechoslovakia was still debating its future as a single country. Hungary's apparent political stability masked deep apprehensions over economic change. At the centre of all these changes lies the development of capital markets, progressing at an agonisingly slow pace for the East Europeans, but compared with the evolution of these markets in the West, at remarkable speed.

The less fortunate members of the reformers' club faced even greater problems. Albania's social stability, fragile at the best of times, was near collapse at the end of 1991 as the economy daily drew near to chaos, with shortages increasing and the government desperately trying to implement reforms without going all the way and embracing market economics, private property and the other trappings of the reforms taking place elsewhere in Europe. Yugoslavia had disintegrated into bloody conflict which made a nonsense of reform efforts. While the fighting continues, little progress can be made; once the fighting stops, the country — or countries — will need significant help in rebuilding and repairing war damage. Trying to regain economic balance in such a situation will be difficult and the West will need to help both with money and people.

Bulgaria's elections in autumn 1991 were seen by the opposition as a great victory, but in reality were a marginal popular mandate to pursue reform. What the country desperately needed was debt rescheduling which would end the moratorium declared in March 1990 and which had since then scuppered any attempt at significant trade credits or international financial help for the country.

Romania at one stage almost looked a haven of stability and tranquillity. That did not last long, as political instability — together with rioting miners in September 1991 — rocked the country's fragile democracy. Immediate prospects looked grim at the end of the year, with the West again shunning the country, waiting for signs that things had really changed. Romania's immediate future was a likely deterioration of the economy bringing with it serious social problems and continued political trouble.

The chaotic breakup of the Soviet Union, coupled with its disastrous economic performance — and the possibility of a human flood of political and economic refugees — presented a less than optimistic scenario for future prospects. Its uncertainty was felt throughout the region, as Eastern Europe watched uneasily to see if the former empire could pull itself together, or collapse, causing even more economic and political instability internally and externally. Meanwhile, the newly independent Baltic states of Estonia, Latvia and Lithuania began their own reform programmes, with varying degrees of success and assistance from abroad.

This was Eastern Europe at the end of 1991. Not the thriving capitalistic paradise many yearned for and certainly the economic reality was a far cry from the heady optimistic last days of 1989.

Economic theories have begun colliding all too frequently with the stubborn facts of life in Eastern Europe. Economists, aid agencies, financial institutions and Western governments all agree, together with their East European counterparts, that a market economy is the solution. Everyone thinks he knows how to get such a system in place, but no one has yet been able to perform the miracle. Some, like Hungary, appear to come close to it at times. Others, like the Soviet Union and Albania, appear so far away that the smallest sign of progress is greeted with over-enthusiastic optimism by the West.

Before the dust of the 1989 revolutions in Eastern Europe had settled, the countries were struggling to find their own way to build a market economy. The intention was to introduce reforms to establish as quickly as possible a society that resembled Western Europe.

High expectations from populations that thought the end of communist rule would also mean the end of poor living standards had a rude awakening. In their attempts to rebuild markets and damaged economies the countries in the region were forced to free prices, lower living standards and for the first time in decades face serious unemployment. Each country has tried to find its own way to cope with the turmoil, and expectations of its population. None have found it easy, and so far no one has been declared a winner in the race to be the first to succeed in recreating a market economy.

In trying to examine how the reform process and the development of capital markets are progressing, each country needs to be taken separately. But there are a few important generalisations that can be made about all the countries in the region, despite the widely varying pace of reform or the development of their economies.

After 40-plus years of communist (mis)rule and central planning no one had a healthy economy. All the countries are experiencing deep recession or are perilously close to sustained depression. While trying to catch up with the West economically, they are also trying simultaneously to establish democratic institutions to protect the fledgeling market. This is being done more often than not in an atmosphere of confusion and, in too many cases, violence.

Industry is too fat and inefficient. There is over-manning and low productivity throughout all sectors of these economies. Shortages are endemic. They occur in every country, sometimes less obvious (Hungary, Czechoslovakia) than in others and in a few countries are acute (Albania, Soviet Union, Bulgaria).

Nowhere is there a healthy private sector. In too many cases the old black marketeers have tried to make the transition to a legally-based free market. They have often failed and in some cases the past misdeeds and shameful speculation has given all of the private sector a bad name. The private sector is undeveloped and hindered by a lack of domestic resources and know-how.

All the countries in the region have suffered from isolation: political, economic and technological. Restrictions imposed by the West and constraints of the former communist regimes have, in one way or another, helped to hinder economic and social development. Society has been hurt by this. Travel restrictions, hard currency shortages, limited scope for contact with the real business environment have left behind a legacy of confusion, misunderstanding and sometimes even mistrust.

The invisible fence between Western and Eastern economies has taken its toll. Management in the region is not equipped to deal with the cutting edge of market economics. Organisational skills in the region were geared towards an environment where shortages abounded and supplies were often dominated by monopoly (state) agencies. Hard currency was tightly controlled. In such a climate, enterprise directors became adept at wheeling and dealing in a system gone crazy. But faced with the intricacies of international markets, their skills are useless.

Western high-flyers are baffled by what they find in Eastern Europe. The complex barter and swap arrangements which internally kept factories producing, look too much like illegal deals to the West. International accountants called in to value Eastern companies shake their heads at the inadequate accounts of companies now offering themselves up to Western buyers. Eastern workers are scared and shaken by the too harsh reality of markets. The would-be new Western managers are worried that staff is 'too unionised' and lazy.

Misunderstandings abound. Both sides are confused and floundering. It is not just the East that needs time to adjust to the new systems. Too often the Western advisers are keen to destroy old ways, but putting in place new systems and rebuilding the market will take decades. This is not and will not be a fast or easy process. Most governments hope to show their populations some kind of visible improvement in living standards after five years of hard slog. The next generation should begin to reap the rewards of the revolutions. But an entirely re-educated generation will have to grow up before the region hopes to resemble in all aspects Western Europe.

This is not cause for pessimism, however. The fact that the rebuilding can and has started is cause for celebration and hope. The potential of the region has been under-exploited for decades. Now, the West, together with the newly emerging democracies, can work together to develop a market that without the Soviet Union doubles the size of the European Community.

One of the keystones of the development of market economies in the region is the formation of capital markets. All the countries have begun the process, but each is going at its own pace and faces its own unique problems. Controversy surrounds almost every aspect of the reforms and there is much confusion over the process, both within the countries and from the Western business and financial community.

There will be winners and losers in this process. Some countries will develop faster — and better — than others. Nevertheless, the developments will affect all of Europe now and in the future. Businessmen, financial institutions and governments all have a role to play in helping Eastern Europe develop capital markets.

Explanation of text

As Eastern Europe continues its evolution, it is impossible to include every piece of information. This book contains much of the information available by autumn 1991, but of necessity cannot include everything.

Each chapter looks at a specific country, beginning with Albania. Not every chapter covers all the aspects of developing capital markets, mainly because information is not available yet on all the countries or because the situation was still unclear or in a state of flux. Therefore, the chapters include as much information as could be gathered by the time of publication. The laws which are reproduced in each chapter have been paraphrased for ease of understanding and reading. The translation of the Polish privatisation law was supplied by the Central and East European Privatisation Network from its publication *Privatisation in Eastern Europe*.

As a result of the conflict within Yugoslavia, only Slovenia is covered. This state has begun significant reforms designed to develop capital markets and has initiated a privatisation programme. As the republic has avoided significant war damage on its territory and appears to be somewhat isolated from the problems of Yugoslavia as a whole, a summary of its attempts to transform itself into a market economy is included.

The Soviet Union is excluded from the book. By autumn of 1991, the republics of the former union were still not sure of how, if at all, they would remain together. Economic reform programmes and privatisation plans were far from being formulated in many republics or were too unclear for analysis. The three Baltic states of Estonia, Latvia and Lithuania had succeeded in breaking away from the union, but their individual reform and privatisation programmes were also unclear. For these reasons, discussion of the USSR and Baltic states has been deleted from this study.

In the three appendices, readers will find information supplementing that contained in the chapters. Appendix I covers insurance throughout the region and contains information supplied by Salomon Brothers, New York. Appendix II looks at the role of the International Finance Corporation, an affiliate of the World Bank, the European Community's Phare programme, the European Bank for Reconstruction and Development and the Central East European Privatisation Network, which are all involved in the development of capital markets in Eastern Europe. The third appendix lists useful addresses for some of the countries.

Chapter 1

ALBANIA

Albania's development of capital markets has been minuscule. So far the country has not managed to put together a coherent economic reform programme. Politically the country remains unstable with the reformed communist party still in many key positions. Continued civil unrest and the potential that the troubles in neighbouring Yugoslavia could spill over into Albania do not bode well for the future.

The country can ill afford any more problems. As the poorest, and most repressed, of the East European countries, Albania's road back to a market economy is going to be tough. The small size of the country — just over 3m people — and its continuing political problems have made it difficult for international financial organisations to do much to help the country. Western business has not been impressed with the reform process so far. Only a few investments have been made and most interest centres around exploitation of natural resources such as oil and gas and chrome.

Albania at present has little to attract business or international organisations. The decades of isolation from the rest of Europe have taken a heavy toll. The population is ill-equipped to enter the international business community. Economists have little idea of what market economics are all about.

The people, half-starved and repressed for so long, have little concept of what building a market economy entails. It is difficult to see, too, how the West or any Albanian government in future could ask the people to suffer even more hardship before relief comes to them.

The country is littered with crumbling factories. The largest factory in the country produces spare parts for 1950s machinery which the Albanians still try to operate. Albania's industry and population appear stuck in a 1950s time warp. Many Western businessmen think it might just be easier to scrap all the factories and start again. Reconstruction would be time-consuming and costly. All the factories need substantial improvements, ranging from putting glass back into the windows to new machinery.

The people themselves have little to work with. Private trade was completely wiped out under the communist regime. A few private businesses have begun and a handful of international businesses have set up joint ventures. Farmers are being encouraged to sell more products on a free market and dozens of small, family businesses — mainly snack bars, and services — have opened since the summer of 1990. Under present law, however, entrepreneurs cannot hire people from outside their own family. A tax and company law structure are needed before large-scale business can develop.

A reform of sorts began after the death of Enver Hoxha in the mid-1980s. Under the then leader, Ramiz Alia, the country began gradually opening, restoring diplomatic links and ending its isolation by re-joining at least some international organisations, such as the Conference on Security and Co-operation in Europe (CSCE). The country has applied for International Monetary Fund membership and approached the European Bank for Reconstruction and Development. Talks were at a very early stage with the European Community in autumn 1991 on some sort of trade agreement which would also extend financial aid to the country. Help from the Group of 24 industrialised countries had not yet encompassed Albania. Individual countries, like Italy, were trying to help, mainly through emergency food aid.

The delay by the West in helping Albania recover from communist politics and damaging central planning economics was understandable. With so much else going on in Europe in 1991 — revolution in the USSR, war in Yugoslavia — Albania's half-hearted attempts at reform brought little applause from the West. Countries surrounding Albania were more interested in finding ways of keeping Albanian refugees out than in funding reconstruction programmes inside the state. Albania itself was giving the West little to work with.

Reform plans

The country did not announce any real plans to boost the role of the market until January 1990. Even then, little happened. However, the exodus of Albanians desperate to leave their country for the more prosperous regions of Europe (mainly Italy and Germany), prompted more liberal reforms at home and was a signal to the West that if something was not done, more refugees would follow.

With one eye fixed on the emerging democracies in Eastern Europe and the other on expanding links with Western Europe, the government ordered a fundamental overhaul of the Albanian constitution. It passed an election law allowing secret ballots and a choice of parliamentary candidates. Free elections were held in March 1991, but the outcome was far from satisfactory. The reformed communist party (known as the Albanian Workers' Party) won all the parliamentary seats in the countryside, while the opposition movement (Democratic Party) won almost all the votes in the cities. The result was increasing polarisation between the city and countryside, political instability as the old communists tried to hang on to power, and more popular unrest and violence. This mixture finally led to the resignation of the government which was replaced by a non-partisan coalition which had good intentions to start reform, but had little chance of doing so. Continuing political turmoil and renewed attempts by disgruntled Albanians to leave the country, ensured little was done to start development of a stable economic environment.

If one of the first prerequisites for developing capital markets is a manageable, stable economy, Albania has failed at the first hurdle. As Europe's poorest country, with over 50 per cent of its population engaged in agricultural work, there is little chance of dramatic economic changes over the short term. The private sector completely disappeared by 1989 and the co-operative sector was severely limited under the communist government.

Private enterprise

It was not until July 1990 that private enterprises were again permitted to operate, but only in services, trade and the retail sector. By the end of July 1990, decrees were passed on foreign investment and joint ventures. Banking reforms have begun, but rather half-heartedly. The State Bank of Albania is to change into a central bank. A commercial banking sector is being formed. The first private commercial bank — a joint venture Albanian-Swiss bank, named Iliria, set up to help finance construction and assist foreign Albanian joint ventures in trade and financial services — opened in January 1991.

Privatisation

The policies of the government now include privatisation of small enterprises and some land. A crisis programme was published in autumn 1991 which aimed to introduce a market economy which would:

- allow foreign enterprises, banks and foreign nationals to set up companies in Albania;
- safeguard those investments against expropriation or nationalisation;
- guarantee the right for foreign investors of full repatriation of profits in hard currency.

As part of the programme, parliament began work on a new tax system.

Foreign trade

Significant restrictions on foreign business remain. Foreign companies are not allowed to own or buy property, but they are allowed to rent and lease it. The privatisation law, which was expected to be passed sometime in 1991 is unlikely to engender much enthusiasm from the international business community.

Albania began a substantial liberalisation of its foreign trade in October 1991.

Exports and imports of goods were freed, except for a limited number of items subject to quotas and licensing. The Foreign Trade and Economic Ministries will decide each year which goods will be subject to quotas. Import and export licences will be issued by the Foreign Trade Ministry, which is also responsible for drafting regulations concerning the licences and for supervision of the quotas.

At the same time, Albania set up a Foreign Investment Agency to co-operate with foreign investors. The agency, which began work on 1 October, is to publicise Albanian foreign trade opportunities abroad and encourage foreign investments. The agency will be the state body which studies applications for foreign investment, although it can only pass on its opinion to the Foreign Trade Ministry, which gives the final approval for any foreign investment project or joint venture.

As part of the decree setting up the agency, Teknoimport Foreign Trade enterprise was liquidated and its work transferred to other enterprises that are under ministries or other central institutions. Staff, financial plans (including hard currency allocations) and other assets of Teknoimport have been transferred to the Foreign Investment Agency. The agency will be financed from the state budget until the end of 1991. From 1992 it will work on a self-financing basis.

Currency reforms

Albania is to allow the Tirana branch of Savings Bank to perform foreign currency operations. Initially the bank will exchange foreign currency at the set rate of the new Lek 30 to the dollar, cash cheques, buy lek and foreign currency cheques, make payments on money orders received from abroad, change foreign bank notes into smaller denominations, receive foreign currency for savings, open banking accounts in foreign currency and transfer foreign currency abroad. All Albanian and foreign citizens will be allowed to deposit foreign currency with the bank. Eventually all district branches of the Savings Bank will provide such services.

The Albanian Finance and Economy Ministries, together with the State Bank, issued a decree in 1991 under which the Albanian currency, the lek, is to be related to the European currency unit (Ecu). From 10 September 1991 the exchange rate of foreign currencies in relation to the lek was set at Lek 30 to Ecu 1. Under the decree state enterprises will have the right to keep a proportion of their foreign currency earnings, although the bulk of hard currency must be sold to the State Bank at the current commercial exchange rate.

Physical and legal persons are allowed to buy foreign currency at the bank, using leks. The bank has the right to dispense foreign currency on credit. Priorities for the supply of foreign currency will be decided by a commission made up of representatives of the banks, the Ministries of Finance, Economy and Foreign Trade. Input from other relevant ministries and other state institutions will be taken into account.

IMF membership

Albania was admitted to the International Monetary Fund and made a member of the World Bank in October 1991.

Conclusion

With elections scheduled for 1992, more political turmoil is forecast. The economic situation is expected to become much worse before it shows any signs of improving.

The country comes last on the list of potential winners in the race to create a market economy. If and when the country finally pulls itself together and manages to attract sufficient Western aid and interest to help with reform, Albania could begin its transformation. Until then, there will continue to be intermittent good news coming from the country, mixed with large doses of political upheaval and civil unrest.

Even after real reform begins, the development of capital markets in Albania will take several years. The population is in desperate need of training and education in all sectors, ranging from small business to international finance. The existing factories in the country are hardly worth privatising and certainly there is little likelihood that Western investors will be that interested in the crumbling plants that exist. Of more interest will be exploitation of natural resources, development of the tourist sector and other projects — all of which will need substantial outside funding.

Economic activity of foreign capital in Albania (Decree 7407)

Chapter I: General provisions

ARTICLE 1
In Albania, enterprises with participation of foreign capital may exercise their activity in various sectors of the economy, in accordance with the objectives outlined in the plans for the present and future development of the country's economy.

ARTICLE 2
An enterprise with participation of foreign capital (referred to as 'enterprise') is a juridical person residing in the territory of Albania, and is set up under a contract in which one party is an Albanian juridical person residing in Albania and the other part is an Albanian or foreign person, physical or juridical, residing outside the territory of Albania (referred to as 'foreign person').

ARTICLE 3

The enterprise pursues the aims of:

- modernising the existing plants or the establishment of new ones working on the basis of advanced technology for the extraction and processing of local raw materials;
- increasing exports or reducing imports;
- diversifying the production of consumer goods;
- creating new jobs;
- introducing modern methods of organisation and management of production, services and other commercial aims.

ARTICLE 4

The purpose and activity of the enterprise are set out in the contract and its constitution.

ARTICLE 5

The activity of the enterprise, the relations stemming from the contract under which it is established and its relations with other Albanian juridical persons are governed by Albanian law.

ARTICLE 6

The state protects the economic activity of the enterprise, as well as the investments made therein by foreign persons, and ensures to them the same conditions as those ensured to Albanian juridical persons.

Through provisions by the Council of Ministers, special limitations may be imposed on foreign persons of those states which apply similar limitations on the activity of Albanian persons.

ARTICLE 7

The enterprise exercises its activity after being issued the relative authorisation by the competent state body.

ARTICLE 8

The enterprise meets its commitments with its own funds: it is liable neither for state commitments nor for commitments of other juridical persons. The state and other juridical persons are not liable for the commitments of the enterprise.

ARTICLE 9

The term of the activity of the enterprise is specified under contract.

ARTICLE 10

In accordance with its constitution, the enterprise determines the annual and five-year programme of its economic and financial activity.

ARTICLE 11

By 31 March of the successive year, the enterprise submits the report on its activity and its annual balance to the local financial bodies.

Chapter II: Authorisation for concluding a contract

ARTICLE 12
At the request by the Albanian juridical person, the authorisation for concluding a contract or its amendment is granted by the Council of Ministers of Albania, through the ministry covering the sector to which the enterprise will extend its activity.

In the field of banking operations, the authorisation is granted by the State Bank of Albania.

The Council of Ministers examines and decides on an application for authorisation within two months from the date of its presentation.

ARTICLE 13
The application or authorisation should comprise:

(a) the name of the enterprise, the centre of its activity and its concerning foreign persons;
(b) the purpose of the activity of the enterprise;
(c) the subjects and forms of the enterprise;
(d) complete studies, including technical and economic analyses, of the activity of the enterprise;
(e) the basic capital, the shares of the individual participants, the form and currency of the payments, the mode of distribution of profits, the coverage of losses and the minimum amount of the reserve fund;
(f) the draft constitution and draft contract.

ARTICLE 14
Authorisation is granted for a period of up to 10 years. Requests for prolonging its duration are notified a year prior to the termination of the validity of the authorisation in force.

Chapter III: Management of the enterprise

ARTICLE 15
The enterprise conducts its activity in compliance with the contract and its constitution. It is free to establish, within the territory of Albania, economic relations for carrying out its activities, by concluding contracts with local enterprises.

ARTICLE 16
The enterprise is supplied with primary and other materials under competitive conditions. Its material-technology supply from within the country or from imports is done in the currency specified in the contract.

ARTICLE 17
The enterprise is free to decide on the form of its relations with its partners

abroad. Within the limits permitted by the legislation of Albania, it may conclude contracts with them independently, or co-operate with Albanian foreign trade enterprises in carrying out its exports and imports.

Chapter IV: Financial management

ARTICLE 18
The enterprise determines the following funds:

(a) a reserve fund to cover losses or risks and to finance oscillations in the management of the enterprise, both in Albanian and foreign currency;
(b) cultural, social and remuneration funds according to the general rules envisaged in the constitution.

ARTICLE 19
At the end of each calendar year, after paying all taxes, the enterprise allocates not less than 5 per cent of its profits to the reserve fund, until it reaches the sum specified in the contract.

After paying taxes and putting aside the monetary means according to Article 18 of this decree, the enterprise is free to establish a fund destined for its further development or for other purposes.

ARTICLE 20
The funds established by the enterprise cannot be blocked. It is free to dispose them for the purpose it has established them.

ARTICLE 21
After paying taxes and allocating funds, profits are shared among participants.

ARTICLE 22
The annual balance of the enterprise and its annual financial report are approved according to the rules stipulated in the constitution of the enterprise.

Chapter V: Administration of currency

ARTICLE 23
The enterprise is self-financed in leks and in foreign currency.

ARTICLE 24
The enterprise opens accounts in foreign currency with the State Bank of Albania. In agreement with the bank, such accounts may also be opened with a foreign bank.

ARTICLE 25
The foreign person is free to transfer its part of profit abroad.

ARTICLE 26
The conversion of Albanian currency into foreign currency and vice versa is effectuated at the exchange rate fixed by the State Bank of Albania.

ARTICLE 27
The enterprise is free to take credits in foreign currency from the State Bank of Albania. Likewise, in agreement with the State Bank of Albania, it may also take such credits from a foreign bank.

Chapter VI: Economic conditions

ARTICLE 28
The enterprise establishes a system of economic information in compliance with the legal provisions applicable to Albanian enterprises.

ARTICLE 29
The enterprise keeps accounts in Albanian currency in conformity with the relative legal provisions applicable to Albanian enterprises. Exceptions to this rule are subject to approval by the Finance Ministry.

ARTICLE 30
The enterprise provides the competent Albanian organs with accounting and statistical data on matters bearing on the mode and conditions stipulated in the legal provisions applicable to the Albanian enterprises.

ARTICLE 31
The profits of the enterprise are subject to taxation. The taxation rate is fixed by the Finance Ministry.

ARTICLE 32
When during a fiscal year the economic activity of the enterprise incurs losses, it may pay its taxes from its profits in the following three years.

ARTICLE 33
That part of the profit that, under a contract of donation, is transferred to an Albanian social, cultural, scientific or educational organisation, or goes in funds allocated for the assistance of victims of natural calamities, is not subject to taxation.

ARTICLE 34
The enterprise is obliged to keep its accounts according to the rules set by the competent Albanian state organs. At the request of the relevant fiscal organs, it will every year produce information on its accounts and economic activity.

ARTICLE 35
Annual profits are declared within a month after drawing up the annual balance, but not later than 31 March of the following fiscal year.

The Finance Ministry issues the relative taxation rules, within a month after the declaration of the profits of the enterprise has been submitted.

ARTICLE 36
Primary and other materials and equipment imported by the enterprise and destined for production for export are not subject to customs duties.

Materials, machinery, equipment and other goods which are imported for reinvestment are not subject to customs duties.

Chapter VII: Labour relations

ARTICLE 37
Labour relations in the enterprise are regulated through the labour contract.

Parties to the labour contract may agree to pay part of the salary of the foreign staff of the enterprise in convertible currency.

Claims by workers employed by the enterprise are settled by the Albanian court of justice. When the claimant is a foreigner, the claim is settled by the organ specified in the labour contract.

Claims not envisaged in the labour contract will be subject to the provisions of the Albanian labour legislation.

ARTICLE 38
Albanian workers of the enterprise are insured according to Albanian legislation on social insurance. Foreign staff are insured according to the rules set forth in the constitution.

ARTICLE 39
By special provisions, complementary stipulations may be added about the salaries of the Albanian workers engaged in the enterprise.

ARTICLE 40
The interests of the workers of the enterprise are protected by Albanian legislation.

Chapter VIII: Closure of the enterprise

ARTICLE 41
The enterprise is closed in the cases stipulated in the contract.

ARTICLE 42
The enterprise is dissolved according to the rules stipulated in its constitution.

ARTICLE 43
This decree comes into force immediately (Tirana: 31 July 1990).

Protection of foreign investments in Albania (Decree 7406)

ARTICLE 1
Enterprises, firms and foreign or Albanian physical persons residing outside the territory of Albania can make investments and carry out related economic activity in the territory of Albania, in compliance with the legislation governing these activities.

Foreign investments in Albania enjoy full protection and security.

ARTICLE 2
The term 'investment' denotes:

(a) real and personal property;
(b) shares in the economic activity with the participation of foreign capital;
(c) monetary commitments for the creation of economic values or any kind of commitments with economic value;
(d) investments in trade, the exploration, extraction and mining of natural assets and other kinds of investments.

ARTICLE 3
Foreign investments in Albania will not be subject to expropriation, nationalisation and any other measure similar to expropriation or nationalisation, except for specific cases made for public purposes and always against the payment of damages.

Damages for the cases mentioned in the first paragraph of this article are equal to the value of the investment expropriated on the day of the notification of the other party. Damages are effected without delay, at the current banking interest rates on the paying date. They are fully realisable and freely transferable.

In case of a delay in the payment of damages, they are paid with an amount that places the investor in a position not less favourable than he would have been if damages were paid immediately on the date of expropriation. The clauses on the mode of payment of said damages should be set prior to the time of expropriation.

ARTICLE 4
The legitimacy of expropriation, nationalisation, or any other similar measure, and the amount of damages will be subject to examination by a lawsuit.

ARTICLE 5
The enterprises, companies or foreign physical persons, whose investments suffer losses in Albania due to war, state of emergency and natural elements such as earthquakes, floods and other similar acts are accorded the same treatment regarding damages and compensation as its own enterprises.

ARTICLE 6
Payments under Article 3 are effectuated without delay, at the current exchange rate on the date of payment.

ARTICLE 7
Reinvestment of profits enjoy the same protection as investments.

ARTICLE 8
Albania will promote the spirit of understanding and co-operation for the rapid and correct settlement of disputes that might arise among the investing parties. Failing which, upon the request of one party, the case is submitted to the arbitration assigned by them.

ARTICLE 9
Albania will publish all laws, regulations and procedures dealing with or affecting investments.

ARTICLE 10
This decree comes into force immediately (Tirana: 31 July 1990).

State Bank of Albania (Law 7377)

This law is enacted in order to enable the State Bank of Albania to play an active role in the development of the economy and to raise its effectiveness through the currency, credit and the strengthening of financial discipline and dynamic monetary control.

ARTICLE 1
The State Bank, as a central state institution, implements the economic policy for the economic and financial development and strengthening of enterprises, institutions and agricultural co-operatives and exercises monetary control to prevent any action in contravention of the plan and finance discipline.

ARTICLE 2
The State Bank has the following duties and obligations:

(a) to issue the currency;
(b) to provide credits in local and foreign currency;
(c) to finance the fundamental investments and constructions and to exercise control over the study of their profitability on the basis of documentation deposited with it;
(d) to carry out transactions of the treasury and hold the funds for the state budget;
(e) to carry out juridical transactions regarding valuable metals and precious stones and foreign currency;

(f) to concentrate the accounts of payments and encashments by enterprises, institutions and social organisations, and to carry out payments and encashments and collection of monetary means;
(g) to exercise control over the circulation of currency and the allocation of payment funds, credits and investment funds, over the foreign currency and valuable metals, over transactions of the state budget fund and the encashments and payments effectuated among enterprises and institutions, as well as over their foreign relations;
(h) the bank is answerable for the stability and raising of the purchasing power of the currency, the correct allocation and effectiveness of credits in local and foreign currency, and for the enforcement of discipline in the financing of investments, in encashments and payments.

ARTICLE 3
The State Bank issues and puts into circulation banknotes and metallic coins, which the state guarantees with commodities, gold, other valuable metals, foreign currency and banking operations.

The monetary unit in Albania is the lek.

The Council of Ministers defines the type, quantity and values of banknotes and metallic coins, as well as the rules for taking them in and out of the country.

ARTICLE 4
The State Bank participates in all state activities and agreements of an economic and financial character of our country with the foreign world. It establishes relations and enters into banking agreements with foreign banks, and keeps the deposits and accounts of foreign banks as well as its own deposits and accounts with them.

The State Bank keeps the accounts in foreign currency of other foreign and Albanian juridical and physical persons, and carries out exchanges of foreign currency inside and outside the state for its own needs and those of its clients.

ARTICLE 5
The State Bank trades in securities in foreign currency and financial and commercial documents. It issues and accepts bank guarantees on the basis of criteria adopted by itself.

ARTICLE 6
The State Bank guarantees the secrecy of all relations with its clients regarding their deposits and accounts and the transactions it carries out with them.

ARTICLE 7
The State Bank extends short- and long-term credits, provided they are allocated for the original purpose, are guaranteed with material values, and are returned when they fall due.

The State Bank charges interest rates on the credits it extends.

The resources for extending credits are formed by the instruments of the bank and the rest of the monetary means of the state budget, enterprises, institutions, social organisations and individuals, which are temporarily free and accumulated in the Bank.

The State Bank pays an interest rate to the enterprises, institutions and individuals for the monetary instruments they deposit with it.

ARTICLE 8

Short-term credits are provided to enterprises as additional means of circulation to enable them to carry out their productive activities.

Long-term credits are provided to enterprises for new productive investments and technical and technological reconstruction of the existing production plants and services.

The bank extends credits on definite terms to working people residing in the city for the improvement of housing, as well as partial credits for the fulfilment of needs for new houses.

ARTICLE 9

The State Bank participates actively in the process of study and planning, and provides opinions on the inclusion of investments in the plan and the order of priorities for their execution.

Prior to extending credits for investments, the bank examines and controls the studies, designs and estimates, and approves the provision of credit on the basis of the indices of economic and social profitability. It checks up on and controls the execution of works according to designs and estimates, their putting into operation in due time, and the fulfilment of the indices of effectiveness, until the credit is repaid in full.

Whenever it observes violations of the rules and deviations from the purpose or destination of the investment, the bank suspends financing operations, orders the interruption of works, and notifies the relative organs.

ARTICLE 10

Whenever the State Bank observes that the credit is not allocated to the original purpose, it immediately suspends a further flow of the credit, demands the reimbursement of the credit before it falls due, and informs the relative ministry and the executive committee of the people's council of the district on which the responsible enterprise depends.

When the credit is not returned when it falls due, or is not guaranteed with material values, the bank suspends or limits the further extension of the credit, or demands its immediate reimbursement. Failure to reimburse credits in due time entails higher interest rates than those charged for ordinary credits.

ARTICLE 11

The criteria governing the planning of funds in cash, the use of wages' fund, credit and financing of investments and the bank interest rate are determined under specific provisions by the Council of Ministers.

ARTICLE 12
The State Bank has the following funds:

(a) establishment fund of Leks 750m;
(b) reserve fund of Leks 250m;
(c) main instruments fund.

ARTICLE 13
The State Bank is organised according to the principle of independent accounting. Ninety per cent of the planned net income and 70 per cent of the part of it above the plan are deposited in the state budget. The rest is allocated to the strengthening of the funds of the bank, investments, etc., according to the criteria determined under specific provisions.

The annual balance of the State Bank is approved by the Council of Ministers.

ARTICLE 14
The state guarantees all obligations of the State Bank resulting from operations carried out on the basis of this law.

ARTICLE 15
The State Bank is a juridical person with its centre in Tirana and branches in the districts; it depends on the Council of Ministers and is answerable to it. The general director of the State Bank has a staff which discharges its duties.

The general manager of the State Bank runs the Bank, is answerable for its activity and represents it, or authorises other people to represent it.

ARTICLE 16
The general director of the bank sets up the council of the State Bank as a consultative organ which is presided by the general manager of the State Bank, who approves the membership of this council.

ARTICLE 17
The district branches depend on the general director of the State Bank and, in carrying out their functions and duties, are controlled by and answerable to the director and to the executive committee of the people's council of the district.

ARTICLE 18
Ministries, other central institutions and enterprises present the financial plans, balance sheets and other information necessary for study, analysis and control of an economic and financial character, to the State Bank at its request.

ARTICLE 19
On the basis of the provisions of this law and those of the Council of Ministers,

and for their implementation, the General Director of the State Bank gives instructions which are binding on the ministries, other central institutions and the organs depending on them.

ARTICLE 20
When the provisions of this law are violated, the State Bank is empowered to charge the authors of said violations with administrative and material responsibilities, according to the rules defined under specific provisions.

ARTICLE 21
The State Bank has its seal with the signs of Albania.

ARTICLE 22
This law came into force on 1 January 1991.

Chapter 2

BULGARIA

Bulgaria's break with its communist past was not a clean one. At the elections held in 1990, the reformed communist party, now known as the Bulgarian Socialist Party (BSP), won a resounding victory, which later proved to be rather hollow, as the opposition umbrella movement, the Union of Democratic Forces (UDF), complained loud and long of a return to the bad old days of communist rule. Street protests and strikes throughout 1990 followed.

By the end of 1990, the BSP government was forced to resign and a coalition government was formed. Parliamentary elections were held in October 1991 in which the UDF won a marginal majority and formed a government.

What the political turmoil hurt most was economic reform progress. Political squabbling delayed implementation of radical reform measures. It was not until February of 1991 that the coalition government finally set out its blueprint for change. Radical in concept, the package of measures included macroeconomic stabilisation and price liberalisation.

Banking reform

Part of Bulgaria's commercial debt rescheduling agreement included a reform of the banking sector. The government wanted to restore credibility to the country's banking sector and a reform seemed to be the answer. A two-tier banking system was introduced in 1990, but there was little progress in solving the general undercapitalisation of the banking sector which comprises the State Bank, eight specialised commercial banks and 60 universal banks.

Some rules on non-remunerated minimum reserve requirement on deposits and minimum equity to assets ratio as well as exposure to a single borrower has not had much affect. Banks found it easier to keep lending the money, rather than go bankrupt themselves.

Banking law

In June 1991 Bulgaria's parliament, the grand national assembly, adopted the Law on the Bulgarian National Bank. The Law on Banks and Crediting, expected to be approved by parliament by the end of 1991, will update the legal framework of banking activity in the country. International experience, including direct consultations with foreign experts was used in drafting the present laws.

Existing banking rules and regulations are being revised. A special regulation has been written to determine the procedure for setting up and the functioning of exchange bureaux licensed to purchase and sell foreign currency. A regulation on payments and other basic documents regulating its use related to the refinancing of commercial banks by the National Bank, the system of the minimum reserves held by banks with the National Bank, the functioning of the inter-bank money market and other matters are being prepared.

National Bank

The Law of the National Bank, the first law of a central bank in Bulgaria, sets up the basis of an independent central bank, directly subordinated to parliament. The changes in the bank began in the second half of 1990 when the bank was reorganised with new departments set up, including a foreign exchange department, the state credits department and others. Since then the National Bank has undergone substantial organisational changes. An inner structure for the bank corresponding to the functions of a central bank have been built up with the consultancy and expert advice of the International Monetary Fund's central banking department.

Functions of the National Bank

Government foreign exchange reserves have been transferred from the Foreign Trade Bank to the National Bank. Government credit operations were transferred from one of the commercial banks to the National Bank. Five National Bank branches (Sofia, Plovdiv, Varna, Bourgas and Pleven) have been opened, performing mainly issuing functions.

The monetary policy of Bulgaria is now conducted by the National Bank, but the number of instruments it uses is relatively limited. This is mainly due to the specific circumstances of the transitional period. Discount and open market operations are to be introduced in 1992. Some Lombard operations were started in 1991.

Considerable work needs to be done with on-site checks of regulations and activities of exchange offices. At the end of June 1991, licences for practising the purchase and sale of foreign currencies were granted to eight state-owned companies and 18 private ones which had opened 80 exchange offices by late 1991.

Commercial banks

The first commercial banks were created in 1987 but the largest of them have been emerging since 1990 when the ex-branches of the National Bank were transformed into individual banks. By mid-1991 there were approximately 70 commercial banks operating in Bulgaria. As a result, the National Bank has set higher requirements for granting licences permitting the setting up of new banks. The minimum authorised capital must total Lev 50m of Bulgarian banks and $20m for foreign banks.

New commercial banks

Five new banks have been set up: the Central Co-operative Bank in Sofia, the Agro-Business Bank in Plovdiv, the Bulgarian Postal Bank in Sofia, the Credit Bank in Dragoman and Suedinenie Commercial Bank in Sofia. They have been constituted by protocols of the board of the National Bank. Other proposals, including those made by foreign companies, were under consideration at the end of 1991.

There are important problems in this sector and restructuring of the commercial banks is needed. A project for doing this has been prepared and will be implemented with help from the World Bank. The main idea of the project is to merge existing state banks into 10 to 15 large banks and at the same time start their privatisation. The major shareholders in the commercial banks are state-owned enterprises and the National Bank.

This ownership will be gradually transferred to private owners, including foreign ones. Another problem is how to clean up the balance sheets of the commercial banks. One part of the bad loans will be taken up by the state budget. The banks themselves and their clients are expected to come to some agreement over the remaining outstanding debts.

The existing commercial banks in Bulgaria are not independent financial intermediaries, working on the principles of liquidity, solvency and profitability. Their own capital and reserves are small and limited, their own deposit basis is insufficient and they have been refinanced quasi-automatically by the National Bank. They have risky portfolios because they are extending large loans to the shareholders or to specific sectors of the economy. The deposits made with the commercial banks are not guaranteed because there is no system or institution for insuring bank deposits. Most of these banks are regional institutions without a developed network throughout the country.

Foreign banks

Foreign banks in Bulgaria have not had an important role to play. One private bank was set up in 1991 with two others where the majority of shares were owned by private companies. There was in 1991 one joint venture bank, American-Bulgarian, with equal foreign and Bulgarian participation, and one co-operative bank.

State Savings Bank

The State Savings Bank was created in 1951 as a specialised institution for banking services to the population. This bank receives deposits from the population and provides some loans especially for buying homes. The Savings Bank usually had a positive balance which was transferred to the National Bank or to the budget. A part of its funds cannot be repaid now because of the large budget deficit and the debts owed by state enterprise. The Savings Bank has been developing its operations and now resembles more a commercial bank. Compared with the other banks operating in Bulgaria, Savings Bank has a relatively larger and better developed network all over the country.

Financial markets

Some elements of financial markets are being created in Bulgaria. The inter-bank money market and the foreign exchange market are both being developed. The money market is a market for short-term deposits with the commercial banks having as participants the banks themselves and the National Bank. This market was complemented in 1991 by an auction for one-month deposits. Through this market the commercial banks are supplied with liquidity. The National Bank is to offer Lombard operations, as a transition to open market operations. There is a basis for Lombard operations as there are government securities already issued and held by the population, the banks, the Savings Bank and enterprises. The amount of these issues is not large, but they can serve as collateral for the first refinancing operations.

The lack of a secondary market for government securities hinders the public confidence in these institutions and is influencing their initial prices.

Foreign exchange market

In February 1991 a foreign exchange market began operating. This is an inter-bank market with commercial banks and the National Bank as participants. Each bank buys and sells foreign currency, fixing its own rates of exchange. On the basis of these rates, a National Bank rate is fixed and announced every day.

The rates float depending on the demand and supply of foreign currency. The foreign exchange market is one of the most important achievements in the field of Bulgaria's economic reform because there was a multiplicity of exchange rates in the past, determined arbitrarily by the central authorities. The leva rate was artificially high and this distorted international trade relations.

Insurance

Bulgaria's insurance industry is governed by the Law on the State Insurance Institute (first passed in 1946, redrafted in 1969), the Law on Contracts and Obligations and various other parliament, state council and government acts and ministerial regulations.

The insurance industry in Bulgaria was nationalised in the 1940s and a state monopoly established. There are two state insurance companies with universal operations and one private insurance company. According to existing law, the State Insurance Institute has the sole right to carry out all kinds of insurance operations in Bulgaria. Foreign insurance and reinsurance is carried under rules set by the Council of Ministers (the government). In 1961, using this law and Decree 155, the State Insurance Institute through the operations of its foreign insurance department created the Bulgarian Foreign Insurance and Reinsurance Company. Bulstrad was established as a joint stock company in 1961.

Supervision

Both the State Insurance Institute and Bulstrad are under the supervision of the Finance Minister. There is no insurance supervisory office since there is no insurance market. No market statistics are collated or published.

The State Insurance Institute has a head office in Sofia and 106 branch offices throughout the country, of which 28 are regional offices, situated in the previous district cities of Bulgaria. The total number of employees is about 2,500, of which about 120 are in the head office. The State Insurance Institute also has another 2,500 agents working full time on commission. Insurance brokers are not mentioned in the acts and by virtue of monopoly status under the law, little competition is expected in the near future.

The State Insurance Institute carries out all kinds of insurances as well as the obligatory insurances prescribed by laws, decrees or government acts.

Policies

In Bulgaria motor third party liability is unlimited and its insurance is compulsory. In respect of Bulgarian physical and juridical persons the Law on Insurance of Properties applies. Under this law, all fixed and movable property (including cars, but excluding the contents of private homes), industrial buildings, machinery, other fixed property, stock, goods in transit, agricultural produce (including plants and crops) and livestock are compulsorily insured with the State Insurance Institute. In voluntary insurances personal lines (life and personal accident) predominate. These are sold mainly through agents.

Insurance reform

Moves began in 1988 to reform Bulgaria's insurance sector. At that time basic principles of improvement of the insurance system were drafted jointly by the State Insurance Institute and Bulstrad. It was suggested then that the insurance monopoly be abolished, and that an insurance market be created, together with the necessary supervisory body.

Bulgaria needs a new insurance law. Recommendations for changes have been accepted, but the drafting of the new law has been postponed. The government's heavy legislative programme has further delayed changes in the sector. Also, new laws on health and social security are needed and should be co-ordinated with any new insurance laws.

In January 1989, Decree 56 was published, under which a new way of management of the economy was adopted. The existing state enterprises were to be reorganised into firms (companies), which could be state firms, joint stock companies, limited liability companies and unlimited liability companies. Private companies were allowed. The decree dealt with insolvency and liquidation of companies, state regulation of economic activity, economic activities of foreign and mixed companies in Bulgaria and other matters. On the basis of this decree the State Insurance Institute started carrying out insurance operations in foreign currency and reinsurance, which until recently were the monopoly of Bulstrad.

A fresh attempt was made to reorganise the State Insurance Institute into a joint stock company in 1990. This necessitated an amendment of the Law on the State Insurance Institute to the effect that the sole right on all insurance operations was repealed, as well as necessary amendments of various other laws and regulations. It was suggested by the Ministry of Economy and Planning that this amendment could be done by a Decree of the State Council. Although the preliminary work was done, the changes were at the bottom of a legislative queue and were never passed.

Mutual societies

Under another decree of the state council on agriculture, issued in May 1989, formation of insurance co-operatives (mutual societies) was allowed. One such co-operative, specialising initially in mutual pension insurance of private self-employed persons was formed.

Under present legislation, co-operation with Western insurers is only possible in the field of reinsurance. Bulstrad maintains good connections and exchanges business with companies on the French market. The State Insurance Institute, dealing at present only with outgoing reinsurances of its marine hull and cargo business in convertible currency, has also placed a share of its reinsurance treaty business with French companies through Le Blanc de Nicolay Réassurances, Paris.

Deregulation

Under proposed new legislation, insurance will be deregulated and an insurance market created, together with the necessary supervisory office. Compulsory insurances, except motor third party liability, are expected to be scrapped.

The market is very much underdeveloped. Opportunities exist particularly in industrial, fire, machinery breakdown, loss of profits, contractors/erection all risks, pension insurance and other areas. The emerging private sector will provide a market for insurance business.

Once the insurance industry is deregulated, the possibilities for Western insurers and brokers to open branch offices, establish wholly-owned subsidiaries, form joint ventures, buy shares of existing companies and other activities should open. However, a lot will depend on the economic situation, especially the possibility to repatriate premiums and profits, earned not only in foreign currency, but also in domestic currency.

Stock market

A stock market, although initially quite primitive, is vital for the revival of the economy and for the transition toward market structures. For a couple of years there have been common stocks in the portfolios of some economic agents, but they have been frozen there without any possibility of reselling them. A new amount of securities has been added to these stock, but were frozen in the hands of their holders. This is a potential basis for development of the financial markets in Bulgaria. The creation of a secondary securities market will be facilitated and speeded up by adopting a special law on the operations with securities and the stock exchange.

Bulgaria has been late in setting up sound financial institutions and appropriate financial markets. A part of the delay was caused by the inertia of the former communist party and partly by measures undertaken in the course of the economic reform, neglect and bad co-ordination of some important steps towards a market economy, such as privatisation, demonopolisation and the creation of financial markets.

It will take a long time to create a variety of financial institutions. For a small country like Bulgaria, some of these institutions may appear unnecessary.

Stock exchange

The first step in setting up Bulgaria's stock exchange was made in late 1991 with the appointment of Victor Parazov as chief executive of the First Bulgarian Stock Exchange. The exchange, funded by 10 Bulgarian shareholders, has an initial capital of Lev 10m (almost $600,000 at the exchange rate in November 1991). Investors in the exchange include Credit Bank, Bulgaria's first private bank, an insurance company in Sofia and an industrial trading company. The exchange is expected to grow quickly once the privatisation process begins. At the same time, a new banking law, anti-monopoly laws and a new foreign investment law are needed before the international investors will feel comfortable committing themselves to large investments.

Privatisation

While the small-scale privatisation of trades and services began in Bulgaria in 1991, it did not achieve the success seen in other East European countries. A few auctions were held for small businesses, including the breakup of the monopoly of petrol stations, but there was little excitement generated.

The large-scale privatisation had yet to begin by the end of 1991. In November 1991 the draft law was still under debate in parliament. Many believe that Bulgaria needs to pass legislation opening the possibility of privatisation of large companies before any significant change in the economy will be seen. Some Western business interest has been shown in the country. Western financial groups, such as Price Waterhouse, Ernst & Young and others have begun helping some of the larger enterprises prepare initial privatisation plans. Until a privatisation law is passed, however, it is difficult to see how the country will be able to achieve the much needed transformation process.

Foreign investment rules

Under the new foreign investment regulations, very few sectors of the economy are closed to foreign investors. Restrictions apply only to a limited number of sectors, including telecommunications, radio and television where investment is permitted after approval. In other areas, registration only will be required. While the law is liberal in its granting of tax holidays and other incentives, there has been relatively little interest in the potential of the country by international investors.

Conclusion

Despite good intentions, Bulgaria's reformers have been able to deliver little.

The political and economic instability of the country has prevented progress on many areas of reform, most importantly in privatisation.

While some major pieces of legislation were passed at the beginning of 1991, including laws on accounting, tax, and ownership of agricultural land, little has been done to begin the development of capital markets. Banking reform has been half-hearted and little has changed. With the deteriorating financial situation in many companies, the existing commercial banks are facing liquidity crisis points.

The moratorium (declared in March 1990) on commercial hard currency debt repayments has severely limited the scope of the commercial banking sector. Few Western banks are interested in setting up in Bulgaria before the rescheduling has been worked out. With the country near bankruptcy, there is little prospect for some form of internal convertibility until rescheduling agreements are signed with commercial bank creditors and a financial package, supported by Western financial institutions, can be put together.

Western investors have grown tired waiting for privatisation legislation. Although some new investment has been made in the country since 1990, there has been no surge in investment. Financial and technical help from such groups as the World Bank, International Finance Corporation, European Bank for Reconstruction and Development and others could help change the situation, but it will take time before Bulgaria begins to have even the basics of a market economy in place and operating.

In the short term there is little to do but wait for a government to pass needed legislation and get the process of transformation moving. Even with the passage of laws on commerce, foreign investment and competition, the country has a long way to go to catch up with the reform leaders (Czechoslovakia, Hungary and Poland).

The country needs help with training staff in the developing market institutions, particularly in banking and insurance. Privatisation should help bring in new management and skills, but there is a lack of good accounting practice and much help from the West will be needed in this area.

Commerce law

Bulgaria's Law on Commerce is a long and complex law. A full text translation of the law (covering 93 pages) is available from the Bulgarian Chamber of Commerce and Industry in Sofia. A summary of the main sections of the law is given here:

- Part One: General Part - Chapter 1, General provisions; Chapter 2, Commercial register; Chapter 3, Business name and registered office; Chapter 4, Enterprises and transactions; Chapter 5, Branches; Chapter 6, Agency; Chapter 7, Account books
- Part Two: Kinds of merchants Division I: Private merchant - Chapter 8,

Natural person as merchant; Division II: State-owned and municipal enterprises - Chapter 9, Public enterprise as merchant

- Part Three: Commercial companies - Chapter 10, General provisions; Chapter 11, Unlimited partnership; Chapter 12, Limited partnership; Chapter 13, Private limited company; Chapter 14, Public limited company; Chapter 15, Public limited partnership; Chapter 16, Reconstruction of commercial companies; Chapter 17, Liquidation; Chapter 18, Commercial groups; Chapter 19, Subsidiary legislation; Chapter 20, Administrative penalties
- Interim and concluding provisions.

Law on foreign investments (unofficial translation)

Purpose

ARTICLE 1
This law will provide for the conditions and order of investment by foreign persons in business activities in the country.

Territorial scope

ARTICLE 2
Foreign investments can be carried out in Bulgaria, including the territorial sea, as well as the continental shelf and the exclusive economic zone.

Foreign investments regime

ARTICLE 3
In regards to foreign persons who invest in the country, the national regime will be applied, unless there have been other provisions made by law or by international agreement.

Investments in business activities

ARTICLE 4
Foreign persons can invest in any business activity, except if it is prohibited by law. Investments and business activities will be performed in observance of Bulgarian legislation, morals and when public health, national security and public order are not threatened.

Foreign persons can invest in the country without permission, except for the following cases:

(a) investments in military industry, banking and the insurance business;

(b) obtaining the right of ownership over buildings and other property rights immovable property;
(c) leasing agricultural lands and forest lands;
(d) investments in particular geographic regions, determined by the Council of Ministers;
(e) investments for the use of the territorial sea, as well as the continental shelf and the exclusive economic zone;
(f) investments in particular sectors and activities, determined by the Council of Ministers, when foreign participation in companies leads to gaining control of these companies;
(g) deals on transferring investments, which are performed with permission (in accordance with this paragraph).

Foreign investments will be registered as established by law for the respective legal form of business activity. Investments for which permission is not required will be declared to the authority (under Article 6, paragraph 1) within a period of 30 days from registration.

Legally performed investments will not be affected by subsequent restrictions or prohibitions.

ARTICLE 5
Foreign persons and companies with foreign participation cannot obtain ownership over land, underground resources, forests and water.

Foreign persons and companies with foreign participation that have invested in the country can obtain the right of use over non-agricultural land for up to 70 years in order to conduct their business activities.

When, in the event of ending foreign participation in the country, immovable property and property rights over it are sold, the right of preference (all other conditions being equal), will belong to the Bulgarian participant, and when there is no such claim — to the Bulgarian state.

Licences

ARTICLE 6
Permissions envisaged by this law will be issued by the Council of Ministers or by its appointed collective authority on the basis of an application, with technical-economic justification enclosed, containing respective data on:

(a) technological and technical renovation of production up to modern standard, creation and realisation of new science-technical products in the field of the respective business activity;
(b) establishing and expanding production of competitive products, and stimulating production by using local raw materials, other materials and energy resources in the respective business activity;

(c) creating new jobs;
(d) restoring and protecting the environment.

Permission for foreign investment in banking will be issued by the managerial council of the Bulgarian National Bank on recommendation from its chairman.

Permissions will be issued within 45 days from the day the application is submitted. Permissions and refusals will not be subject to appeal.

When the application has been declined, permission can be requested again if there are no changes in the proposal, with the reasons for denial being taken into consideration.

Forms of business activities by foreign persons

ARTICLE 7
Foreign investments in business activities in the country can be performed in all legal forms, established by the national legislation for local nationals.

Absence of restriction

ARTICLE 8
The maximum amount of foreign participation in newly established and previously existing companies will not be restricted.

Protection of foreign investors' property rights

ARTICLE 9
Investments of foreign persons will not be subject to administrative confiscation in favour of the state, if the act is not subject to court appeal.

The immovable property of foreign investors cannot be expropriated, except for important state needs, which cannot be fulfilled otherwise.

In the event of expropriation, the foreign person will be compensated. If within a period of 90 days from notification of the decision to expropriate an agreement has not been reached, the type and amount of compensation will be determined by the district court, on request by the interested party.

When the compensation is monetary, it will be paid immediately after the expropriation becomes executable and it will be freely transferable abroad. The expropriated property cannot be taken over by the state before due compensation has been paid in full.

Concessions

ARTICLE 10
The areas, conditions and order of giving concessions to foreign persons for studying, planning, developing, extracting and using natural resources, as well as for business activities, over which state monopoly has been established, will be determined only by virtue of a special law for each concession.

Transfer of earnings and compensations

ARTICLE 11
Foreign persons, who have invested in the country, can transfer abroad profits, interest, dividends and other income made in foreign currency from their investment.

The Bulgarian National Bank will sell convertible currency in exchange for leva at the central exchange rate, when the foreign person who has invested in the country exports:

(a) compensation, received in local currency, for expropriated investments;
(b) a portion of this liquidation quota, received in leva, up to the amount of the foreign currency deposits in capital.

A foreign person, who has invested in the country, can change profits, earned salary and liquidation quota made in leva from his investment, by buying foreign currency at the market exchange rate from any bank that performs such operations, and can transfer abroad foreign currency bought in this way.

Transfers as outlined above will be performed not later than 30 days, from the day on which the foreign person submitted the application for transfer to the Bulgarian People's Bank. In the event of delay, a market interest for current deposits will be due.

Employment and social security

ARTICLE 12
Labour relations, arising in connection with investments by foreign persons in a business activity including joint investments with local nationals, will be provided for by the labour contract.

Labour disputes, when a Bulgarian citizen is a party, will be resolved by the Bulgarian courts, and when a foreign person is a party — as agreed in the labour contract.

For issues unprovided for by the labour contract, provisions of the Bulgarian labour law will apply.

Bulgarian citizens, who are employed (as under paragraph 1), will have mandatory insurance, in accordance with Bulgarian law. Foreign workers will be insured as outlined in the labour contract.

Administrative sanctions

ARTICLE 13
A foreign person, who has invested in a business activity without registering or getting permission if it is required, will be liable to a fine, equal to or double the amount of profits made in the country, as established by the tax authorities, but not less than 50,000 leva. In such cases, the activity will end. Violations will be determined by the Finance Minister. Fines and ending the activity will be enacted by the Finance Minister and will be appealed in the order of the Law on Administrative Violations and Penalties.

Additional provisions

The Council of Ministers can decree that the provisions of this law not be applied in part or in whole for investments in business activities by foreign persons from countries, in which discriminatory measures are being applied to Bulgarian companies.

In cases under Article 4 (paragraph 3), as well as in transferring nominal shares and stakes of foreign persons in Bulgarian companies to other foreign persons or local nationals, the respective authority performing registration will be obligated to notify immediately the authority under Article 6 (paragraph 1) by sending a copy of the registration document.

Under this law, foreign investments will be investments by foreign persons in a business activity by:

(a) founding their own enterprise or obtaining exclusive ownership over an enterprise;
(b) expanding their own enterprise;
(c) long-term investment credit to an enterprise (five or more years), not received through the bank.

The minimum amount of investment (under paragraphs 1, 3 and 4 above) cannot be less than $50,000 or the equivalent in another convertible currency at the exchange rate on the day of registration.

Payments made by foreign persons (under the preceding paragraphs) to the foundations, funds and other organisations with non-commercial purpose, including when a business activity is performed to attain the aims of these organisations, will not be regarded as investments.

Foreign person under this law will be:

(a) legal entity or company, which is not a legal person, registered and with a seat abroad;

(b) foreign citizen, regardless of whether or not he has permanent residence in the country;
(c) Bulgarian citizen permanently residing abroad.

Under this law, foreign control means an investment or participation of a foreign person in an enterprise, which secures him the right or ability to determine directly or indirectly decisions or activities of the enterprise.

Transitional and concluding provisions

The provisions under Article 4 also apply to companies with foreign participation registered in the country.

This law revokes Articles 99-106, 119, 120, 121, 123, 124, 125, 126, and paragraph 11 of the Transitional and Concluding Provisions of Decree 56 on business activity.

Foreign investments in duty-free zones will be provided for by a separate law.

The Council of Ministers will confirm the lists under Article 4, (paragraph 2, items 2 and 4) within a period of three months from the law coming into force.

The implementation of this law will be entrusted to the Council of Ministers.

The law was passed by parliament on 17 May 1991. Published: Durzhaven Vestnik, No 47/1991: correction: DV No 18/1991, page 28.

Bulgarian foreign investment encouragement bill (draft)

ARTICLE 1
This bill specifies the order for the investment of foreign capital in Bulgaria.

The aim of this bill is to encourage, protect and facilitate foreign parties in the investment of foreign capital and aid the development of the national economy.

ARTICLE 2
For the purposes of this bill foreign parties denotes:

(a) corporate bodies seated outside the country;
(b) foreign citizens, who immediately before becoming engaged in economic activity in the country, were permanent residents of a foreign country.

Foreign capital denotes:

(a) capital in the form of foreign currency;
(b) machinery, equipment, tools and similar goods, machine components and spare parts, materials and other necessary goods and facilities;
(c) payments under licensing agreements, for know-how, patent and trade mark rights;

(d) income converted into capital through reinvestment as listed in Article 8;
(e) income from foreign capital and private foreign loans.

The stipulations of this bill concerning foreign parties apply equally to all Bulgarians who are permanent residents of a foreign country.

ARTICLE 3
Foreign parties may invest in the country by:

(a) the acquisition of equity (shares) in a going concern (which may be a state-owned firm in the process of transformation or privatisation, a joint venture, or a private-owned Bulgarian business);
(b) setting up a new joint stock company with a Bulgarian company or a Bulgarian corporate body;
(c) setting up a new joint stock company owned completely by the foreign party, or by the acquisition of shares by one or more foreign parties. In this case, a foreign party may not own more than 49 per cent of the equity of another joint stock company in the country.

ARTICLE 4
Foreign investments in Bulgaria enjoy protection and security.

Damage suffered by a foreign party from action which affects that party's property rights will be indemnified in toto in the currency of the investment. The indemnity will be effected by the administrative body which has caused the damage.

ARTICLE 5
All activities concerning foreign investments in pursuance of this bill will be carried out by the Agency for the Encouragement of Foreign Investment (AEFI), which is an arm of the Presidency of the Republic of Bulgaria.

The Agency's activities will be regulated by a separate bill.

AEFI will issue all permits related to foreign investment in Bulgaria, including the purchasing of stock, the setting up of joint ventures and wholly foreign-owned joint stock companies, subsidiaries and their economic activity on the condition that these will:

- contribute to the country's economic development without establishing a monopoly or special privileges;
- not engage in activities prohibited or restricted by Bulgarian laws and statutory legislation; or contravening the environmental-protection laws; or concerning major state projects; or in energy-intensive production exceeding the permissible levels; or materially-intensive production exceeding the permissible levels; or projects which threaten the lives of citizens; or projects related to the defence of Bulgaria; or projects which run counter to public morals.

In addition, AEFI will issue all permits concerning any increase or decrease in an investment or equity share, or changes in the terms, quantities and spheres of activity, or in the value and ratio of the different kinds of shares. It will approve all agreements concerning licensing, know-how, technical assistance, and others, between Bulgarian and foreign companies and joint ventures, as well as all short- and long-term credit agreements involving foreign investment and the acquisition of bearer shares by foreign parties — the agency will issue the work permits for foreigners employed by companies with foreign capital.

ARTICLE 6

No AEFI permission will be required for joint stock companies with less than 50 per cent foreign capital. In such cases the foreign party will present to AEFI its application for registration before the respective civil court and a copy of that court's ruling which will be given to AEFI not later than two weeks from the date on which the court issues its ruling. If AEFI find a violation of Article 5 (para. 3), it will request a new court ruling.

If foreign capital in a joint stock company exceeds 50 per cent of the equity, AEFI will issue a permit within:

(a) 20 days if foreign capital does not exceed \$3m;
(b) 30 days if foreign capital exceeds \$3m.

If permission (as above) is not denied within 90 days of the submission of the application, it will be considered issued.

Applications for permission are submitted before AEFI in the form contained in an Appendix (attached to this bill).

The Commercial Act and this bill will apply to all joint stock companies with foreign capital.

ARTICLE 7

A foreign party will be free to transfer abroad its share of the foreign-currency profit and its share of the foreign-currency part of the liquidation quota.

The Bulgarian National Bank will exchange Bulgarian leva in the original currency of the investment whenever a foreign party:

(a) takes out of Bulgaria indemnity for expropriated investments;
(b) takes out its liquidation quota from a joint stock company with foreign capital, which will not exceed the initial foreign currency investment;
(c) reports profit in Bulgarian leva from transactions with other companies in and outside the country;
(d) applicable to all foreign-exchange operations will be the current rates at which the Bulgarian National Bank auctions foreign currencies.

ARTICLE 8
A foreign party is free to reinvest all or part of its income in the original founding capital or in another joint stock company (Article 2, para. 2).

ARTICLE 9
Foreign parties will register with AEFI (at the Ministry of Finance) any acquired share in a Bulgarian company within seven days of acquisition.

ARTICLE 10
A joint stock company with foreign capital will pay income tax, value added tax (VAT), duties, excise tax, rates and fees at the same rate as all Bulgarian joint stock companies, as outlined in existing national legislation.

Exemption from taxation will be given to:

(a) any income used to buy shares or bonds in the country;
(b) licensing fees;
(c) fees for technical services rendered in connection with the delivery of complete plant, research, production or commercial equipment;
(d) the income of a joint stock company with foreign capital on the territory of a free-trade zone.

A joint stock company with foreign capital will be exempt from income tax for the first five years following its registration, if engaged in a high-technology area of activity, as defined by AEFI.

A foreign party will not pay import duty on raw and prime materials and equipment delivered for the purpose of export-oriented production by a joint stock company.

A foreign party will register itself with the municipal tax authority by the procedure described in the Appendix attached to this bill.

ARTICLE 11
On liquidation of a joint stock company with foreign capital, the Bulgarian shareholder will have first option to buy the company's immovables and property rights thereon. All immovables will be sold to local buyers on liquidation of a subsidiary company or a wholly foreign-owned company, or when the Bulgarian shareholder has refused to exercise his option.

ARTICLE 12
Any rights, concessions and privileges granted to national capital or form of economic activity will apply equally to foreign investments and identical economic activities.

This bill will come into effect on the date of its publication in Durzhaven Vestnik (State Gazette).

Protection of Competition Act

Chapter I: General provisions

ARTICLE 1
Aims

The aims of this act are to create conditions for free enterprise in manufacture, distribution and services as well as free pricing and the protection of consumer interests. To ensure these aims the act provides protection against the misuse of monopoly market position, unfair competition and other actions which may have a restrictive effect on domestic competition.

ARTICLE 2
Commission for the protection of competition

A commission for the protection of competition will be set up as an autonomous budget-financed institution. The commission will comprise a chairman, two vice-chairmen and eight members to be elected for a term of five years and relieved of office by parliament. Half of the commission members will be qualified lawyers who have served a minimum of 10 years in this capacity.

Chapter II: Position of monopoly

ARTICLE 3
Definitions

A person is in a monopoly position in the national market when he:

- holds the exclusive right to carry on a particular business of manufacturer of goods and/or services, distributor agent, purchaser, creditor, insurer and others;
- independently or jointly with other dependent persons, holds over 35 per cent share in the market of any particular business as listed above.

ARTICLE 4
Ban on the establishment of monopoly

Central and local government authorities will not adopt decisions explicitly or implicitly where a monopoly is established or when such decisions result in the establishment of a monopoly or if free competition and/or pricing is severely restricted.

ARTICLE 5
Ban on grouping and merger

If grouping, subordination and merger of companies leads to such consequences as those under Article 4, the action is banned.

A company is subordinated when another company is the holder of equities or shares in a proportion which ensures majority voting power of that other company to adopt or prevent the adoption of decisions by the company.

Equities or shares may not be acquired by transfer between dependent persons.

ARTICLE 6
Notification and consent

Persons in a monopoly position and those who by acquisition of equities or shares obtains such a position, will submit to the commission for the protection of competition prior notice of the acquisition of equities or shares in a competitor company of subsidiary status and also of any decision to contain or limit the growth of production, sales, investment or technological development.

Actions or transactions as listed above will be subject to consent by the commission for the protection of competition or the commission's acquiescence, which will be deemed granted if the commission does not make an objection within 30 days of notification.

ARTICLE 7
Ban on the misuse of monopoly

A monopoly position will be deemed misused where a person (Article 3) acts in a manner that restricts competition or prejudices consumer interests by:

- hindering other persons from carrying on a business if that restricts the growth of a market or access to it;
- applying distinctly inequitable standards in dealings with various counterparts or inequitable contract terms, including unjustifiable imposition of limited or expanded liability or by imposing goods and services on a market that are below common quality standards;
- creating a shortage of goods and services by withholding, destroying or damaging such goods and services or by the unjustifiable recycling of such goods, buying up competitors' goods and other such actions;
- concluding or implementing a contract conditional on a counterpart's acceptance of additional terms which are unrelated to the subject or the implementation of the contract;
- resorting to economic constraint to cause other companies to dissolve, split up, merge or transform;
- imposing monopoly prices that over a period of some considerable duration are considerably above costs related to the production and distribution of particular goods and services.

Chapter III: Ban on the restriction of competition

ARTICLE 8
Banned agreements and decisions

Agreements (cartels) will be null and void and decisions made by companies, groups, alliances or persons which explicitly or implicitly propose setting up a domestic monopoly or would effectively result in such.

Contract terms will be banned that restrict a choice of market, sources of purchasing, buying, selling or using, unless such a restriction is warranted by the specific nature of contracts and where it does not prejudice consumer interests.

ARTICLE 9
Control of marketing agreements

Subject to consent by the commission for the protection of competition, agreements can be made to adopt unified contract terms of sale, manufacture, service, shipment, credit, settlements and other areas if such agreements do not affect free pricing, do not restrict competition and do not prejudice consumer interests.

ARTICLE 10
Exclusive distribution rights

Contracts will be banned if one person becomes an agent for or is given exclusive rights for buying or selling goods and/or services which:

- are supplied by competitors where this would lead to restriction of domestic competition or to a monopoly market position;
- fall under the contract's monopoly in production, consumption or distribution.

Chapter IV: Unfair competition

ARTICLE 11
Ban

Unfair competition is banned.

ARTICLE 12
Acts of unfair competition

An action or business behaviour will be deemed to constitute an act of unfair competition when it contravenes commercial practices and prejudices or might prejudice competitors' interests vis-à-vis one another or vis-à-vis consumers.

The following will constitute unfair competition:

- damage to the good reputation and credibility of competitors and those of the goods and services supplied by them or to competitors' credit worthiness by claiming or by circulating false facts as well as by distortion of facts; by commercial advertising or in any other way attributing non-existent features to goods and services in comparison with competitors' goods and services;
- non-avowal or concealment of essential deficiencies of, or hazards arising from, goods and services offered;
- misleading consumers about essential features or the usage of goods by claiming false facts or by interpreting facts in a misleading manner;
- supply or commercial advertising of goods and services whose appearance, packaging, labelling, name or other distinctive features mislead or might serve to mislead, consumers about the origin, manufacturer, seller, way and location of manufacture, source and manner of acquisition, quantity, quality, nature, user benefits and other essential characteristics of such goods and services;
- use of a corporate identity, trade mark, brand name, special legend and symbols in a manner such as might serve to mislead the consumer;
- use of legends which might create wrong ideas of non-existing features of goods and services;
- commercial advertising of goods and services which are not available on demand or which are available only in short supply by overall quantity and by variety range;
- misleading quotation of prices, discounts and other special offers of goods and services;
- non-compliance with, or unilateral termination of, a contract in order to conclude a similar contract with third parties, that reduces the competition capability of the original party;
- resort to constraint or any other unlawful method of influencing customers in order to make them buy or use a particular product or service;
- provision of incomplete or false information on essential elements of a credit or hire-purchase contract.

ARTICLE 13
Ban on soliciting termination or breach of contract

Actions, such as under Article 12, are banned if they are intended to attract customers and where such actions result in termination or breach of contract with competitors.

ARTICLE 14
Ban on the disclosure of production or commercial secrets

Also deemed as acts of unfair competition will be the possession, use or disclosure in contravention of bona fide commercial practices of others' production or commercial secrets.

Production and commercial secrets will mean business-related decisions and data such as might, if possessed, used or disclosed by others, prejudice the business interests of the rightful owner.

Possession of production or commercial secrets contravenes bona fide commercial practices, and where gained by eavesdropping, breaking into premises, unauthorised access to correspondence, filming or studying documents or other materials kept so as to limit access to them and by fraud or by corruption of persons whose access to such secrets is authorised under official status or contract.

Use and disclosure of others' production or commercial secrets is banned when possession has been gained or granted under the condition that such secrets may not be used or disclosed.

Employees in all enterprises and organisations and government departments will not, even after the relevant contract expires, disclose production or commercial secrets which they have knowledge of through official authority, for a period of five years unless a longer period has been specified by employment or another relevant contract.

ARTICLE 15
Unfair competition by employees

A person may not simultaneously, and for a period of three years after having been relieved of office, be on the governing or controlling bodies of competing companies.

An employee may not, without his employer's consent, on either his own account or on that of some other person, carry on a business the same as his employer. Acquiescence will be deemed granted where at signing of the relevant employment contract the employer knew of such a business being carried on by the person concerned and where an explicit provision to end the same was not made. In the event of a breach of this ban, the employer can terminate the employment contract without prior notice.

Persons as explained above may not engage in competition with their employer for a period of three years after terminating the contract unless otherwise provided for in the contract of employment.

An executive officer may not participate in a company or be a member of a governing or a controlling body if that might interfere with the fulfilment of his official duties.

Chapter V: Government action to prevent establishment and misuse of monopoly and unfair competition

ARTICLE 16
Mandatory prices

When a monopoly position is misused, the Council of Ministers or another body authorised by the council can (subject to advice by the commission for the protection of competition) enforce maximum and/or minimum prices on a person in a monopoly position.

ARTICLE 17
Import and export quotas

Where import or export quotas exist for certain goods and services, the authority assigned to control compliance with such rules will announce such quotas and provide persons concerned with equal opportunities to participate in a competitive tender for the allocation of sub-quotas.

ARTICLE 18
Terms of reference of the commission for the protection of competition

The commission for the protection of competition will:

- following the relevant procedure make submissions to the effect that administrative enactments of government organs be repealed where found to contravene this act;
- take legal proceedings to impose sanctions where a monopoly position is unlawfully established or misused or where unfair competition is practised or competition is restricted.

ARTICLE 19
Appeal

A ruling by the commission for the protection of competition, under Articles 6 and 9, will be subject to appeal before the Sofia City Court within a month of announcement. Where a commission has not granted permission within a month of request pursuant to Article 9, such permission will be deemed refused.

ARTICLE 20
Mandatory co-operation

Executive officers of enterprises and administrative authorities will as required by the commission for the protection of competition, provide information and documentation and submit written statements on matters within the commission's terms of reference.

Chapter VI: Responsibility

ARTICLE 21
Claims

Where the bans or restrictions provided by this act have been violated and depending on the nature of the offence, claims may be lodged with courts by:

- persons whose interests have been prejudiced or endangered by the offence;

- the commission for the protection of competition and district attorneys.

A court can establish whether an offence has occurred; rule the termination of activity until non-compliance is overcome; declare transactions and decisions to be in contravention of this act null and void; and instruct the offender to stop non-compliance. A court can also rule the confiscation as state revenue of profit made in contravention of this act. A state revenue fee will not be required for claims under this article. Such fees will be assigned at closure of the case pursuant to civil procedure.

ARTICLE 22
Jurisdiction

Claims under Article 21 will fall under district court jurisdiction.

ARTICLE 23
Penalties

Offending companies and enterprises under Articles 4, 5, 7, 10 and 13 as well as companies and enterprises acting without due permission under Article 9 will be liable to fines (between Lev 20,000 to Lev 1m). Penalties will range between Lev 20,000 and Lev 1m where offences

- under this act are repeated within a period of three years;
- as above are exceptionally grave and lead to significant adverse consequences in the market and for consumers or the national economy;
- fall under Articles 6, 8, 12 and 14;
- where implementation of agreements or decisions which were declared null and void or actions have been taken which were banned by a court ruling.

In minor cases penalties will range from Lev 500 to Lev 5,000.

ARTICLE 24
Administrative responsibility

Persons who have committed or were allowed to commit offences under this act, if the offence does not constitute a crime, will be liable to a fine of Lev 10,000.

ARTICLE 25
Enforcement of penalties

Where offences are committed for which offenders are liable to fines under Article 23, the commission for the protection of competition will draw up a statement, under the administrative offences and sanctions act, which will then be referred to the local district court. Where an offence has been committed over areas of jurisdiction of two or more district courts, the statement will be referred to the Sofia City Court.

Court hearings, rulings and appeals will be subject to civil procedure.

Establishment of offences under Article 24, issuance, appeal and execution of the relevant penal statement will be subject to administrative offences and sanctions act.

Transitional and final provisions

As under Article 3, the Council of Ministers within three months will submit a bill on businesses that can carry on monopoly activities in the national market.

Within a month of the date of this act coming into force, the chairman of the commission for the protection of competition will approve rules and the organisation and procedure for the commission.

This act is referred for execution to the commission for the protection of competition and the courts.

This act was voted into law by parliament on 2 May 1991.

Law of the Bulgarian National Bank (unofficial translation)

Chapter I: General provisions

ARTICLE 1

Bulgarian National Bank is the central and the issuing bank of Bulgaria. It is a legal person.

The Bulgarian National Bank will account for its activity before the national assembly (parliament).

ARTICLE 2

The main task of the National Bank is to exert influence in maintaining the internal and external stability of the national currency unit. For this purpose it will develop and carry out the national monetary and credit policy.

The National Bank will have the exclusive right of issuing banknotes in this country and will contribute to the creation and maintenance of efficient mechanisms of payment.

The National Bank will regulate and supervise other banks' activities in this country for the purpose of maintaining the stability of the banking system.

ARTICLE 3

In defining the general trends of the monetary and crediting policies, the National Bank and the Council of Ministers will inform each other about their intentions and actions.

ARTICLE 4
In connection with the performance of its entrusted functions, the National Bank will have the right to demand from banks and other financial institutions to submit any documents and information, as well as to carry out the respective examinations.

It is obliged not to spread and not to transmit to other persons the information obtained which is of confidential character for the banks and the other participants in the money turnover and the credit relations.

ARTICLE 5
The National Bank may participate organisationally and financially in international institutions which aim at promoting international co-operation in the sphere of foreign currency, monetary and credit policy, as well as to take part in the measures and activities carried out by these organisations when Bulgaria has interest.

ARTICLE 6
The National Bank will have its head office in Sofia. It may have branch offices and representative offices.

The National Bank will have a seal with its name and an image of the state coat of arms.

Chapter II: Statutory fund and reserves

ARTICLE 7
The statutory fund of the National Bank will be Lev 200m.

The amount of the bank's own capital by which it exceeds the statutory fund provided for in the preceding paragraph at the time this law enters into force, will constitute the reserves fund of the bank.

ARTICLE 8
The reserves fund will be built up from deductions amounting to 25 per cent of the annual net profit of the bank. These resources will be used for covering bank's losses.

After deducting the amount for the reserves fund and for non-collectable or doubtful receipts, the necessary amounts for special funds, set up under a managing board's decision, will be allotted from the annual positive profit/loss account of the bank.

The account of the state budget will be annually credited by the remainder of the net profit of the bank within four months after the end of the fiscal year.

ARTICLE 9
Whenever the bank's balance sheet shows that the amount of its assets is less than

the amount of its liabilities and statutory fund paid, the Finance Minister will grant ownership to the bank over negotiable, interest-bearing securities, issued by the Council of Ministers, at the amount which is necessary for covering the negative balance. The granted securities will be paid from the positive balance of the profit/loss account of the bank.

Instructions covering a negative balance will be applied only in cases when the resources of the reserves fund of the bank have been exhausted.

Chapter III: Management, administration and officials

ARTICLE 10
The management and administration of the National Bank will be carried out by a managing board, a plenary council and a president.

ARTICLE 11
The managing board will consist of the president of the bank, three vice-presidents and five heads of departments (directors) of the bank. The members of the managing board will be only Bulgarian citizens.

ARTICLE 12
The president and the vice-presidents of the National Bank will be elected by parliament for the term of five years. The other members of the managing board will be appointed by the president of Bulgaria at the proposal of the president of the bank for the term of five years.

The President cannot be elected for more than two terms of office.

ARTICLE 13
At inauguration, the president, the vice-presidents and the other members of the managing board will swear a solemn oath to observe strictly the legislation in this country and whenever necessary to assist in the implementation of the functions entrusted to the bank and to keep the bank's commercial secrets.

The president and the vice-presidents will swear a solemn oath before parliament while the other members of the managing board will swear an oath before the president of the bank.

ARTICLE 14
The members of the managing board will not take part in any other paid activity with the exception of their occupation as assistants in scientific institutes and university professors.

ARTICLE 15
The president of the bank, the vice-presidents and the other members of the managing board may be dismissed during their terms of office only if they have been sentenced for committing a crime of general character with malice prepense or are prevented from performing their functions for more than a year.

Where a member of the managing board leaves before his term of office expires the competent authority under the provisions of Article 12 will appoint a new member to take up office until the end of the term.

ARTICLE 16

The managing board will hold a session at least once a month. It will be convened by the president or upon the request of no less than three of its members by written invitation.

The sessions of the managing board will be chaired by the president of the bank. In his absence it will be chaired by the vice-president.

ARTICLE 17

The managing board will:

- discuss and take decisions regarding the implementation of the monetary and credit policies;
- adopt legal acts concerning this bank's activities;
- fix interest rates for this bank's operations;
- define the amount of minimal reserves to be held by the banks and confirm the conditions and requirements regarding their fulfilment;
- define regulations and requirements regulating banking activities;
- define the structure of this bank, the tasks of its departments and the competence of its officials;
- take decisions about introduction or cessation of separate functions of the bank and about issuing of securities;
- set up and close branches of the bank;
- adopt decisions for issuing new banknotes, setting time limits after which banknotes cease to be legal tender and within which banknotes called in have to be exchanged;
- define the type of securities and the conditions at which they could be accepted for securing;
- define the system and competence for the transfer to losses of uncollectable receipts of the National Bank;
- adopt decisions for the participation of the bank in international institutions and the initiatives and activities undertaken by such institutions;
- take decisions on issuing or depriving of licences for performing banking and crediting activities in this country;
- consider and resolve other issues of the activity of the bank.

ARTICLE 18

The managing board can be in session if more than one half of all its members are present.

Decisions will be adopted by a simple majority of votes of the members present. In the event of equal split of votes the president will have the casting vote. In his absence the vice-president will chair the managing board.

Abstention from voting on questions raised before the managing board will not be permitted.

ARTICLE 19

The plenary council of the National Bank will consist of the members of the managing board of the bank together with six leading experts in monetary, financial, economic and scientific spheres for the term of three years.

The plenary council of the bank will define the main trends for the monetary and credit policy and will approve the annual report and the budget of the bank.

The plenary council will be convened by the president or at the request of one-third of its members.

The plenary council may hold a session if two-thirds of its members are present.

The provisions of Articles 15 and 18 apply to the plenary council.

ARTICLE 20

The president of the National Bank will organise, direct and supervise the activity of the bank, represent it at home and abroad. He may delegate some of his rights to other officials.

ARTICLE 21

The managing board may set up standing or interim consultative councils consisting of representatives from the industrial, agricultural, commercial, banking and other business activities.

ARTICLE 22

The internal auditing of the financial activities of the bank will be implemented by a chief auditor, appointed by the managing board and approved by the chairman of the chamber of accounts.

The chief auditor may be assisted by experts hired or engaged for a special purpose, or by special companies for bank auditing.

The chief auditor will:

- check the annual financial report and the periodical reports prepared by the bank;
- make an evaluation of the balance sheet and the budget of the bank;
- audit the bank's books, vaults and safes of the bank;
- submit to the managing board the reports after auditing and make recommendations for undertaking corrective measures.

ARTICLE 23
Officials of the the National Bank in entering office will sign a declaration, that with all their actions they will faithfully serve its interests and will keep bank and commercial secrets.

The bank officials will be obliged to observe secrecy concerning the negotiations, the bank transactions, the bank clients' deposits and their operations, the information received by the bank's and its clients' activities which represent official or commercial secrets for them.

The remuneration of the bank officials will be determined by the managing board, but it cannot be lower than the average remuneration in the national banking system for officials with similar functions.

Chapter IV: Monetary unit, banknotes and coins

ARTICLE 24
The national monetary unit of Bulgaria will be the lev, divisible into 100 stotinki.

ARTICLE 25
The National Bank will have the exclusive right to issue banknotes and to mint coins.

The banknotes issued by the bank will be the legal tender and will be received for payment in their full face value without restrictions.

The National Bank will ensure the issuing of banknotes and the minting of coins, will guarantee the safe storage of notes and coins not yet in circulation, as well as keeping and destroying, when banknotes and coins are withdrawn from circulation.

The banknotes and coins put in circulation by the bank will have a nominal value, coverage, form and design, determined by the Council of Ministers.

Before putting into circulation a new banknote or coin, the bank will publish their exact description in the State Gazette and the mass media.

ARTICLE 26
The National Bank, after informing the public through announcement in the State Gazette and the mass media, may demand the withdrawal from circulation of its issued banknotes and coins by paying their nominal value. After a deadline set by the bank, but not shorter than one year, such banknotes and coins will be considered out of circulation and will cease to be legal tender.

ARTICLE 27
The terms under which damaged banknotes will be exchanged at partial or full nominal value, will be specified by the bank.

Coins punched, cut, deformed, or having a private sign or whose design is indistinguishable, will be exchanged by the bank on its own discretion.

ARTICLE 28
Money put into circulation by the bank will be fully covered by the international reserves as determined by Article 38 and by the following assets:

- credits guaranteed by the state;
- securities in the commercial portfolio of the bank;
- credits to banks granted against mortgage;
- cheques owned and kept by the bank and due to be collected.

Chapter V: Bank's operations

ARTICLE 29
The National Bank will have the right to carry out:

- broking of exchange bills and discounting of cheques;
- credit operations against mortgage;
- securities operations, including issuing and operating securities of its own;
- operations with precious metals;
- foreign exchange operations;
- operations with deposits and financial investments;
- operations connected with the money turnover;
- commission operations;
- bank operations abroad.

ARTICLE 30
The bank may:

- discount bills of exchange and promissory notes consigned by the banks and financial institutions for trading purposes payable in this country within three months and bearing the signatures of at least two indebted persons of proved solvency;
- extend credits to banks and financial institutions against gold, securities, foreign currency and other assets, determined by the managing board, for a period of no longer than three months.

The managing board of the bank will determine the type of the accepted securities, the conditions at which they will be accepted, the part of the nominal value which could be covered by credit and the maximum amount of the possible credit to be extended against acceptance of securities at their trading value instead of the nominal value.

The bank can give to other banks unsecured short-term credits on conditions, determined by the managing board, only when such credit is extremely necessary for meeting the demands for liquidity of the bank — receiver of credit.

ARTICLE 31
The bank may refuse discounting of securities or extending credit against securities without explaining the reasons that have led to the refusal.

ARTICLE 32
Where a credit received against securities is not repaid at the contracted maturity, the National Bank will have the right to sell the securities without judicial intervention. The amount received will cover the bank's receipts regarding the principal part of the credit, the interest and the expenses; the current account of the debtor will be debited with the balance.

The bank may not sell the securities against an unpaid debt and instead set up a claim against the debtor who is responsible with all his property for the amount due.

ARTICLE 33
The National Bank will have the right while implementing its monetary and credit policy to:

- buy and sell securities properly put in circulation at the open market, including government and local government securities accepted by the managing board as equivalent regarding the bank operation at the open market;
- put in circulation its own securities for the needs of its own operations.

ARTICLE 34
The National Bank will set and maintain under conditions periodically stipulated by the managing board, an international reserve consisting of all or some of the following assets:

- gold;
- foreign currency in cash of banknotes and coins, bank balances kept abroad, in currencies and countries stipulated by the managing board of the bank;
- internationally acknowledged reserve assets;
- bills of exchange and promissory notes denominated in foreign currency, as well as Treasury bills and other securities in foreign currency issued or guaranteed by foreign governments;
- other similar assets set for the purpose by the managing board;
- reserves will be kept at a level corresponding to the international transactions of the state.

If the reserve has diminished or the bank considers it a danger to decrease to an extent which could impair the necessary correspondence, the bank will submit to the Council of Ministers a report on the state of the reserve and the reasons which have caused or can cause such a decrease; it will be accompanied by recommendations for measures considered necessary for preventing or eliminating the decrease.

The bank will periodically submit such reports and recommendations until the reserve reaches the necessary proportion.

ARTICLE 35
All bank profits arising from changes in the valuation of the bank assets or liabilities in, or denominated in gold or foreign currencies, in result of change of the price or the exchange rates of gold or the foreign currencies to the lev, will be kept in a special reserve account.

Losses arising from changes provided for in the preceding paragraph will be covered by the balance of the special reserve account; if the balance of this account and balance of the reserve fund account are not enough for covering such losses the government will grant to the bank negotiable and interest bearing securities at the amount of the shortage/margin. The securities granted will be covered from the annual active balance of the profit/loss account.

ARTICLE 36
The National Bank may:

- buy and sell gold coins and bullion or other precious metals;
- buy, sell or make deals for foreign currencies using to this end all means traditionally used;
- open and maintain accounts with international financial organisations, central banks and other financial institutions, outside this country;
- open and maintain accounts or act as representative or correspondents of international financial institutions and central banks and other financial institutions outside this country.

ARTICLE 37
The National Bank will accept precious metals, securities and other valuables for safe-keeping at conditions defined by the managing board. It will have the right to put an end to its obligations of depository unilaterally by informing the deponent 14 working days in advance by a written notification, after which it may transfer at deponent's expense and risk the valuables left to the common public warehouses.

ARTICLE 38
The National Bank may accept from banks, financial institutions, the government and municipalities monetary deposits at current or time deposit accounts, at conditions announced by the managing board.

The bank may turn down a request for opening a current or deposit account, as well as to close such an account, after sending a written notification fourteen working days in advance to the titular, without explaining the reasons having caused such an action.

ARTICLE 39
For the purpose of facilitating non-cash payments the National Bank may

organise and participate in a clearing office and adopt rules for carrying out of this activity.

As a commissioner the bank will have the right to carry out collection of payments.

Chapter VI: Relationship to banks

ARTICLE 40
The National Bank will:

- determine the obligatory minimum reserves the banks should hold with the National Bank up to the amount of 15 per cent of all assets, as well as the method of their calculation;
- define other terms and conditions aiming at the maintenance of the stability of the credit system.

A bank not complying with the obligatory minimum reserves will have to make punitive interest payments over the amount of the shortage until its full covering at a rate not exceeding the doubled interest rate at which the National Bank extends credits to the other banks.

ARTICLE 41
The bank will have the right to demand and examine the accounts, files and books of each person who is duly considered to have extended or to be extending credits.

ARTICLE 42
The National Bank will determine:

- rules regulating gold and foreign exchange operations of the banks in conformity with the foreign exchange legislation of this country for the purpose of protecting the national currency;
- the ceiling of the assets in gold and foreign exchange which the licensed institutions can keep in deposit with them;
- the maximum amount allowed of the open foreign exchange positions of the banks and the other financial institutions, as well as the set of rules for calculating and debiting non-interest bearing accounts with itself of the minimum obligatory reserves, securing these positions;
- the exchange rates at which it sells, buys or transacts gold and foreign currencies and set the central exchange rate of currencies to the lev.

ARTICLE 43
The National Bank will compose the balance of payments of this country, in connection with which it will closely watch the international payments, the carrying out and the condition of the direct investments of non-residents in this country and of residents abroad.

ARTICLE 44
The National Bank will carry out the supervision over the banking and credit system. It will collect information, follow banks' activities and carry out periodical auditing and purposeful inspections at the banks and the other financial institutions, necessary for fulfilment of the bank's tasks regarding bank supervision. Statistical data published by the bank will not contain data about separate operations and transactions.

With regard to bank supervision the National Bank may undertake all necessary measures for securing the stability of the bank system.

Chapter VII: Relations between the bank and the state

ARTICLE 45
The National Bank will be the official depository of state funds.

The bank will organise and execute the cash performance of the state budget through commercial and other banks. The operations of the cash performance of the state budget will be carried out by the banks free of charge.

Under terms agreed upon with the Finance Minister, the bank will issue and manage securities of the state or securities guaranteed by the state which are public emission.

The bank may act as representative of the government for purposes and under the terms determined by the bank and the Council of Ministers.

ARTICLE 46
The National Bank may grant to the state temporary credits (advances) with up to three months maturity, but repayable not later than the end of the current year. The maximal amounts, which can become unsettled at any time, will not exceed more than 5 per cent of the annual revenues of the budget, as well as the sum deposits in fixed capital and the resources in the reserve fund.

ARTICLE 47
In performing its duties the bank will be independent from the Council of Ministers and other state bodies.

ARTICLE 48
The National Bank may purchase and sell securities issued or guaranteed by the state which are part of a public emission.

ARTICLE 49
Except in cases provided for by this law, the bank will neither directly, nor indirectly, acquire government securities nor extend any credits to the government or to the municipalities.

Chapter VIII: Accountability and balance

ARTICLE 50
The fiscal year of the bank will begin on 1 January and end on 31 December.

ARTICLE 51
The expenditures of the National Bank will be made in accordance with annual budget approved by the plenary council of the bank.

The administrative expenditures will be made by decision of the managing board.

The reports on the budget expenses of the bank, together with the appropriate documents, will be audited by a commission appointed by the chairman of the chamber of accounts, which will prepare a special report on the results of the audit. The report on the budget expenses of the bank will be submitted to parliament together with the annual report.

ARTICLE 52
The bank will publish in the State Gazette:

- the state of assets and liabilities as at the end of each month;
- the annual balance sheet and profit/loss account of the bank within the four months after the end of the fiscal year.

The monthly balance of assets and liabilities of the bank will include:

- on the assets side: cash in Bulgarian coins; cash in foreign currency; participation in international institute; cash in foreign securities; credits granted to banks; credits granted to the state; securities; other assets;
- on the liabilities side: fixed capital; amount of banknotes in circulation; current and deposit accounts; other liabilities.

The annual balance sheet of the bank will be prepared in leva as of 31 December of the respective year. Precious metal stocks and asset items in foreign currency will be calculated at market exchange rates as of 31 December. All securities will be calculated at prices which will neither exceed the acquisition price nor the market price as of 31 December.

ARTICLE 53
Twice a year the National Bank will submit to paliament and publish a report containing:

- proofs of the reasonability of the monetary policy it intends to pursue during the following six months;
- description of the principles the bank intends to follow while elaborating and implementing the monetary policy during the following two years or another longer period set by the bank;

- review and evaluation of the monetary policy followed during the past six months.

ARTICLE 54

The National Bank will submit to parliament its annual report, balance sheet and budget report not later than 30 April of the next year.

Chapter IX: Property sanctions and criminal responsibility

ARTICLE 55

In cases of discovered violations of banking operations rules, of obligatory minimal reserves and other normatives and established accountability determined by the bank, the National Bank will impose on the banks and other financial institutions property sanctions in the amount from Lev 10,000 to Lev 250,000.

When the violations under paragraph 1 are repeated within one year or have led to considerable damaging consequences, the property sanction will be from Lev 20,000 to Lev 500,000.

ARTICLE 56

Persons who have committed violation of this law, if the act does not constitute a crime, will be punished with a fine up to Lev 10,000.

ARTICLE 57

Statements for discovered violations under Articles 55 and 56 will be drawn up by the authorities of bank control, and the punitive decrees will be issued by the president of the National Bank or by an official authorised by him.

Drawing up statements, issuing, appealing and execution of the punitive decrees will be as provisioned in the Law on Administrative Violations and Punishment.

Chapter X: Other provisions

ARTICLE 58

Attachments, mortgages and forced action on money and securities deposited with the bank will be allowed only if they do not infringe upon the rights of the bank connected with these possessions.

ARTICLE 59

The National Bank may make deductions with its receipts still not fallen due when a bank or another financial institution has begun procedure of liquidation of its activities or has stopped payments on its debt, as well as in cases when the National Bank has the right to get its receipts before falling due.

ARTICLE 60
The National Bank will not acquire property and property rights over it, except for:

- securing premises for the performance of its activity and housing for the staff;
- protecting itself from losses connected with credit transactions.

The bank will be obliged to relieve itself from ownership of immovable property (as detailed above) within a period of five years.

ARTICLE 61
The National Bank will be exempted from paying taxes to the central and local government, as well as duty on import and export.

ARTICLE 62
The National Bank will issue regulations and decrees for application of this law.

Additional provisions

Under this law, the term 'financial institution' will mean, not counting the banks, all institutions which attract resources from other persons through selling or marketing of bonds, certificates, bills of exchange and other securities, and use these resources wholly or partially for lending credits or for investment at own expense and risk.

Transitional and final provisions

All operations having been stated by the date of entry into force of this law which are in contradiction to its provision will be obliged to be finished within five years from the date of its entry into force.

This law will repeal:

- Statute of the National Bank (published in the State Gazette, Issue 94 from 1956; amendments and additions: Issues 11 from 1957, 104 from 1958, 32 from 1959, 20 from 1961, 99 from 1963, 65 from 1965, 48 from 1989);
- Decree for reorganisation of the banking system (published in the State Gazette, issue 3 from January 1967);
- Decree for the right of the National Bank when liquidating its receipts and for penalties for breaching government instructions about bank's activity (published in the State Gazette, Issue 51 from 1951; amendments and additions: Issues 12 from 1952, 94 from 1956, 5 from 1957 and 57 from 1961).

The implementation of this Law will be delegated to the managing board of the National Bank.

This law was passed by parliament on 6 June 1991.

Chapter 3
CZECHOSLOVAKIA

On 1 January 1990, the State Bank of Czechoslovakia passed its commercial banking activities to three state-owned financial institutions: the newly created Komercni Banka, Prague; Vseobecna Uverova Banka, Bratislava; and the existing Investicni Bank, Prague. A two-tiered banking system was established with the State Bank acting as the central bank and the commercial banks providing banking operations on a commercial basis. Since 1 January 1991, new commercial banks, including private banks, have been permitted to be set up. The regulatory process accelerated, especially in the last half of 1990 and in 1991, with the registration of 26 commercial banks.

Foreign bank participation

Czechoslovakia allows foreign banks in three possible forms:

- representative office representing the interests of foreign banks, but not engaging in banking activities;
- participation in joint venture banks;
- independent subsidiaries of foreign banks, founded as joint ventures with 100 per cent foreign ownership.

By January 31 1991, there were 31 representative offices, five joint venture banks and three subsidiaries of foreign banks operating in Czechoslovakia. The number of representative offices, joint venture banks and foreign banks are growing. A foreign bank does not need any permission in order to open a representative office, but after opening, registration is required.

Joint venture banks

Joint venture banks have equal rights to Czechoslovak banks, with no general limitations as to the share of foreign capital. Share volume is subject to negotiation in each case. The process of granting permission for independent activity is granted to foreign banks taking into account three points. Independent foreign banks must:

- be subsidiaries of foreign banks;
- have a minimal capitalisation of $10m or its equivalent in the Czechoslovak or another currency for a universal bank;
- demonstrate the intended range of business and service activities, breadth of branch network and other aspects of activity.

Development of the banking sector

The development of the banking sector includes services and support activities. This includes preparatory work for the foundation of special financial institutions that collect and sell information on individual clients and corporations. The establishment of special banks with state participation as either guarantor of small business loans to the commercial banks or provider of subsidisation of the interest spread between the market interest rate and the small business interest rate.

The development of banking activities will be improved by the planned modernisation of the system of payments and clearing. With the aim of simplifying payments, the State Bank is establishing a clearing centre where all domestic inter-bank payments in local currency will be electronically processed. In the third quarter of 1991 all banks were required to join the system.

A decisive role in the development of the Czechoslovak banking system is planned by the State Bank which is an independent institution responsible for Czechoslovak monetary policy and for the effective functioning of Czechoslovak banking as a whole.

Banking reform

Although at the beginning of 1990 Czechoslovak banks were organised into a two-tier structure — a central bank and commercial banks, including the savings banks — the commercial banks by the beginning of 1991 still had not satisfied the growing demand for banking products and services. There remains a lack of qualified specialists and trained staff in the banking sector. The level of remunerations, compared with the banking sectors of the developed European countries and with other branches of the Czechoslovak economy, is insufficient.

There is a lack of modern technology and techniques for payment systems, accounts and inter-bank information transfer. The continued problems at the beginning of 1991 were tied up with the lack of proper legislation to support the economic transition. In particular a clear banking law was needed to enable the development of banking and the setting up of foreign banks.

Legal changes

The law on banks, which replaces the law 158/89, enables the state monetary institute to be transformed into a joint stock company. The idea is to make the National Bank the supervisory authority, at the same time introducing rules which will conform to European Community legislation. Political debates have held up the introduction of the banking law. The continued political confusion over the Czech and Slovak lands and arguments over the rights and wrongs of two central banks (one for the Czech lands, one for the Slovaks), has hindered the adoption of the banking law.

Basic changes to central bank activities

The National Bank will undergo a change of organisational structure, including strengthening its analytic and research abilities, creating a structural banking supervision and professional training of specialists for this purpose. The bank will create commercial units at the capital and foreign exchange market and gradually implement their activity. The National Bank will modernise its information system for merchant banking and inter-banking information system. It will also create a network of money deposit places, enabling easy supplies of money.

The National Bank is a state central bank responsible for maintaining the currency purchase power, money circulation, national payments and accounts and foreign currency policy. To realise these tasks, a strong, independent and efficient central bank is needed. At present there is insufficient legal framework to allow for this. The bank inherited from the previous, communist system, restrictive working organisational methods, mainly concerning data processing, lack of training in international banking and an imprecise and non-verified practice of currency instruments to steer and float the money and manage commercial and savings bank operations.

Law on the National Bank

The law on the National Bank defines clearly the legal relations and the position of the National Bank regarding its powers, financial and institutional independence. The organisation of the bank began its transformation at the beginning of 1991, partly as a result of the decision of the federal government to have a revolving head of the bank (Czech and Slovak) and to maintain two branches of the bank, one in Prague and the other in Bratislava.

Regulation

Banking is one of the most regulated branches of economic activity. Under the new law, the minimum capital for setting up a bank will rise. Under the old law, founding capital had already been raised from Kcs 50m to $10m or its equivalent in crowns. The terms of granting a licence are to be tightened, with special attention given to qualifications of managers. The foundation of small banking institutions with a lower opening capital will be permitted. Supervision will focus mainly on the smaller banks.

Although competition in commercial banking was introduced in 1990, the sector remained more or less a monopoly controlled by the two republican savings banks and the two republican credit banks, Commercial Bank and Common Credit Bank. (see table below)

Share of the four biggest Czechoslovak banks in total banking transactions at 30 September 1990

	Credit in bn Kcs	*Share in credits in banking (per cent)*
Credits		
Commercial Bank Prague (KB)	301.4	51.2
Common Credit Bank Bratislava (VUB)	120.6	20.5
Czech Savings Bank Prague (CSTSP)	32.8	5.6
Slovak Savings Bank Bratislava (SSTSP)	18.6	3.2
Other banks	115.5	19.5
Deposits		
Commercial Bank Prague (KB)	195.4	43.1
Common Credit Bank Bratislava (VUB)	93.1	20.5
Czech Savings Bank Prague (CSTSP)	75.1	16.6
Slovak Savings Bank Bratislava (SSTSP)	32.3	7.1
Other banks	57.2	12.7

Source: National Bank of Czechoslovakia. Note: Kcs is the Czechoslovak currency, the crown.

Commercial banks

The Commercial Bank and Common Credit Bank are state financial institutions of a similar character. They were created by separating functions out of the National Bank. They both at the beginning of 1991 had a great number of potentially bad loans due to the problems of Czechoslovakia's industrial sector. Both lack services and trained staff. One positive asset is the wide branch network, although organisationally and technically it is not efficient.

Investment Bank Prague

Investment Bank Prague, set up in January 1990, acquired a part of the assets and liabilities of the National Bank. The Finance Ministry is its founder. It is a universal bank whose activity is oriented towards financing, crediting and controlling investments. It has 13 branches. The major problem facing the bank is its lack of own payment and accounts relations and the necessity to keep its identity separate from the two main commercial banks.

Czechoslovak Commercial Bank

Czechoslovak Commercial Bank is a joint stock company with 53 per cent of its shares belonging to the National Bank. It is registered in Prague with six branch offices in Czechoslovakia, four independent representations abroad and three agencies incorporated in foreign commercial representations. It is a universal bank, authorised for foreign currency operations, specially oriented towards international payments and securing the financing of the central foreign currency reserves of the country.

Craft Bank

Craft Bank is a state financial institution founded by the National Bank with an office in Prague and a branch in London. It deals mainly with foreign accounts on behalf of private customers. In 1989 the bank took over from the Investment Bank the branch of securities of foreign issues and of the external secured loans in foreign currency. It serves as an accounting centre for Eurocheques issued for crowns.

Monopoly position by banks

This virtual monopoly by the biggest banks influences the flexibility of deposit interest rates and does not encourage dynamic development or attractive offers for bank deposits. The Commercial Bank and Common Credit Bank, because of their vast network of branches may abuse their position.

One way to break the monopoly and to force the largest commercial banks to respond better to the changing condition is to allow foreign banking activity. There are several advantages to allowing foreign banks into Czechoslovakia. First, they reinforce competition and offer better banking services. They are also better qualified, generally have more working capital as well as technical and know-how advantages. This process has already begun, with several foreign banks opening representative offices in the country. By mid-1991, at least one major joint venture foreign bank had begun operations.

Société Générale joint venture

Société Générale set up the first joint venture bank in Czechoslovakia, Société Générale Komercni Banka (SGKB).

Société Générale's interest in Czechoslovakia began in 1982, when it became the first foreign bank to open a representative office in Prague. After November 1989, the bank began looking for ways of significantly expanding its operations in the country. Komercni Banka — Czechoslovakia's largest commercial bank — has a network of over 80 branches throughout the country and planned to open 100 more in 1991.

The joint bank, SGKB, is owned 75 per cent by Société Générale with the remaining shares held by Komercni Banka.

Foreign banking operations

To open a mixed bank (foreign bank as an office or agent) the minimal starting capital for universal banks is $10m. Founding capital for specialised banking institutions is set individually. The minimal compulsory share of own resources (capital/reserves) in the bank assets is set at 8 per cent. The licence is granted by the National Bank. In principle, mixed banks will not be limited and the assets will be discussed when the licence is granted. Foreign capital will not be limited. Independent foreign banks will also be permitted, with the opening of agencies or branch offices. The authorisation for the opening of a branch office would need special permission. A total of 10 foreign banks are expected to receive a licence in 1991.

Privatisation of banks

The denationalisation and privatisation of the economy will affect banking. The privatisation of banks is expected to boost their economic activity. While rules have yet to be drawn up on the privatisation of the banking sector, the National Bank suggests the following procedure be followed:

- creation of a commission for privatisation, composed of representatives of the founders of all the state-owned banking organisations (including insurance companies) and the representatives of the privatisation ministries. The group would set out a common procedure for the process;
- the transformation of the state-owned enterprises into joint stock companies with a 100 per cent participation of the founders;
- if a decision on the issue of demonopolisation is taken, the creation of an appropriate number of joint stock companies;
- there should be clear rules on the privatisation methods: ie, application of bonuses; sale to employees and domestic investors; sale to foreign nationals;
- there should be a co-ordination of the process and an eventual determination of the state's participation in banking.

Sequencing the privatisation of banks will need to take into account their role in the privatisation of other types of enterprises.

Banking act

In late November 1991, the banking act was approved by the federal government and sent to parliament. Under the law, the state intends to retain a 40 to 50 per cent equity stake in the country's six leading commercial banks. These include two large savings banks and make up the banks hived off from the State Bank earlier in 1991. Foreign investors will, under the law, be allowed to buy up to a maximum 25 per cent of any bank's equity, but no one investor will be allowed to hold more than a 10 per cent share. These restrictions will not apply to smaller banks.

The law also sets out the legal framework for the privatisation of banks. Banks are expected to submit plans or projects for their privatisation by the end of 1991. Part of the plans will probably include the controversial coupon scheme under which equity is distributed to citizens in the form of vouchers. Privatisation of the large banks is expected to begin in spring 1992.

Training

The need to train existing and new staff for the banking system is an acute problem. Secondary, university and postgraduate studies aimed at the banking sector are needed. Together with the World Bank, a banking institute is to be set up in Prague and Bratislava. The institute will provide international teaching and training in banking. An inter-banking committee for banking education will co-ordinate professional training and organise the institute. Czechoslovak banks will be represented on the committee.

Linguistic skills of banking staff are also important. Foreign courses and secondments abroad will play an important role in the education system.

Clearing houses

A clearing house is needed to serve as an intermediary in clearing and distributing the electronic payments in national currency within the banking exchange. A clearing house has been founded by the National Bank, and will become a joint stock company owned by banks and other financial institutions, such as the stock exchange. All the banks are obliged to use the clearing house. Payment and book-keeping relations with clients is determined by the banks themselves. Work on the clearing house began in 1991.

Credit cards

By the end of 1990, at least 35,000 credit cards had been issued. There were 100 automatic cash machines installed and between 1,200 and 1,500 are to be installed in 1991, together with 100,000 cash-desk terminals. Up to 2,000, non-cash payments services will cover three-quarters of the population. But the introduction and use of credit cards and electronic banking facilities depends on the introduction of new payment instruments, technical and financial developments as well as the development of a payment system for the credit cards. This means introducing an inter-bank organisation.

Accounts and statistics

Accounting and statistical practices are to observe the recommendations of the European Community. Indexes will be set so they reflect the financial standing of the bank, its liquidity and quality. New accountancy reports were obligatory from 1 January 1991. The new set of accounts will be introduced — at the latest — by 1 January 1993. From 1991, banks have the choice to adapt their book-keeping to the new requirements or use an analytic organisation of accounts.

Money market

Competition for the Czechoslovak money market is increasing. Banks are now offering private depositors, as well as commercial clients, higher interest rates on deposit accounts.

Capital markets

In 1990 Czechoslovakia issued its first bonds. These were issued by companies and some banks, but there were no state bonds. In 1990 the bond law was also issued. In 1991 Czechoslovakia began preparations on the law of the stock exchange. This project was undertaken jointly by the State Bank and the Finance Ministry. International bodies, in particular the World Bank, recommended that many functions of supervision of the exchange and banking system remain with the State Bank, rather than with the Finance Ministry.

The law on the stock exchange is expected to be passed by the end of 1991. Only a small volume of securities were traded in 1991 as in reality there is no capital market just yet. The value of bonds issued in 1990 was around Kcs 4.2bn but only around Kcs 2bn were traded, and only through banks.

Stock exchange

In 1871 a stock exchange was established in Prague, 100 years after the Vienna exchange began operations. The exchange was closed in 1945. The new exchange operates from the parliament building in Prague.

There are several economic, technical and legislative problems concerning the setting up of a stock exchange in Czechoslovakia. First, there is no law covering the operation of the exchange and second, there is no proper building for the stock exchange. The main legislative questions still to be answered include the activity of trade and financial matters, settling of the investors' protection principles, stock exchange quoting of securities, requirements on prospects and inquiries on issuing houses, principles of advertising the transactions and price quoting, principles of trading listed and unlisted securities, ways of resolving trade litigations, principles of keeping some information confidential and insider trading.

Securities law

There is some controversy over the preparation of a securities law. The State Bank would prefer to see a separate securities law while the Finance Ministry wants only a bond law and a law covering the stock exchange. The Ministry thinks it will be sufficient to put rules for securities within the commercial law, which is expected to be completed in 1991. The Finance Ministry wants all trade and deposits and questions of capital markets put in the commercial law, rather than a separate securities law. The practice throughout Europe is to have separate laws on the stock exchange and securities. Until the laws are written and passed, the State Bank will continue to license the operations of stock exchange dealers, as most of these activities are done by banks, which are under the supervision of the State Bank. Brokers at present are only found in the banks which trade with the securities. There is as yet no division of the banking sector into commercial and investment banks, but that is expected in future.

The Finance Ministry wants to set up a stock exchange commission to supervise the operations of the exchange and to license its dealers. There are no plans in the initial stages to separate the banking and brokerage activities. It appears the Czechoslovaks will rely on their own experience before deciding what to do.

Most expect the Czechoslovak exchange to end up similar to the Frankfurt exchange. The Finance Ministry is preparing a stock exchange law which follows German law, although other major exchanges, in particular New York and London, are being studied. The general opinion appears to be that an order-driven system where an official broker sets the price as opposed to market markers (London and New York) would be more appropriate to Czechoslovakia.

The joint stock company law and the state enterprise law are to be combined into a new commercial (company) law.

Secondary market

Czechoslovakia's secondary market will operate as an auction organised by the State Bank together with the some of the commercial banks. At the same time, an organisational preparatory committee is working on setting up the stock exchange.

Auctions

Auctions began in February 1991 and were to continue, twice a month on Wednesdays, until the stock exchange was functioning. Every bank will have a seat at the auctions through an agent. The agent will buy and sell the securities for clients. Only agents for the commercial banks and the State Bank will be able to take part in the auctions.

The State Bank and commercial banks will act as an official broker, setting prices of shares and securities (bonds). The problem is not securities at present. The primary market will not trade for some time, although the government hopes to start it in earnest in 1991.

The preparatory committee is to decide the regulation of the stock exchange. The group consists of 10 banks: the major nine commercial banks plus the State Bank. The task of this committee is to prepare the establishment of the exchange, choose people to run it and send them to developed West European countries for training on their exchanges. The State Bank has already contacted stock exchanges in Europe as well as in the US for training. About 30 people will be trained for up to two months in the first programme. Frankfurt, Brussels, Amsterdam, Milan, Vienna, Paris and London are all involved. There is also contact with some companies which are advising. Coopers and Lybrand Deloittes is acting as adviser together with the Toronto Stock exchange, one of the official advisers. Other firms are expected to help.

Trading volume

Trading volume of securities increased gradually after the first auction. To begin with only bonds of Komercni Bank and Vseobecna Uverova Banka were traded. The traded price of bonds stabilised at their face value. Bonds of Tos Kurim enterprise appeared next on the market. Tos Kurim's sale of bonds was handled by Atlantic Holdings of the US. The nominal value of the issue totalled \$50m. The bonds, in values of \$1,000, \$5,000 and \$10,000, were on sale in Prague and Kurim in August 1991.

The number of banks present at the auctions increased to five by autumn 1991, from an initial four. The provisional secondary market started operating in autumn 1991.

Auction funds

The proceeds from the auction sales are transferred to a special account of the Ministry of Privatisation of the Czech republic, kept with the Czech State Saving Bank. The same procedure applies in the Slovak republic where the special account is with the Slovak State Saving Bank. Another source of income of the accounts may be the final proceeds from the liquidation of state enterprises.

Over the first nine months of 1991, the State Bank decided what kind of information and training systems together with clearing and settlement operations will be used by the fledgeling exchange.

The country has considerable political problems in setting up an exchange. As a result of political tensions, two exchanges will operate: one in Prague (the Czech republic) and one in Bratislava (the Slovak republic).

Investment funds

A law on investment funds is being written by the Finance Ministry. Investment banks have been set up in Czechoslovakia and by the end of the first quarter of 1991, three mutual funds were established. These funds are joint stock companies.

In 1991 the authorities are confident that the stock exchange will begin operation, but only a small volume of shares and bonds will be traded at the start, and probably mainly using an auction method. There are plans to use both Vienna and Budapest exchanges at the beginning. The Hungarian Investment Bank of Budapest has set up a subsidiary in Prague (with connections to Merrill Lynch), and is expected to help Czechoslovak companies prepare for share listing on the Budapest exchange. By the end of 1992/beginning of 1993, the authorities expect volume to be higher and a physical building will be needed. Preparations for opening an exchange continued in 1991.

Privatisation

The large-scale privatisation bill, effective from 1 April 1991, establishes the National Property Fund which took over all the debts and liabilities of enterprises prior to their sale. It will hold shares of enterprises not immediately privatised. Members of the fund will be proposed by the federal government and approved by parliament.

The fund will be responsible on behalf of the federal, Czech and Slovak governments for the privatisation process. Federal law covers the details of how each individual privatisation should proceed. The Czech and Slovak funds will carry out the privatisation. Proceeds from the majority of privatisation sales will go to the Czech and Slovak governments, rather than to the federal government.

The governments have three months to draft the guidelines for privatisation. Property which is subject to restitution claims will not be included in the privatisation.

Enterprise privatisation plans

Under the law, each enterprise will determine its own plan for privatisation, which has to be approved by the ministries of industry and privatisation of the Czech or Slovak republics. A time limit has been placed on the completion of privatisation. The first step will be the transformation of state enterprises into joint stock companies, followed by an asset valuation.

Methods of privatisation

Various methods will be allowed for privatisation. The controversial coupon or voucher scheme is to play a small part in the process. The coupons are to be distributed by the Finance Ministry and not by the State Bank.

Vouchers

By the end of 1991 property assessments were defined, giving guidance on how to price capital assets and land. Also by the end of 1991, each individual enterprise to be privatised was expected say how much of its shares are to be distributed through the voucher system.

Restitution claims will be settled through a Restitution Fund. Shares of these funds will be offered at a nominal value equivalent to the restitution claim to those persons whose property claims are legally upheld. It will be difficult to define beforehand how much of the privatised enterprise will go to the Restitution Fund. Each privatisation project must earmark at least 3 per cent of its shares to meet eventual restitution claims. The Restitution Fund were set up by the respective national property funds by November 1991.

The quota for the vouchers to be distributed will depend on the circumstances of each individual enterprise. The owner of vouchers may appoint someone to act as a proxy or use an intermediary, mainly financial institutions such as banks, to buy and trade the vouchers.

As there is still no legislation on investment funds, the use of financial institutions by voucher holders is not yet clear. Nevertheless, some investment funds already exist in Czechoslovakia. The Privatisation Investment Fund is to be set up and function under present rules. The fund will buy shares of various joint stock companies using vouchers transferred to it by its shareholders.

Postponement in Czech lands

In October 1991, the Czech republic decided to postpone the coupon privatisation plan. The move met with significant criticism from the federal Finance Ministry which said the move was "disloyal" and would cost the economy millions of dollars each month in delay. Later in November, the Czech government decided to postpone privatisation of the republic's largest companies.

Czech privatisation

Property to be privatised in the Czech republic alone is estimated to be worth Kcs 550bn. Out of this, Kcs 360bn worth of property represents industrial enterprises under the supervision of the Czech Industry Ministry. The majority of these enterprises will be sold to private persons in the course of the large privatisation programme. Within the jurisdiction of the Czech Industry Ministry there are 1,321 enterprises earmarked for privatisation. Annual turnover of these companies ranges from \$50m to \$500m. Enterprises which have been chosen for the small privatisation (auction) as well as those under threat of liquidation are not listed.

In the Czech republic by the end of September 1991, over 19,760 businesses were approved for privatisation. Out of this number, 9,514 were privatised and 8,310 sold through auctions which raised Kcs 6.879bn. Over 1,110 businesses were leased, worth Kcs 163m. Eighty-seven businesses were given back to the original owners.

The highest number of businesses approved for privatisation, about 3,500, as well as those privatised (about 1,500) were in northern Bohemia. The lowest number were in southern Bohemia where only 1,500 enterprises were approved for privatisation and 750 actually privatised.

Slovak privatisation

Ivan Miklos, the Privatisation Minister for the Slovak republic, admitted in the autumn of 1991 that privatisation in Slovakia had not proceeded at the expected pace, both for the small- and large-scale privatisations. The Slovak government approved in August 1991 a list of enterprises earmarked for privatisation where foreign capital could participate. Out of the total number of around 2,000 state enterprises and organisations, 736 were in the preliminary selection for the first wave of privatisation which will begin in January 1992 and last until June 1992.

Around 562 enterprises are listed for the second wave of privatisation, to start in the second half of 1992. Over 600 enterprises will not be privatised, including those where property rights have not yet been clarified. Some enterprises are expected to go bankrupt while others may survive to enter the "third wave" of privatisation. In the first phase of privatisation in Slovakia, the total value of state property amounts to around Kcs 166bn. Different privatisation methods are to be used, including the voucher scheme which is expected to account for about Kcs 101bn worth of property.

In the second wave, the total value of property to be evaluated is set at Kcs 208bn, out of which over Kcs 97bn will be sold through the voucher method. Enterprises were expected to have submitted privatisation projects for approval to the Slovak ministry by the end of October.

Bratislava exchange

A commodity stock exchange has been registered in Bratislava. Known as Bratislava International Stock Exchange, it names among its founding shareholders the Moscow Commodity Exchange, Finvestbank of Moscow, Bizniscentrum of the Russian Federation, Prior Bank of Minsk, Delakt Moscow and the Austrian company ORWZ.

Initial capital is Kcs 50m. A broker's seat costs Kcs 200,000. Organisation is similar to the Moscow Commodity Exchange.

Auction privatisation

By November 1991, 3,000 small businesses and shops had been privatised through auctions. Over 15,400 small businesses, worth a total of Kcs 11.6bn, were approved under the small privatisation scheme in the Czech republic alone in 1991. Out of this number, 7,092 were sold for a total of Kcs 5.8bn by October 1991.

In the Czech republic in the first six months of 1991, proceeds from the sale by auction of small privatisations amounted to over Kcs 3.118bn. During the same period, funds were used from the account to cover the expenses of the work of the privatisation commission.

At the end of June 1991 in the Slovak republic, the overall proceeds kept on special account reached over Kcs 475m with expenditures of over Kcs 1.2m.

Exemptions

Privatisation will not affect certain specific organisations, such as testing laboratories for precious metals and technical apprentice establishments. The large-scale privatisation of industrial enterprises will take place in two stages. Projects for the first stage must be worked out and submitted to the industry ministry by 31 October 1991 and for the second stage by 31 May 1992. Over two-thirds of the industrial enterprises would like to be included in the first wave of privatisation. This will not be possible due to the sheer number of companies being privatised. In most cases, a combination of privatisation methods and techniques will be used, including vouchers, property restitution and direct sales to original owners as well as auctions, foreign capital investment and transformation initially into wholly-owned state joint stock companies.

Privatisation of shares owned by the state will be linked mainly with restructuring through direct investments. Modernisation of major industrial enterprises in the Czech republic will not be able to take place without substantial foreign capital participation. Direct investments by foreign companies should also include managerial and employee share sales at preferential rates.

Foreign investment

The Czech industry ministry has a programme for direct foreign investments. The implementation of this programme will be carried out with help from foreign consultants including Bankers Trust International, Arthur D Little, Arthur Andersen and Squire, Sanders & Dempsey. The team is now helping select the enterprises most suitable for foreign capital participation.

Law on conditions on which state property is transferred to other persons

Part I: Subject and scope

ARTICLE 1

This act determines the conditions by which state property administered by state enterprises, state banking institutions, state insurance groups and other state organisations (hereinafter referred to as 'enterprises'), including their participations in the entrepreneurial activities of other juristical persons and the conditions under which this property of the state is transferred to Czechoslovak or foreign juristic or natural persons (hereinafter referred to as 'privatisation').

This act also applies to the property of the foreign trade enterprises and purpose-made organisations of foreign trade (foreign trade organisations) and their property participations in the entrepreneurial activity of other juristic persons.

The condition stated in this act under which state property is transferred will not apply to property which according to the constitutional acts or special acts is deemed to be the ownership of the state only.

ARTICLE 2
For the purposes of this act, the property of the enterprise includes both the physical and financial means administered or owned by the enterprise or the rights, assets and obligations of the enterprise.

ARTICLE 3
This act applies to the property which is to be returned to juristic persons under special rules (1).

This act does not apply to the property under the ownership of the churches, monastic orders, congregations and religious societies which was transferred to the state administration after 25 February 1948.

The property which natural persons can claim according to the provisions of special rules (2) can be the subject of this act if such a person did not claim his or her property rights by the last day of the fixed term or if such claim was refused.

ARTICLE 4
The property cannot be transferred according to the act if such property was proposed or determined to be transferred from the state to the ownership of other juristical or natural persons under special rules (3) until the decision is made not to register the property in the list of operational units designed for such transfer or excluded from the list (4).

Part II: Privatisation projects

ARTICLE 5
The transfer of property according to this act is carried out on the basis of approved privatisation projects drawn up by the enterprise or when there is an approved privatisation project for the state participation in the entrepreneurial activity.

ARTICLE 6
Privatisation project of the enterprise

The privatisation project of the enterprise is understood to include economic, technical, property, time and other data containing:

(a) indication of the enterprise and the scope of the property designed for the privatisation referred to as 'privatisation property';

(b) data concerning the manner in which the state acquired the privatised property;
(c) data stating the part of the property not suitable for entrepreneurial purposes (for example uncollectable bills, non-used stocks and production);
(d) valuation of privatised property;
(e) the manner of transferring privatisation property, including the settlement of claims;
(f) the legal form in case of the establishment of a company;
(g) in case of the establishment of a joint stock company, the manner in which the shares are divided, the amount of shares, the kinds of shares and the data concerning the use and possible use of investment coupons;
(h) in case of sale, its form, setting a price and payment terms;
(i) in case it is governed by Article 11, paragraph 3, the fixing of shares of privatised property according to Article 11, paragraph 4;
(j) the manner in which the industrial rights or other intellectual property approved by the Federal Institute for Inventions are transferred, if such rights are the property of the enterprise;
(k) a time schedule for the privatisation project.

The privatisation project of the enterprise (besides the requisites stated above) can also contain:

(a) a recommendation concerning the sphere of entrepreneurial activity;
(b) information on the persons who are interested in the purchase of the enterprise or involved in the establishment of a company using the property of the enterprise or in the purchase of shares of the newly established company;
(c) data on the position of the enterprise in the market, existing or supposed;
(d) information giving the number and the structure of employees.

The privatisation project may concern only a part of the enterprise, the whole enterprise or the property of several enterprises.

ARTICLE 7

The founder (referred to as "the founder") to whom the privatisation project proposals of the enterprise are passed, is responsible for the carrying out of the privatisation project.

The privatisation project is worked out by the enterprise itself. If the privatisation project is worked out by the founder or someone outside the enterprise, the founder will receive the proposal from the enterprise.

The founder can tell the enterprise to work out the privatisation project and set the appropriate terms for its realisation.

The enterprise will inform the competent trade union authority about the privatisation proposal.

ARTICLE 8

The founder will consider the privatisation project passed to him and, together with his statement, submit them without unnecessary delay to be approved by:

(a) the Federal Finance Ministry, if the founder is a central agency of the federal state administration;
(b) the competent agency of a republic administration in all other cases.

The founder, in accordance with Article 1, will submit all proposals, including those which are not recommended by him, together with his statement.

ARTICLE 9

Privatisation project on property participation of the state in the entrepreneurial activity

The central agency of federal state administration which exercises the rights of the state concerning the property of the entrepreneurial activity of juristic persons is responsible for working out the privatisation project on such property participations within a term stated by the Government of Czechoslovakia and submitting it to the Federal Finance Ministry.

The republic agency of state administration or municipality, which exercises the right of the state arising from property participation in the entrepreneurial activity of juristic persons is responsible for working out the privatisation projects in such property participations within a term stated by the government of the Czech republic or the government of the Slovak republic (hereinafter referred to as 'republic governments') and submitting them to the competent republic agency of state administration.

The privatisation project (referred to as 'privatisation project on participation') contains appropriate requisites of the privatisation project of the enterprise.

The proposal of the privatisation project on participation works out juristic persons concerned hereof as a rule. The procedure stated in paragraphs 7 and 8 will apply appropriately.

ARTICLE 10

The act of approval of privatisation projects

The privatisation project of the enterprise and the privatisation project on participation are approved and published by:

(a) the Federal Finance Ministry if the central agency of federal state administration is a founder or exercises the rights of the state concerning property participation of juristic persons;
(b) the competent republic agency of state administration in other cases.

The Czechoslovak Government or the republic governments may withhold approval of the privatisation project of the enterprise and the privatisation project on participation.

When there is a direct sale, apart from a public competition or a public sale, the approval of the privatisation project is governed by the provisions of paragraph 2.

Part III: Transfer of privatised property to funds and the use of the property of funds

ARTICLE 11

In accordance with an approved privatisation project, the founder ends the enterprise without winding up or excluding a part of the property of the enterprise.

If by the time of the winding up the founder of the enterprise is the central agency of federal state administration, the privatisation property will be transferred to the Federal Fund of the National Property set up under this act according to Article 29 (hereinafter referred to as "Fund") on the day on which the enterprise ceases to exist or the day on which a part of the property is excluded. This is not valid in cases detailed in Article 42.

If the founder of the enterprise is a republic agency or a municipality on the date on which the enterprise ceases to exist, or a part of the property is excluded, the privatised property will be transferred to the Fund of National Property of the Czech Republic or the Fund of National Property of the Slovak Republic (referred to as "republic funds") which are governed by the national council's acts.

The following will be transferred to the competent republic fund according to paragraph three:

(a) the part of the privatisation property which is situated on the territory of the appropriate republic;
(b) the financial means and property consisting of titles and obligations and activity;
(c) the financial means and property consisting of titles and obligations which are not owned by the property to be privatised are transferred to the appropriate republic fund according to paragraphs (a) and (b).

Before the property is transferred according to paragraphs 2 and 3, the enterprise deals with a part of non-used property (Article 6, paragraph 1, part (c)) in accordance with approved privatisation project.

The founder will not exclude part of the property of the enterprise to which industrial rights or intellectual property ownership rights are adhered to or which is created by them (Article 6, paragraph 1, sentence (j)). These rights are transferred by means of a contract.

If all property of the enterprise is transferred to the Fund or the republic funds, the establishment of the company or the sale of the property is to be held on the same date on which the extinction of the enterprise without winding it up takes place.

On the date fixed in the approved privatisation project, the central agency of federal state administration will transfer all rights concerning these participations to the Fund and the republic agencies of state administration and the municipalities will transfer them to the competent republic fund.

ARTICLE 12

The property of the Fund and the republic funds (referred to as 'funds') does not go to the state budgets. It may only be used for the purposes specified by the law.

The property of the funds may be used in accordance with the approved privatisation project in the following ways:

(a) for the establishment of a joint stock company or other companies (5) and for the disposal of property participation in these companies;
(b) for sale of the property of the enterprise or its parts;
(c) for transfer of the privatisation property to municipalities;
(d) for transfer of the privatisation property to old age pensions and health insurance purposes.

The disposal of the property may be carried out without authorisation according to special rules (6).

Any claims of entitled persons may be covered from the property of the funds according to the special rules (7).

The obligations of the enterprises designed for privatisation may be covered by using the property of the funds.

ARTICLE 13

In selling the property of the funds, no advantage will be granted. In selling the shares, only the advantage granted under the Joint Stock Companies Act will be granted.

ARTICLE 14

The sale of the privatised property will be carried out by the funds on the basis of a contract concluded with the purchaser or in a public auction. If the sale is carried out in a public auction, the provisions of special rules (3) governing the transfer of the property to the state apply.

If the privatised property has invested capital in a company, the proceedings of such funds is governed by the special rules (3).

ARTICLE 15

If the privatised property is sold or if it is invested to the capital stock of a business company, the title of ownership as well as other rights and obligations connected with the privatised property will be acquired by the date on which the contract enters into effect.

The transfer of outstanding debts is governed by the provisions of the special rules concerning the assignment of claims.

The creditor's consent is not required in case of transferring of the obligation. However, the Fund stands with its assets for the obligation of the acquirer of privatisation property.

The acquirer is obliged to inform the creditors without delay on his assumption of the obligation.

ARTICLE 16
The industrial rights or intellectual property ownership rights are transferred on the basis of a contract concluded between the acquirer and the enterprise.

ARTICLE 17
Rights and obligations of the enterprise arising from labour law relations to employees of the enterprise or its organisational unit applying to the privatisation shall pass on to the acquirer.

ARTICLE 18
In case all the property of the enterprise is privatised and no other arrangements arise from a contract or a legal act through which the property of the enterprise is invested to the capital stock of a business company, the title to use of the commercial name passes to the acquirer if it is not contrary to the law governing the usage of commercial name. Transferring this title will not be prevented by the amendment of the addition to the commercial name which defines legal form of the enterprise.

ARTICLE 19
Within the date of the effectiveness of a contract or an investment, the Fund is obliged to deliver and the acquirer is obliged to accept the delivery of the items belonging to the privatised property. The protocol on the acceptance of the things upon delivery will be drawn up and signed by both parties.

The ownership of the physical objects and the risks to this property will pass to the acquirer on completion of the transaction.

To acquire ownership of immovables, registration under special rules (8) is required.

ARTICLE 20
The protocol of the acceptance of physical objects upon delivery (Article 19, paragraph 1) will list any missing or damaged objects. Unless the contract provides otherwise, missing things which were not transferred to the acquirer, although according to the contract they form a part of the property, are transferred. The defect will be considered with regard to its ability to be used in

the operation of the enterprise and with regard to the period of use of the thing according to the accounting records.

ARTICLE 21
On the transferring of physical objects and drawing up the protocol of the acceptance of physical objects upon delivery, the Fund is represented by the persons entitled to act in the name of the enterprise on the day on which the enterprise ceases to exist or a part of the property of the enterprise was excluded. These persons are responsible.

Part IV: Investment coupons

ARTICLE 22
An investment coupon (referred to as 'coupon' for the purposes of this act) is deemed to be a security registered in the name of its owner, giving the owner the right to buy the shares which are designed for purchase using the coupons. The coupon may not be transferred and rights pertaining to it may be transferred to a specified heir only.

The coupon may not be declared invalid.

ARTICLE 23
The requisites of the coupon are:

(a) the name of the citizen and birth certificate number;
(b) designation of the agency which issued the coupon;
(c) acquiring price;
(d) validity period;
(e) date of issue.

Coupons are issued by the Federal Finance Ministry.

The net yield of the sale of coupons will be transferred to appropriate republic fund according to the place of residence of the acquirer of coupons on the day on which the coupons were acquired.

ARTICLE 24
Each Czechoslovak citizen who resides in the territory of the republics and who is 18 years of age on the date of issue, is entitled to acquire the coupons.

ARTICLE 25
The coupons may be used for:

(a) the purchase of shares of any joint stock company included for this purpose in the list of privatisation projects, provided the citizen asserts his claim within the period of time stated in such list;
(b) obtaining participation in companies specially set up for this purpose. Prior consent of the competent republic agency is necessary.

The provisions of paragraphs 1 and 2 may be applied parallely.

ARTICLE 26
The owner of coupons may deal with coupons being represented by a natural or a juristic person on the basis and to the extent of written authorisation.

Part V: Federal Fund of National Property

ARTICLE 27
The Federal Fund of National Property is being set up as a juristical operation. The Fund is registered in the register of companies.

The organs of the Fund are the presidium, the executive committee and the supervisory board.

The property of the Fund consists of the property transferred to the Fund according to Article 11, paragraph 2, and the profit of the Fund gained by the participation in the entrepreneurial activity of business companies.

The details of the organisation of the Fund and its activity are given in the statute approved by the presidium of the Fund.

ARTICLE 28
According to an approved privatisation project, the Fund concludes contracts in its own name and performs other legal acts:

(a) establishes joint stock and other companies or participates in their establishment and investments;
(b) acquires the shares based on its participation in the entrepreneurial activity of joint stock companies and performs the rights of a shareholder and attends the general meetings;
(c) performs the right of a partner participating in other than joint stock companies;
(d) participates in economic results of a company; it takes part in the entrepreneurial activity of such a company and bears the consequences (profits or losses);
(e) sells the joint stock shares or other company shares;
(f) participates in the winding up of the company to the extent of its participation in the activity of the company if the company is wound up;
(g) concludes contracts for sale of the enterprises, their organisational units and their property parts, using the public competition;
(h) rents these assets during limited period until they are used for the privatisation.

The Fund employs the specialists who are awarded upon the consent of the presidium.

ARTICLE 29

The Fund acquires the rights and assumes obligations arising from the activities outlined in Article 28. The Fund is entitled to claim its rights by the court or other competent body. The Fund may be accused of not meeting its commitments and other obligations for which it stands with its assets.

ARTICLE 30

The highest organ of the Fund is the presidium which will have nine members. The chairman and vice-chairman and the members of the presidium are elected on a proposal of the Czechoslovak Government by the Federal Assembly for a period of five years. The members of the Czechoslovak Government, the members of the government of the Czech republic and the government of the Slovak republic, deputy of the Federal Assembly, the Czech National Council and the Slovak National Council will not be elected as a member of the presidium.

ARTICLE 31

The presidium is competent to:

(a) appoint and rule the executive committee and supervise its dealings;
(b) approve the statute of the Fund;
(c) approve the rewarding of the members of the executive committee;
(d) work out the proposal of the budget of the Fund and submit it to the Government of the Czech and Slovak Federative Republic for discussion;
(e) approve the order of proceedings of the presidium and the executive committee;
(f) discuss annual financial statement and submit it to the Czechoslovak Government for discussion;
(g) discuss by 30 April at the latest the annual report of activities of the Fund concerning the previous year.

After being discussed in the Czechoslovak Government the budget proposal and the annual financial statement are submitted by the Fund to the Federal Assembly for the approval.

ARTICLE 32

The presidium is capable of dealing if its meeting is attended by more than half of its members including the chairman or vice-chairman. The decisions are made at least by a clear majority of present votes. In case of equality the chairman has the casting vote.

In the name of the presidium the chairman and in his absence the vice-chairman signs the documents.

ARTICLE 33

The activity of the Fund is directed upon the instruction of the presidium by the executive committee of the Fund (referred to as 'committee').

The committee acts in the name of the Fund to the extent limited by the statute. The statute defines which of the written legal acts will be signed by two members of the committee. Statute determines when and to which extent of their powers the members of the committee act in the name of the Fund and grant the appointment to act in the name of the Fund to the third persons. The members of the committee who are entitled to act in the name of the Fund will be entered in the register of companies.

ARTICLE 34
The committee consists of nine members appointed by the presidium for a period of five years. Before the expiration of this period the presidium may suspend the member of the committee in case he breaches his duties or is not able to perform his function properly.

The chairman of the committee, and not more than two vice-chairmen are elected by the members of the committee.

The members of the committee are the employees of the Fund.

ARTICLE 35
The supervisory board of the Fund (referred to as 'board') supervises the activity and the management of the Fund, its presidium and committee. The board advises the presidium, the Czechoslovak Government, Federal Assembly, and any other competent agency of any discrepancies.

The presidium is obliged to discuss the budget proposal and the annual financial statement in the board before submitting the same to the Czechoslovak Government.

ARTICLE 36
The board consists of five members elected by the Federal Assembly for a period of five years. The Federal Assembly may suspend a member of the board prior to the end of his function period. The election and the suspension of the members of the board is carried out by secret voting.

The members of the board may not be the employees of the Fund.

ARTICLE 37
The chairman and the vice-chairman are elected by the members of the board.

The provisions of Article 32 will apply.

ARTICLE 38
The functions of the members of the presidium, the committee and the board are incompatible.

ARTICLE 39
The members of the presidium, committee, board and the employees of the Fund will not carry out the activities which are against the interest of the Fund.

They will not be the members of the joint stock company organs in the business activity in which the Fund participates. The members of the presidium, committee and board will not acquire the property of the Fund with the exception of shares bought for coupons.

ARTICLE 40

The Fund reimburses the costs connected with its activity from its assets beyond the scope of its budget approved by the Federal Assembly.

Part VI: Special, interim and final provisions

ARTICLE 41

For the purpose of the privatisation and using the coupons, the Czechoslovak Government and the governments of the republics will work out the fundamental articles within three months from the effectiveness of this act. On the basis of these principles the competent central agencies of state administration and the municipalities will submit lists of enterprises and the lists of the property participation of the state in the entrepreneurial activity of other juristic persons implied to the privatisation to the appropriate government for its approval.

The lists of enterprises submitted for the approval contain namely the commercial name of the enterprise, the seat of the enterprise, the founder, appraisement of the property and the number of employees of the enterprise. The lists of the property participation of the state in the entrepreneurial activity of other juristic persons submitted for approval contain namely the name of the juristic person, its legal form, the sphere of its entrepreneurial activity and the scope of the property participation of the state in such activity.

The Czechoslovak Government and the governments of the republics will set the period of time for working out the privatisation projects.

ARTICLE 42

The property of foreign trade enterprises, purpose-made organisations of foreign trade, state banking institutions (with the exception of the Czechoslovak State Bank and the state savings bank established by the day on which this act comes into effect) will be, according to the privatisation project of enterprise, transferred to the fund of national property of those republics on whose territory the enterprise to be privatised is located and be invested to the capital stock of joint stock companies established by the Fund.

If the property of a privatised enterprise passes to the Fund of National Property of the Czech republic, one-third of the shares of the established joint stock company will be transferred to the Fund of National Property of the Slovak republic by the former Fund. If the property of a privatised enterprise passes to the Fund of National Property of the Slovak republic, two-thirds of the shares of the established joint stock company will be transferred to the Fund of National Property of the Czech republic.

If the enterprises mentioned in paragraph 1 either converted to the joint stock companies or were established as joint stock companies before the day on which this act came into effect, the participation of the state on the entrepreneurial activity of the said companies pass in the scope of two-thirds on to the Fund of National Property of the Czech republic and in the scope of one-third to the Fund of National Property of the Slovak republic on the day of the approval of the privatisation project.

ARTICLE 43

The provisions of this act concerning the central agencies of federal state administration shall apply to the Czechoslovak State Bank.

ARTICLE 44

The appraisement of the property of the enterprise contained in approved privatisation project substitutes the assessment of the non-monetary contribution to the capital stock of a joint stock company made by the sworn expert and required according to the special rules (9).

ARTICLE 45

Outside the scope of normal business enterprises may not conclude the contracts on the transfer of ownership title to the property administered by them, dispose of their property participations in the entrepreneurial activity of juristic persons, nor such persons establish.

The exceptions from the provision of paragraph 1 thereof may be granted in reasonable cases by respective government. The granted exception substitutes the authorisation issued according to the special rules (6).

Property participations of the state in the entrepreneurial activity of juristic persons may be disposed upon approved privatisation project only.

The provisions of paragraphs 1 and 2 will not apply to juristic persons stated in Article 1, paragraph 2, and to the budget-financed and the contributional state organisations.

ARTICLE 46

Legal conditions of the republic funds, their activity and the manner of using their property will be regulated by way of National Councils' Acts. These acts shall also specify the cases in which the property of the republic funds may be used for purposes different from the privatisation.

The Czechoslovak Government, upon the consent of the republic governments, will state by way of a government decree the manner of issuing of coupons, different kinds of coupons, acquiring price of coupons, the manner of expressing the extent of a claim for shares and the manner of using a coupon.

ARTICLE 47

In case the withdrawal of the ownership title to the privatised property or to its part was made under the proceedings provided in Article 2, paragraph 3, of Act No .../1991 Coll. on out-of-trial rehabilitations, the persons entitled upon the said act therefrom will claim their title in a way stated in the privatisation project connected with the respective property.

The entitled person is obliged to claim own title within six months from the date of the effectiveness of this act by the agency competent to approve the privatisation project according to Article 10, paragraph 1, otherwise the title will be extinguished.

ARTICLE 48

The following regulations are repealed: Article 28 of the Act No 111/1990 Coll. on state enterprises; and Legal Measure No 384/1990 Coll. on disposal of state enterprise property.

ARTICLE 49

This act comes into effect 1 April 1991.

Notes

(1) For instance, Act 298/1990 Coll. on governing material relations of monastic orders and congregations and of the Archbishop of Olomouc.

(2) For instance, Act 403/1990 Coll. on moderation of consequences resulting from some material injuries, in the wording of the Act 456/1990 Coll.

(3) Act 427/1990 Coll. on transfers of state ownership of some things to other juristic or natural persons, in the wording of Act 541/1990 Coll.

(4) Czech National Council Law 500/1990 Coll. concerning the competence of agencies of the Czech Republic in cases of transfer of state ownership of some things to other juristic or natural persons.
Slovak National Council Law 474/1990 Coll. concerning the competence of agencies of the Slovak Republic in cases of transfer of state ownership of some things to other juristic or natural persons.

(5) Act 104/1990 Coll. on joint stock companies.
Act 109/1964 Coll., the Economic Code as amended on later occasions.

(6) Act 173/1988 Coll. on the enterprise with foreign property participation in the wording of Act 112/1990 Coll.

(7) Act 40/1964 Coll., the Civil Code.
Act 109/1964 Coll., the Economic Code, in the wording of subsequent provisions.

Act 101/1963 Coll., On Legal Relations Arising in International Business Transactions (the International Trade Code).

(8) Act 95/1963 Coll. on state notaries and procedures before state notaries, in the wording of subsequent provisions.

(9) Act 104/1990 Coll. on joint stock companies.

Chapter 4

HUNGARY

The State Property Agency, together with the Ministries of Trade and Industry and Agriculture, published in December 1990 the second privatisation programme. Organisations carrying on business and state enterprises which had more than 50 per cent of their assets invested in companies had to convert themselves into companies within two years. As under the first privatisation programme, the SPA entrusted the privatisation process to advisers.

To accelerate the process of privatisation, the SPA gave investors an opportunity to make an offer for the purchase of state enterprises of their choice or shares in companies which constitute the property of the state. Such opportunities were open to both domestic and foreign investors.

Spontaneous privatisation

Spontaneous privatisation is a procedure under which privatisation is initiated by the enterprise itself. The privatisation procedure initiated by the investor follows an announcement by the SPA confirming that any individual or corporation or groups constituted by them may submit an offer for investment in any state enterprise or any share in state enterprises or specific assets which can be severed from a state enterprise except the following:

- state-owned companies under Law LXXIV of 1990 on the privatisation of the retail trade and services;
- companies in the privatisation programmes of the SPA;
- companies whose transformation into association has been earlier determined either by the SPA or by the company itself;
- public utilities;
- financial institutions;

- companies that dominate over 40 per cent of the domestic market regarding their main activity.

The offers are considered by the SPA on a competitive basis and consequently the prospective investors must be prepared to bear the consequences of their offer being subject to scrutiny according to market forces.

The SPA published a brochure containing the terms, conditions and particulars under which investors prepare and submit their initial offer. The brochure also sets out the proceedings whereby the SPA offers and how one offer is made to compete with other offers.

Property management

The SPA has organised a system of management of the property under its control. The purpose of the property management is further to advance the progress of privatisation in a way that secures the preservation and the increase of the value of the property in question.

The SPA invited tenders for the management of the state-owned property. The tenders contain a definition of the asset packages under the particular management control and the terms and conditions of the management and the remuneration. According to their nature, tenders may be open or closed. The management contracts are made for a fixed term and may contain provisions for transferring ownership in the property involved.

Domestic and foreign enterprises can bid on equal terms. Non-residents may only enter into such contracts if they agree to the formation of a company for this particular purpose in Hungary.

Depending on the characters of the property to be put under such management, the SPA expects to attract the interest of commercial banks, of companies (holdings) already engaged in property management, of brokerages, of professional advisers and of investment funds.

The information sheets dealing with property management generally and brochures dealing with public tenders may be purchased at the Privatisation Programme Office.

SPA regulation

The SPA is regulated by Act VII of 1990 and Act LII of 1990 (parliament placed the SPA under the supervision of the government from July 1990, instead of parliament itself exercising the supervisory function) and the day-to-day functioning of the SPA is controlled by the State Audit Office.

Since its establishment on 1 March until December 1990, the SPA dealt with 182 cases of privatisation. In 1990, 145 final decisions were made. Of these, 115 privatisation schemes were approved by the SPA and 84 of these were made under the agency's jurisdiction by virtue of the act regarding the Protection for

State Assets. The total value of assets involved amounts to Forint 38bn. Non-resident participation amounts to 42 per cent. In 23 further cases, the SPA approved, respectively participated in the formation of companies pursuant to the act dealing with the transformation of state enterprises and in these cases the state assets involved have been revalued to not less than Forint 35bn. Participation of the state in these companies amounts in the average to 81.5 per cent whereas non-resident participation amounts to about 11 per cent.

In addition, the SPA consented to eight submissions representing altogether Forint 1.8bn. In these cases state assets forming part of the companies involved were the subject of alienation. It is estimated that the Treasury received Forint 1.7bn in the course of such transactions.

In 30 cases the SPA rejected the applications. The greater part of the negative decisions involved the protection of state assets.

In the course of 1990, the SPA started to initiate privatisation programmes.

Protection of state assets

Act VII of 1990 contains the provisions for the protection of state assets allocated to state enterprises. Under the act, state enterprises must report their intention to enter into certain categories of contract to the SPA. Such contracts are the following:

(a) contribution towards the capital of a business other than in cash provided the total value of the contribution exceeds Forint 20m or 10 per cent of the value of the tangible assets of the state enterprise (the forint is Hungary's national currency);
(b) the alienation of rights and privileges belonging to the state enterprises of money or monies worth or the alienation of the equity participation in a company of the state enterprise provided the asset value exceeds Forint 30m;
(c) the alienation of real property belonging to the state enterprise (including a leasing contract) provided the subject matter exceeds Forint 30m in value;
(d) the alienation of other capital assets of the state enterprise provided the value of the same exceeds Forint 50m;
(e) any other contract as a result of which more than 50 per cent of the tangible assets of the company would be vested in a third party, including the use of utilisation or collecting income from such utilisation of the alienated assets.

According to the act, the state enterprise will be at liberty to enter into a contract provided the SPA will not signify its refusal to consent to the transaction pursuant to the provisions of the act within 30 days from lodging the application. The ambit of the act does not extend to the transformation of state enterprise into companies pursuant to Act XIII of 1989.

Pre-privatisation

The government's Programme of National Renewal includes what is officially referred to as pre-privatisation, a programme in which units of state-owned home trade and catering, hotels and consumption-related services are either privatised or leased out for entrepreneurs. The legal framework is contained in Act LXXIV of 1990. The subject matter of the act includes business, workshops including business premises for consumer-related services which presently function on a lease basis or other similar contractual basis and where the number of staff does not exceed 10 when dealing with retail trade, and 15 in catering trade and when offering accommodation or consumer-related services or petrol stations where turnover is within a set limit.

The SPA was given the task to initiate the alienation or a transfer of such businesses to the hands of private entrepreneurs within two years of the act entering into force — 25 September 1990.

Only resident private individuals or partnerships with the participation of resident individuals (including limited partnerships) or private companies with limited liability may benefit under the scheme.

It is the duty of the SPA to establish the value of the business by professionally qualified experts. The SPA has to sell a unit to that entrepreneur — or it has to sign a contract of use with that entrepreneur — whose bid is found the most favourable in a publicly advertised and publicly held auction or at a competitive bidding which is attended by a notary public. The entrepreneur has to be given the right of pre-emption to the premises where the unit concerned will operate.

According to the pre-privatisation programme, the alienation of trading and service units will become a continuous process. One hundred and fifty shops belonging to 25 companies were evaluated by January 1991.

First privatisation programme

The first privatisation programme's objectives are to:

- facilitiate the smooth and rapid transfer of relevant enterprises to the private sector;
- improve markets and competition;
- extend capital and stock markets;
- create funds for the Treasury;
- encourage small investors in Hungary;
- facilitate the growth, profitability and efficiency of the privatised companies;
- enhance technological and management skills.

Within the privatisation process, several criteria must be met. The establishment of a fair value for the selected enterprises is of critical importance.

The first programme focused on creating competition based on international procedures of tender in order to determine the value of the enterprise selected. In cases where the environment, national or cultural interests of Hungary are involved, foreign investment was limited to a minority stake.

When Hungarian investors are concerned, preference is given to the smaller individual investors, to the emerging pension funds and to institutional investors indirectly representing the individual investors.

Hungarian small investors wishing to participate in the privatisation programme are supported through two separate funds — one being special loans available from the National Bank of Hungary and the other being the Existence Fund. The initial shareholder will be the SPA. It is hoped that the majority of the shares will be sold to the private sector, both in Hungary and abroad. The expected sale proceeds for the Treasury on successful completion of the first programme are expected to total Forint 25bn to Forint 40bn (between $385m and $615m).

Selection of enterprises

Enterprises earmarked for privatisation were selected on the basis of recent performance, support of the managers and employees, requirement of potential investors and the extent of preparation for privatisation. The list of enterprises earmarked represented enterprise from manufacturing, trade and transport, hotels and tourism.

Methods of privatisation

Three main methods of privatisation were proposed. The first was the public offering of shares and listing on a stock exchange. In this process the company selected will be incorporated as a joint stock company, offering its shares to the public and seeking a listing on a stock exchange — normally on the Budapest exchange — but in certain cases listing on a foreign one may also be applied for.

To achieve a stock exchange listing, the company will be required to have audited accounts, a prospectus and an asset valuation. This method will be used for the purpose of attracting individual small investors.

A second privatisation method was a competitive tender open or limited to pre-selected bidders. On an open basis the whole or parts of the company will be offered for sale. The letter of invitation to the tender will describe the conditions and requirements for participation and restrictions if any that may be placed on the further use of the assets in question. This method will be applied mainly for selling shops and transportation equipment.

Tenders on a limited basis include a pre-selected number of bidders expected to be particularly desirable in cases where the identity of the future owner(s) would be of importance to Hungary's longer-term interest, avoiding the sale of state assets to bidders whose intentions are not known.

Other methods of privatisation could include: employee-share ownership schemes which result in transforming employees to owners. For the majority of the selected companies, employees could own over 5 to 15 per cent of the entity. A higher proportion of employee ownership may be possible in cases where the number of employees is relatively small, the employees have a direct benefit in the performance of the entity and there is little prospect of attracting external investors.

Employee share ownership schemes will have the support of various funds which offer financing at reduced rates.

The first privatisation programme was announced and list of companies published in 1990. The SPA invited tenders for advisers for planning and implementation of privatisation for each of the selected companies.

Self-privatisation

The self-privatisation scheme applies to small state companies, says the State Property Agency.

Companies with assets and annual turnover of less than Forint 300m and a staff of under 300 will qualify. These companies will be privatised by consultants commissioned by the SPA.

The agency expects most of the companies to be sold to present management and workers.

Second privatisation programme — 'shell companies'

The second privatisation programme concentrates mainly on the privatisation of Hungary's 'shell' companies. These are holding companies which have under them a series of individual enterprises which may be split off and sold separately. If the 'shell' company is seen to be of real economic importance, and not simply stripping assets from its subsidiaries, it will probably remain. Otherwise, the shell company will be closed down and its separate enterprises sold off under the programme.

Taking part in this second programme will be foreign investment banks and consultants, who are eagerly awaiting the SPA's publication of the list which is expected to include between 70-80 companies, although the SPA intends to begin privatisation in only 15.

Foreign investment banks, however, will only take part in the second stage of the privatisation of these companies, after the legal structure of the 'shells' has been sorted out by the SPA and its advisers.

Acceleration of privatisation

Hungary accelerated its privatisation programme in the second half of 1991. The third and fourth privatisation programmes are designed to speed up the process and transfer as quickly as possible state assets into the private sector.

Further privatisation programmes

Hungary has already started on the third programme and the fourth and fifth programmes are under preparation. The main form of privatisation will now be a modified form of 'spontaneous' privatisation — a process which came in for sharp criticism in 1990. Investor-initiated privatisation means that any foreign investor can buy part or all of an enterprise. The SPA will organise a quick tender or order a valuation but otherwise not hinder the process.

Fourth privatisation programme

Under the fourth privatisation programme, the method will be even simpler. The SPA will require management to ask for a consultant or a financial bank to act as an independent counterpart to the management sale of the company. A list of SPA-approved consultants and banks (both foreign and domestic) which must be used when managements privatise, will be issued as soon as the programme has been approved.

The role of SPA will be one of an overseer rather than instigator. The SPA will stand above the general process, acting more like an arbitrator in case of dispute and keeping an eye open for any breaches of law or shady dealings. There are plans for the SPA to act more as a manager of state property, rather than behave as owner. The SPA wants to divest itself of its ownership by assigning a consultant from an investment bank or banks to handle the properties left in state hands.

Under a legal contract the SPA would sign up consultants and banks (both domestic and foreign) to act as portfolio managers, charged with disposing of the remaining state share in some companies or in managing the shares remaining in state hands.

The intention is to keep privatisation on a commercial footing. The government's stake in companies, which will be kept to a minimum, should be managed by professionals on behalf of the state. The SPA, acting on behalf of the government, will sign contracts specifying the terms under which shares can be sold and also expecting revenues from share sales and dividends.

No vouchers

No voucher scheme is expected to emerge in Hungary, although there are plans to introduce legislation that will allow for employee share ownership schemes. A law went to parliament in autumn 1991.

Retained state ownership

Only a narrow list of companies will remain with a majority state interest. The state's holdings in such companies will be managed through a holding company format which is likely to be administered again on a contract basis with consultants and investment banks.

Bidding

The State Property Agency is to make it possible for bids from both Hungarian and foreign investors to be made for state-owned companies or shares in associations or for the assets of such organisations.

The 'investor-led' privatisation should help boost sales. The SPA will give private individuals or legal entities or their groups a chance to submit an investment offer for any state-owned company or state-owned interest. The SPA will compare the bids.

First the investor sends the bid to the SPA which registers receipt of the written intention and the conditions of acceptance. The SPA can then grant an advisory company participating in the transaction a one-off commission. The privatisation procedure starts with the registration of the offer and the appointment of the adviser.

The SPA then agrees the conditions of the privatisation with the relevant ministry, local government and the company to be privatised. If a self-governed company does not agree with the privatisation, the board of directors of the SPA can put the company under state administration.

The company, under the direction of the appointed adviser, prepares a prospectus and financial statements, usually taking between 30-90 days.

The SPA can use newspaper advertisements or direct contacts to try to find more potential investors and create a competitive bidding environment.

Employee buy-outs

Under the new rules, employee buy-outs must follow the same basic procedure. But there are some differences. For example, during the tendering, the SPA or the adviser will require counter-offers from financial or strategic investors. The SPA can examine the financial background of employees or management to make sure they are in a position to purchase the company.

The valuation of the company will be prepared with the direct participation of the SPA. Workers and management can partially cover the required financing of the privatisation from a special credit fund and other credits from the National Bank.

Buy-out offers will be accepted for any state-owned company, interests in a state-owned association or for shares in a state-owned company. Such sales will be affected by Law LXXIV (1990) on the privatisation of retail trade and services. Exceptions will also be made for companies under the SPA's privatisation programme, companies that were transformed into associations by the SPA or the company itself, and for public utilities, financial institutions and companies whose main activity dominates over 40 per cent of the domestic market.

Over 60 applications were received for consideration under the investor-initiated privatisation scheme. Potential investors included several foreign businessmen of Hungarian origin.

Privatisation of foreign trade organisations

The privatisation of Hungary's 25 largest foreign trade companies is to be speeded up. The State Property Agency and the Foreign Trade Ministry have jointly decided to accelerate the process.

The sale of state-owned stakes in foreign trade companies which are no longer 100 per cent state owned is also under consideration. The 25 companies referred to in the latest statement from the ministry account for 51.8 per cent of Hungary's total imports and 37.13 per cent of exports.

New privatisation law needed

The Finance Ministry wants a new, comprehensive privatisation law in place by 1 January 1992. The ministry's proposal has been discussed by the government's economic cabinet, has put forward amendments. The Finance Ministry wants to raise the ratio of foreign ownership in the Hungarian economy from the current 3 per cent to 30 per cent by 1994, reducing the proportion of state property from the current 90 per cent to under 50 per cent. The ministry would also like at least 75 per cent of the income from the sale of state property used to reduce the state budget deficit.

Insurance privatisation

The privatisation of the State Insurance Company (AB) should be completed by the end of November 1991. AB has a 53 per cent share of the Hungarian insurance market and handles 8m policies. Morgan Grenfell is AB's privatisation adviser, and will determine the purchase price and optimum ownership from selected companies.

Banking privatisation

Privatisation of Hungary's banks was expected to begin by the end of autumn

1991. Foreign capital is expected to be involved in the Commercial Bank (formerly the National Commercial and Credit Bank), the Hungarian Credit Bank, Budapest Bank and the Foreign Trade Bank. Hungary's parliament passed a banking act — one of the most significant parts of the reform — in late November 1991. The bill introduces modern banking regulations and sets the legal foundations for selling state-owned banks. The law limits any one shareholder, including the state, to a 25 per cent stake in a bank. The law sets out capital requirements to fit with Bank for International Settlement norms.

Under the act, commercial banks will be able to start operations with a minimum capital of Forint 2bn while a specialised financial institution and investment bank needs Forint 500m. A savings bank can begin with Forint 100m capital. Preliminary approval from the government will be needed to set up wholly or partially foreign-owned banks or for a foreign investor to obtain shares in an already operating Hungarian bank. No government approval is needed if the total foreign stake in a bank remains under 10 per cent. The new law sets a limit of 25 per cent for foreign investment stakes in a bank.

Budapest Stock Exchange

The Budapest Commodities and Stock Exchange, inaugurated in 1864, made a substantial contribution to the country's dynamic economic expansion during the closing decades of the 19th century. The exchange was closed in 1947 when the nationalisation of the economy began. The re-opening of the Budapest Stock Exchange (BSE) was the result of almost 10 years' effort by a small group of economists and lawyers.

Starting in the early 1980s, the Hungarian Government began reforms aimed at recreating a securities market. Progress in the first years was slow, with only the issue and trading of debt securities such as bonds and debentures issued mainly by large public corporations and local authorities.

Parliament passed a new securities law on 1 February 1990 which allowed the formation of the Budapest stock exchange in June 1990 by 41 founding member organisations. The opening of the exchange coincided with the official listing of the shares of Ibusz. This was then followed by another five securities introduced during 1990 and four more in 1991. Securities contained in the securities list prior to 21 June 1990 trading on the exchange was permitted until 31 December 1990. The issuers were supposed to meet the requirements laid down in the listing requirement by that time.

Under existing laws only limited companies may run a business in securities. Brokers must be licensed either as agents, acting for a client and earning a commission, or as a principal dealer, allowed to act as principal.

The exchange itself is an independent, non-profit organisation founded by broking firms. At 30 June 1991 a total of 14 shares were traded on the exchange with a total market capitalisation of Forint 29bn. The minimum capital of a new company to be listed is Forint 200m. A company must offer at least 25 per cent of its issued share capital for public trading, although shares in public companies may be listed on international markets.

Trading

Trading takes place in a traditional, open outcry fashion, where bidders set the price on the floor. Most transactions are spot deals, although the exchange provides facilities for options and future trading. The exchange operates five days a week from 11am to 12.30pm. Licensed representatives of traders registered with the exchange give their offers and bids orally and the final price is set following an oral auction. Any traders may join the auction at any time.

Transactions carried out on the exchange are cleared partly through the stock exchange and partly through the National Bank of Hungary. Since January 1991, the exchange has been acting as a depository while the National Bank has been operating as a financial clearing centre. Clearing is done in a rolling system on the fifth day following the day of the transactions through multilateral netting out of the financial and security positions.

Brokers

Brokers are grouped together in the Association of Brokers and in 1991, securities trading companies formed the association of Brokerage Firms in order to facilitate their efforts and co-operation amongst traders.

At the end of 1990, 460 companies were formed and registered as share companies with only 12 per cent having issued or sold shares publicly.

The trading volumes on the exchange compared with other emerging stock exchanges are promising. The proportion of the average daily turnover in relation to the total market value of all shares (turnover ratio) is similar to that of the Portuguese and the Chilean markets. The Budapest exchange also compares favourably with regard to the average daily turnover per security.

The State Securities Supervisory Board watches over the operations of the exchange and licences securities dealers, authorises new listings and supervises other related activities.

Most buyers on the exchange are foreign investors, individuals and institutional. The exchange index is a composite basket of six listed companies. The council of the exchange decided in April 1991 that the exchange would publish an index, on an experimental basis, reflecting general trends of the market. The index reflects changes of the market value of the companies in the 'basket' with a base of 1,000 as at 2 January 1991. The index basket contains the shares of certain companies, the liquidity and trading volume of which meet selected criteria. On 31 May 1991 the basket included Elso Magyar Szovetkezeti Sorgyar, Fotex, Ibusz, Muszi, Skala-Co-op and Sztrada-Skala. The index basket is open and if some other shares meet the requirements the number of index securities may increase.

Licensing

Only licensed companies are allowed to engage in the dealing of securities. Regulations enable only companies to trade in securities. Licensed traders may not perform activities other than trading in securities. Securities traders may receive two different types of licences: brokers can act only as agent on behalf of their clients while securities dealers can perform transactions on their own account as principal and take part in underwriting securities issues.

In June 1991, 53 companies held permits issued by the State Securities Supervisory Board. The majority (47) of the traders were members of the exchange. A significant number of traders are commercial banks, but under an act of 1990, by the end of 1992, securities traders must run their business in trading securities as their sole activity. Trading banks, currently members of the exchange must establish separate securities trading firms if they want to continue operating on the securities market. Several major foreign banks have founded securities trading companies owned partly or wholly by them, including Giorzentrale, Daiwa and Credit Suisse First Boston.

Assistance for the exchange

The exchange received assistance in its foundation, operation and development from the London, Frankfurt, New York and Vienna stock exchanges. Visits of officials representing a number of different investment and pension funds and major institutional investors for information showed there was an interest outside Hungary in its securities market and trends of development. Various international organisations are also interested in the development of the exchange including the International Finance Corporation, an affiliate of the World Bank and the US Securities and Exchange Commission.

Plans for the future of the exchange

The exchange wants to increase the capacity and efficiency of the operation of the exchange. From the beginning of 1992, the exchange will operate on a new floor which will be larger than the original one and capable of handling trading volumes much higher than in 1991. Another priority is the development of the settlement and depository systems. Both were started in 1991, serving the whole securities market.

Information system

In parallel with the improvement of the trading and settlement systems, the information system of the exchange is to be developed. This will result in the increased range of real time information on issuers and on the market providing more up to date information to the public and professionals working on the exchange.

Measures are to be introduced to stimulate and concentrate demand on securities, including tax preferences of the investors, favourable loan schemes for buying securities, defining the legal framework for the operation of investment funds and other measures to increase the equality of the supply in order to offer attractive investments for the smaller, more risk-reluctant investors.

It is vital to link the Hungarian systems supporting the market to similar systems of national or international market-places. There are two areas where foreign investors would like to see progress. They want fast and reliable information on the market, issuers and speedy and safe settlement. The floor of the exchange is to be directly linked to major international information vendors so information will be transmitted fast. In settlements, system links are to be established with national and international clearing and deposit centres like Euroclear and Cedel.

It is also necessary to widen the knowledge of the people and of professionals on the capital markets. This is particularly important in an environment where a large number of potential and actual participants in the market are not familiar with the nature and operation of the market and not fully aware of the risks involved in investing in various instruments. A nationwide programme is to be set up by the exchange working together with the Hungarian Government.

Hungary's industry and trade development programme 1991-94

Economic policy area: ownership relations, legal framework and guarantees of ownership
State/problem to solve: competence and scope of state ownership not made clear
Objective: establishment of clear ownership relations
Responsible ministry: identification of the range to remain in state-ownership in the long term
Mode of regulation: privatisation strategy of the ministry
Scheduled: 1991
In charge: privatisation department, professional departments

Economic policy area: ownership relations, legal framework and guarantees of ownership
State/problem to solve: competence and scope of state ownership not made clear
Objective: establishment of clear ownership relations

Responsible ministry: putting in order of the right of use and end management of different properties
Mode of regulation: Civil Code, laws on property of the state, local governments, enterprises, co-operatives and the land
Scheduled: 1991
In charge: privatisation department, professional departments

Economic policy area: privatisation of the state's entrepreneurial property
State/problem to solve: transformation and privatisation have started
Objective: acceleration of privatisation and improvement and development of the necessary conditions
Responsible ministry: elaboration of the strategy and programme of privatisation applicable to the given sphere
Mode of regulation: professional guidelines, privatisation strategy
Scheduled: 1991
In charge: privatisation department, professional departments

Economic policy area: privatisation of the state's entrepreneurial property
State/problem to solve: transformation and privatisation have started
Objective: acceleration of the implementation of Act LXXIV of 1990 to have been concluded by mid-1992
Responsible ministry: preliminary arrangements for removing the factors hindering the process of privatisation
Mode of regulation: drawing up of a programme
Scheduled: 1991
In charge: privatisation department, professional departments

Economic policy area: privatisation of the state's entrepreneurial property
State/problem to solve: transformation and privatisation have started
Objective: acceleration of the implementation of Act LXXIV of 1990 to have been concluded by mid-1992
Responsible ministry: establishment of privatisation programme for the building industry
Mode of regulation: elaboration of the professional principles and the techniques of the conduct of the programme
Scheduled: 1991
In charge: building industry department, privatisation department

Economic policy area: institutional and financial promotion of privatisation
State/problem to solve: there is little solvency in relation to the desirable rate of privatisation
Objective: broadening of the legal and financial possibilities of becoming owners
Responsible ministry: operation of the privatisation and existing credit arrangements
Mode of regulation: participation in the preparation and modernisation of the legal regulation
Scheduled: continuous

In charge: National Trade Development Institute, professional departments, legal departments

Economic policy area: institutional and financial promotion of privatisation
State/problem to solve: there is slight solvent demand in relation to the desirable rate of privatisation
Objective: broadening of the legal and financial possibilities of becoming owners
Responsible ministry: further development of the legal framework and rules promoting the attraction of direct investment to the domain of trade
Mode of regulation: participation in the preparation and modernisation of the legal regulation
Scheduled: continuous
In charge: National Trade Development Institute, professional departments, legal departments

Economic policy area: institutional and financial promotion of privatisation
State/problem to solve: there is slight solvent demand in relation to the desirable rate of privatisation
Objective: broadening of the legal and financial possibilities of becoming owners
Responsible ministry: development of arrangement permitting preferential obtaining of shares for employees
Mode of regulation: participation in the preparation and modernisation of the legal regulation
Scheduled: 1991
In charge: privatisation department, legal department, professional departments

Economic policy area: organisational and institutional system for the efficient operation of the enterprises and assets remaining transitory in state ownership due to market or structural barriers
State/problem to solve: current functioning is inefficient, obsolete, unprofessional and enterprise structures are poor
Objective: preparation of the privatisation of the enterprises transitory remaining in state ownership
Responsible ministry: establishment of the institutional order and conditions or the regulation of property management; possibly the creation of state professional property management organisations
Mode of regulation: co-operation in the elaboration of the legal and institutional framework and of the strategy
Scheduled: 1991
In charge: privatisation department and professional departments

Economic policy area: organisational and institutional system for the efficient operation of the enterprises and assets remaining transitory in state ownership due to market or structural barriers
State/problem to solve: current functioning is inefficient, obsolete, unprofessional and enterprise structures are poor

Objective: preparation of the privatisation of the enterprises transitory remaining in state ownership
Responsible ministry: establishment of professional and regional financial holdings
Mode of regulation: co-operation in the establishment of the strategic objectives of the institutional system serving the management of state property
Scheduled: 1991
In charge: privatisation department and professional departments

Economic policy area: separation of state and local government ownership relations
State/problem to solve: the question of the entrepreneurial property of the trading companies founded by local governments is unregulated
Objective: the entrepreneurial property should be separated from the property of local governments
Responsible ministry: settlement through legislation
Mode of regulation: enacting of laws
Scheduled: 1991
In charge: legal department, trade policy department

Economic policy area: institutional system of market economy — encouragement and regulation of competition
State/problem to solve: underdeveloped market economy, conditions, limited competition
Objective: encouragement of competition, demonopolisation, establishment of an enterprise system complying with a competitive market
Responsible ministry: participation in the introduction of legislative and normative regulation of competition
Scheduled: continuous
In charge: legal department, market department, professional departments

Economic policy area: institutional system of market economy — encouragement and regulation of competition
State/problem to solve: underdeveloped market economy, conditions, limited competition
Objective: encouragement of competition, demonopolisation, establishment of an enterprise system complying with a competitive market
Responsible ministry: organisation development and decentralisation
Mode of regulation: organisation development and decentralisation programmes harmonised with privatisation
Scheduled: 1991-92
In charge: professional departments

Economic policy area: institutional system of market economy — encouragement and regulation of competition
State/problem to solve: underdeveloped market economy, conditions, limited competition

Objective: increasing the number of market actors, expansion of private business sector
Responsible ministry: deregulation of the legal rules hindering access to the market and the start-up of ventures
Mode of regulation: deregulation and streamlining of legal rules
Scheduled: 1991
In charge: legal department, market department, professional departments

Economic policy area: institutional system of market economy — encouragement and regulation of competition
State/problem to solve: underdeveloped market economy, conditions, limited competition
Objective: encouragement of competition, demonopolisation, establishment of an enterprise system complying with a competitive market
Responsible ministry: narrowing of the licensing system, making it normative
Scheduled: 1991
In charge: market department

Economic policy area: institutional system of market economy — encouragement and regulation of competition
State/problem to solve: the domestic industry often faces unequal chances
Objective: protection of domestic industry by market methods
Responsible ministry: selective and transitory protection of industry
Mode of regulation: agreements
Scheduled: 1991-92
In charge: professional departments

Economic policy area: institutional system of market economy — encouragement and regulation of competition
State/problem to solve: primitive entrepreneurial infrastructure
Objective: establishment of institutional conditions promoting private business, promotion of equal chances for small- and medium-sized enterprises
Responsible ministry: promotion of entrepreneurial consultancy and information system
Mode of regulation: co-operation in the elaboration of the legal and institutional frames and of the strategy
Scheduled: continuous
In charge: professional departments, National Trade Development Institute

Economic policy area: liberalisation
State/problem to solve: lack of competition in several domains, monopoly position of domestic producers
Objective: establishment of regulation conditions complying with developed market relations and international norms
Responsible ministry: liberalisation of import of consumer goods
Scheduled: 1992
In charge: market department, industry policy department, economic department

Economic policy area: liberalisation
State/problem to solve: lack of competition in several domains, monopoly position of domestic producers
Objective: establishment of regulation conditions complying with developed market relations and international norms
Responsible ministry: replacement of internal trade law by modern trade law adjusted to the international norms regulating trading activity
Mode of regulation: drafting of a bill
Scheduled: 1991
In charge: legal department, trade policy department

Economic policy area: liberalisation
State/problem to solve: non-uniform customs system, deviation from GATT rules
Objective: adjustment of the customs system to market requirements, its perfection in accordance with international obligations
Responsible ministry: lowering of the tariff level
Mode of regulation: law on customs
Scheduled: continuous
In charge: economic department, professional departments, market department

Economic policy area: institutional system of interest co-ordination
State/problem to solve: regulation lagging behind market economy requirements in respect of the protection of consumer interests
Objective: system for the protection of consumer interests complying with market economy requirements
Responsible ministry: creation in the field of trade of the basic principles and institutional conditions of the protection of consumer interests
Mode of regulation: law on the protection of consumer interests
Scheduled: 1991
In charge: legal department, National Trade Development Institute, trade policy department

Economic policy area: institutional system of interest co-ordination
State/problem to solve: ad hoc consultation of interest in the course of government decisions
Objective: creation of harmony between the representatives of interests and the work of the government. Multi-level and multilateral interest co-ordination mechanisms should be established
Responsible ministry: operation of the system of consultation of interests internal trade
Mode of regulation: agreement with the representations of interests
Scheduled: 1991
In charge: employment policy department, legal department, trade policy department

Economic policy area: protection of quality
State/problem to solve: the existence of a system of regulation lagging behind the market economy requirements and norms
Objective: reorganisation of the institutionalised system of quality control in accordance with the European model
Responsible ministry: taking over of the European Community systems
Mode of regulation: co-operation in the establishment of a new regional, attestation of quality, responsibility for product and other areas
Scheduled: 1991
In charge: department for technological development, market department

Economic policy area: government activity aimed at eliminating market disturbances
State/problem to solve: side by side with the self-regulating mechanisms of the market, there will be a need in the long term for the disturbance-eliminating and intervention activity of the state
Objective: establishment of intervention mechanisms and tools complying with market economy relations
Responsible ministry: provision for the norms and financial basis of intervention in trade
Mode of regulation: streamlining legislation
Scheduled: 1991
In charge: market department

Economic policy area: fiscal policy
State/problem to solve: general turnover tax system related to housing is bureaucratic
Objective: introduction of normative regulation
Responsible ministry: elaboration of the conditions of operation
Mode of regulation: elaboration of legal rule
Scheduled: 1991
In charge: department for building industry, legal department

Economic policy area: curbing inflation
State/problem to solve: the price level is rising at an accelerating rate due mainly to the weakness of the environment, the unorganised state of economic relations and the short-term attitude of economic actors and entrepreneurs
Objective: reduction of management and entrepreneurial uncertainties based on inflationary expectations and increasing inflation
Responsible ministry: encouragement of the private sector and competition, elimination of monopoly situations
Mode of regulation: deregulation, streamlining of legislation, privatisation
Scheduled: continuous
In charge: professional departments, market department, privatisation department, legal department

Economic policy area: promotion of international integration
State/problem to solve: disintegration of long-standing Comecon co-operation preparation of accession to European Community
Objective: conclusion of an agreement of association with the European Community, co-operation with other regions, new type relations with the Soviet Union (republics)
Responsible ministry: bringing the industrial customs systems closer to that of the European Community, agreement on trade co-operation with other regions
Mode of regulation: participation in the relevant negotiations, introduction of relevant arrangements in the field of industry
Scheduled: continuous
In charge: department for external economic relations, professional departments, economics department

Economic policy area: promotion of the inflow of direct investment
State/problem to solve: the inflow of direct investment to Hungary increased considerably in 1990 but further development is difficult because of unsettled ownership relations and regulatory contradictions
Objective: acceleration of adjustment to the world market, acquisition of advanced technology and management
Responsible ministry: improvement of supply of information for foreign investments, co-ordination
Mode of regulation: co-operation with the investment agency
Scheduled: continuous
In charge: department for external economic relations

Economic policy area: investments
State/problem to solve: contraction of state investments, shortage of funds for development
Objective: definition of the terms of reference of the ministry, reduction of sectoral and regional disproportions
Responsible ministry: determination of the scopes of decision in accordance with the new structure, improvement of the conditions of lending
Mode of regulation: sectoral adaptation of the budgetary legislation
Scheduled: 1991
In charge: economics department

Hungary's law on the State Property Agency and on the management of property of the state operating in enterprises

Parliament in order to maintain the separation of the executive power and ownership rights of the state, to decrease significantly the enterprising property of the state, and to establish the adequate methods and organisational background and to execute Law 13 1989 on the transformation of economic organisations and economic associations, enacts the law on the State Property

Agency and on the management and utilisation of the property managed by the State Property Agency.

PART I: STATE PROPERTY AGENCY (SPA)

Chapter I: Legal status and supervision of the State Property Agency

ARTICLE 1

The State Property Agency (hereinafter SPA) is a legal entity operating under the supervision of parliament, an organisation financed by state budget that exercises the ownership rights of the state regarding the state property belonging to it.

The budget of the SPA has to be registered separately from the state property under the control of the SPA and from revenues and expenses of the SPA.

The activity of the SPA is monitored by the State Audit office.

ARTICLE 2

Operation of the SPA is supervised by an 11-member board of directors, and its decisions are compulsory for the managing director of the SPA. The board of directors elects a president from among its members.

From among the members of the board of directors six are elected freely and five are representatives of the sectors listed below:

- one member represents the social organisations for environmental protection;
- one member represents the trade unions;
- one member represents the business federation of the employers;
- one member represents the social security system;
- one member represents the property managing organisations.

The board of directors establishes its own operational procedures.

Members of the board of directors should not be employed and should not be hired for work by the SPA on the basis of another legal contract.

ARTICLE 3

The members of the board of directors of the SPA are elected for five years, are relieved of their office and their salaries are stipulated by parliament.

The Planning and Budget Committee of parliament nominates the members of the board of directors, except the members mentioned in Article 2, provision (2).

The organisations concerned elect a person representing their activity from their staff and subsequently they submit their recommendations for the five members to parliament.

ARTICLE 4
Organisation of the SPA is headed by the managing director according to the valid legal regulations, the property policy guidelines (Article 34) and the decisions of the board of directors.

The operational statutes including the rules of procedures of the SPA are approved by parliament.

ARTICLE 5
The managing director of the SPA is elected for five years and discharged by parliament under the recommendation of a nominations committee appointed by parliament. His mandate can be extended. The salary of the managing director is stipulated by parliament on the basis of the recommendations for the first time of the Planning and Budget Committee then of the board of directors.

During their assignment the managing director and the members of the board of directors of the SPA can be relieved of their offices by parliament, if the president of the board of directors or that of the State Audit Office suggests. To relieve them, the qualified majority of the votes in parliament is needed.

ARTICLE 6
The managing director of the SPA and the employees under the operational statutes cannot maintain another job, except artistic, scientific and educational activity, they cannot be leading officers, members of the board of supervision or permanent auditors of an economic association.

Persons listed under paragraph 1 should not participate in decisions on economic associations in which they or any close relatives have any interest (Article 685 of the Civil Code). This provision is also applicable for members of the board of directors of the SPA.

Chapter II: Tasks and operation of the SPA

Title 1: State property managed by the SPA

ARTICLE 7
According to this law the following properties belong to the SPA property of the state-owned enterprises and other state-owned economic units transformed into economic associations under the Transformation Law:

- all business shares and shares that have not been transferred to external entrepreneurs of enterprises, trusts and other economic organisations under state supervision;
- in the case of a state-owned enterprise previously under the control of enterprise councils and the general meeting of employees (meeting of representatives), from the primary capital the business shares with the exception of the right to sell, that can be kept by the economic association for sale on the basis of Article 23, paragraph 1 of the Transformation Law.

Also according to this law, those properties in the economic associations which have been in the possession of the state before and since the Transformation Law came into force and that were not mentioned in the paragraph above.

Properties remaining in state possession after the liquidation of state-owned economic organisations and every kind of state property allocated to the SPA by a separate law or a resolution of parliament.

ARTICLE 8
Properties not belonging to the SPA:

- those properties of budgetary organisations that are in an economic association founded for welfare or operating purposes;
- property of state-owned enterprises and other state economic units that are in economic associations.

ARTICLE 9
Separate laws regulate:

- the ownership in respect of the properties due to the state from property of state-owned economic units established and supervised by local councils and of economic associations transformed;
- the practice of ownership rights of the state regarding the state-owned shares of the National Bank of Hungary;
- exercising of ownership rights of the state regarding the state-owned property not mentioned in paragraph 1a and in Article 7.

Title 2: Tasks of the SPA

ARTICLE 10
Tasks of the SPA include:

- taking over and registration of the state-owned property belonging to it (Article 7);
- exercising rights granted by the Transformation Law and this law to the state property managing organisation;
- providing the exploitation and supervision of utilisation of the state-owned property belonging to the SPA;
- with regard to the state-owned enterprises, exercising the founder's rights in the framework of this law;
- taking the state-owned enterprises, controlled by enterprise council or general meeting of employees (of representatives) under state administration supervision;
- preparation for sale (utilisation) of the companies drawn under state supervision according to the previous item;
- implementing investigations, preparation of decision making, and taking part in execution in connection with the sale of state property;

- exceptional and temporary direct property management;
- working out of a draft for the property policy guidelines, its submission to parliament, execution of the guidelines;
- making an annual report to parliament on the activity of the SPA;
- any tasks in connection with the state property delegated to the SPA by law or by a parliamentary resolution.

The SPA can practise its rights (as in paragraph 1) in accordance with the opinion of the founder organisation.

ARTICLE 11
The SPA is not allowed to carry on any kind of direct economic activity, with the exceptions given by this law. It is obliged to use state property taken over under the most advantageous conditions, as soon as possible.

ARTICLE 12
Rights of the founders belong to the SPA in cases regulated by Transformation Law (Article 16, paragraphs 1 and 2; Article 25, paragraphs 2 and 3; Law VI 1977 on State Owned Enterprises, Article 42/A). The right of liquidation (Article 42, paragraph 2 of the Company Law) can also be practised by the SPA.

While practising the founder's right, the SPA can withdraw the property entrusted to the enterprise, in order to sell it and to establish an association. Doing this, Article 32 of Decree 33/1984 (X.31) of the Council of Ministers does not have to be taken into consideration.

In case of withdrawal of the property, the SPA undertakes to guarantee the effective debts, up to the amount of the property withdrawn and in the ratio of the withdrawal. The responsibility lies with the SPA for the damage caused to the creditors by the withdrawal. These decrees do not influence the rules in Article 27, paragraph 3 in the Law on State-Owned Enterprises.

ARTICLE 13
The SPA gives an opinion about the transformation plan, and the accounting and property balance sheet submitted to it according to the Transformation Law, Article 17, paragraph 2 from the points of protection of the market and ownership rights of the state and makes recommendations if necessary to the transforming enterprise.

If the agreement is concluded between the transforming enterprise and the SPA on the conditions and the way of transformation (Transformation Law, Article 17, paragraph 3) in the time required by law or defined by the parties, the transformation has to be executed according to this agreement which is controlled by the SPA.

If the transforming enterprise deviates from the agreement the SPA may terminate the agreement with immediate effect; in this case the transformation can be executed according to the rules of Transformation Law only.

If the transformation interferes with the interests of the society or it can be detrimental to the national economy the SPA can prohibit the transformation (in 60 days from receipt of the transformation plan). The company (in 30 days from receipt of the decision) can ask the court of justice to review the decision.

ARTICLE 14

If the economic association wants to sell the business shares (shares) within three years after the transformation, in a way that causes prejudice of the ownership rights of the state, the SPA can withdraw the business shares (shares) in question if it pays for the portion belonging to the economic association, as it is in the Transformation Law. This portion has to be defined according to the bidding price.

An intended sale within three years after the transformation has to be reported to the SPA. The sales transaction can be executed under the announced conditions unless the SPA practises its right in paragraph 1 within 30 days from notification.

ARTICLE 15

The Minister of Finance exercises his rights granted by decree of the Council of Ministers (79 XII.7 1988) on state economic rehabilitation in respect of the property belonging to the SPA in agreement with the managing director of the SPA.

ARTICLE 16

If the founder's rights are with the SPA the managing director of the SPA may assign an enterprise commissioner to the economic unit in order to ensure more efficient operation and preparation (reorganisation) for later sale.

(The enterprise commissioner manages the enterprise under the direct control and according to the directions of the SPA.)

Title 3: Revenues and expenses of the SPA; reporting

ARTICLE 17

Income resources of the SPA are:

- proceeds (participation, dividend) of the state-owned property managed by the SPA, excluding the participation of the state in the business shares (shares) kept by the transformed economic association;
- rent receivable from a state-owned property utilised by renting;
- 100 per cent countervalue of the property part, sold by the founder, the trust, the SPA or an appointed property manager from the property of the enterprise used to be under state supervision, from that of the trust and other state-owned economic organisation;
- portion agreed upon (Article 17, paragraph 3 of Transformation Law) or 80 per cent countervalue of the business shares (shares) sold by the enterprise council and the general meeting of the employees (representatives).

ARTICLE 18
The SPA can cover the following expenses from the revenues.

- surrender the proceeds of state properties belonging to the SPA to economic organisations (Article 685, paragraph c of Civil Code) and private entrepreneurs in accordance with the property policy guidelines;
- fee payable to property manager and profit share in the case of surpassing the profit requirement;
- commission after sale;
- expenses of reorganisation (Article 16, paragraph 1);
- expenses of temporarily executed direct property management;
- payment for reduction of state debts, in accordance with the property policy guidelines;
- payment for other purposes stipulated in a separate law.

ARTICLE 19
The managing director of the SPA is obliged to give account annually to parliament, simultaneously with submission of the report on the previous year's budget, on the activity of the SPA, on the state property belonging to it, the results of its utilisation, and on the execution of the property policy guidelines.

The managing director is obliged to present in the report the revenues and expenses of the SPA, separately from its budget. Parallel with the report, a statement should be prepared and submitted on the state property belonging to the SPA.

Opinions of the President of the State Audit Office about the activity of the SPA have to be attached to the report.

PART 2: MANAGEMENT AND USE OF STATE PROPERTY BELONGING TO THE SPA

Chapter III: General rules of management and utilisation

Title 1: Property managers

ARTICLE 20
State property in ventures (hereinafter, the state property) can be managed by any domestic and foreign legal entity, economic association without legal entity and private entrepreneur if they enter into a management contract with the SPA or with an appointed property manager after winning the tender invited for this activity (according to the decree of Title 4 in this chapter).

Regarding foreign parties Law XXIV 1988 must also be applied.

Title 2: Tender system

ARTICLE 21
Assigning the state property into management and leasing, its sale and

authorisation for these activities takes place by a tender. In this case Decree 19 of 1987 on tenders is not to be observed.

ARTICLE 22

The tender is invited by the SPA and announced in two national daily papers at least seven days before the starting date for submission of the applications. The tenders are public unless the board of the SPA approves an exclusive invitation for the tender. In this case the interested parties have to be notified directly about the tender.

The tender invitation has to inform about property part (business shares, shares) to be assigned into management and its value, conditions of the property management requirements of the business policy, as well as place and deadline for submission of the applications which should not be less than 15 days. If the tender is invited for the total partial sale of an economic organisation the announcement has to include the significant data of the balance sheet and the guiding sales price. When securities are sold, the relating regulations are to be applied.

The SPA is obliged to have a registered expert define the value of the announced properties.

The applications are evaluated by the board of directors of the SPA.

ARTICLE 23

The SPA can enter into a contract only with the winner of the tender. If the applicant is a foreigner he has to establish an economic association in Hungary as a prerequisite for a valid contract.

In the case of equal conditions, the applicants have to be ranked as follows:

- the property manager;
- if the property manager's contract has terminated the previous property manager presuming that the property manager cannot be blamed for the termination of the contract;
- the employee, as a private entrepreneur of the economic association in question;
- the economic association or co-operative to be established for the purpose of management by the employees of the economic association in question;
- the participants of an ESOP programme of the economic association concerned.

The SPA announces immediately the outcome of the tender and accordingly the fact of giving into management and leasing of the property assignment for sale or the fact of the sale together with the explanation of the decision in the same two national daily papers. In case of an exclusive tender the applicants have to be informed directly about these data.

Title 3: Ways of property utilisation

ARTICLE 24
The state property can be alienated according to Articles 25-26 or exceptionally, if the conditions of the alienation are disadvantageous or it is otherwise unjustified, can be assigned into management according to Articles 27-30 by the SPA.

ARTICLE 25
The SPA is authorised to sell the state property in the framework of the property policy guidelines.

The state property can be sold to any domestic or foreign natural or legal entity and economic association without legal entity or to a private entrepreneur.

ARTICLE 26
The SPA is authorised to transfer state property into the ownership of the social security fund and other organisations free of charge in accordance with the property policy guidelines. Simultaneously this subsidy from the budget can be cut proportionately.

Title 4: Legal relations of property manager

ARTICLE 27
The SPA enters into contracts (Articles 28-30) with the winners of the tenders for the management of the state property. The parties can freely define the text of the contract within the limits of this law, other legal regulations and the announced tender conditions.

The management contract can be in force for a maximum of 10 years.

ARTICLE 28
In the management entrepreneur contract the property manager assumes, for a fee paid by the SPA, to practise the ownership rights over the property, excluding the right for alienation. He assumes to get proceeds stipulated in advance (dividend, shares) after the property and he is obliged to maintain the contractual value of the property.

The SPA and the property manager can agree that the SPA yields a part of the proceeds to the property manager but this possibility has to be referred to in the tender conditions.

Provisions of the Civil Code regulating entrepreneur contracts are also applicable for contracts concluded according to paragraph 1.

ARTICLE 29
In the management leasing contract the property manager undertakes to pay a fee to the SPA, and to maintain the value of the property determined in the agreement. In return he practises the ownership rights over the property, excluding the rights for alienation.

The SPA and the property manager can agree that the latter yields a certain part of the proceeds of the property to the SPA.

Provision of the Civil Code regulating hiring and tenancy are applicable.

ARTICLE 30
In the portfolio management contract the property manager undertakes to practise the ownership rights, including the right for alienation, for a fee paid by the SPA. The property manager is obliged to get the proceeds and/or property increase stipulated in the contract.

The SPA and the property manager can agree upon the sharing of the proceeds. This possibility has to be referred to in the tender conditions.

Provisions of the Civil Code regulating the entrepreneur contract are applicable.

ARTICLE 31
The property manager treats the proceeds of the property managed by him as if he possessed the property including the proceeds yielded by the SPA.

The property manager can treat the fee, paid by the SPA as an income, and the costs of property management (the fee paid to the SPA) as expenses.

ARTICLE 32
The property manager may purchase the managed property part from the SPA during the existence of the legal contract.

ARTICLE 33
Fulfilment of the obligations in the contract for management of the state property have to be assured by right of pledge, guarantee, joint and several liability or by other means. These guarantees are also applicable together.

PART 3: CLOSING REGULATIONS

Property policy guidelines

ARTICLE 34
For the succeeding year the following have to be defined in the property policy guidelines:

- the framework and conditions of sale of the property operating in state-owned enterprises;
- utilisation of the previous year's revenue of the SPA (portion of payment into the budget, the decrease of state debt and transfer to the economic organisations).

The managing director of the SPA works out, in agreement with the ministers concerned and the leaders of organisations with nationwide authority, and submits the guidelines to parliament simultaneously with the next year's budget.

Parliament passes a resolution on the guidelines.

Temporary and miscellaneous provisions

ARTICLE 35
The founding organisations are obliged to hand over state properties they received from the transforming enterprises before the coming into force of this law with the deadline of 30 April 1990.

ARTICLE 36
Until the election of the first board of directors of the SPA, parliament practises the rights of the board of directors stipulated in Article 42/A, paragraph 3 of Law VI, 1977, on state-owned enterprises. The other rights of the board of directors are exercised by the managing director up to the date mentioned.

ARTICLE 37
The coming into force of the law mentioned in Article 9, paragraph 1 the rights of the state property manager defined in the Transformation Law are exercised by the founder organisation according to this law as regards the property (property shares) in Article 9, paragraph 1.

ARTICLE 38
The property manager is eligible to put 'Fiduciary of the State SPA' on a sign-board and business letters.

ARTICLE 39
Considering the state property managed by the SPA, the second sentence of paragraph 11 and paragraph 12 of Law I of 1987 on Land are not applicable.

COMING INTO FORCE: PARAGRAPH 40
The present law comes into force on 1 March 1990
Modifications are to be made in several laws (detailed in the act).

Hungary's State Property Agency regulations

The State Property Agency (SPA) is a legal entity operating under the supervision of parliament. It is financed by the budget and exercises the ownership rights in respect of the assets vested in the state.

The operation of the SPA is supervised by an 11-man board of directors. The members are elected by parliament on the recommendation of the planning and budget committee and serve for five years.

The following types of assets come under the umbrella of SPA:

(a) Property of state enterprises and other state business entities already reconstructed by virtue of the transformation act; equity participation and shares in enterprises, trusts and other economic organisations under state supervision (other than those already sold). In case of transformation of state enterprises previously under the control of employees' councils and workers' assemblies, 20 per cent of the stock capital which in the balance sheet is referrable to the fixed assets of the enterprise. In addition such fraction of the equity capital (but not including the right of disposal) which may be retained by the enterprise itself for the purpose of future alienation (under Section 23 (1) of the Transformation Act).
(b) Such assets vested in enterprises other than referred to above which were in state ownership both on 1 March 1990 and before the Transformation Act came into force.
(c) Properties remaining in state ownership after the liquidation of state owned business organisations and every kind of state property allocated to the SPA by statute or by resolution of parliament. The law also lists the types of assets not becoming vested in SPA:
    - assets of companies incorporated for welfare or own operational purposes of organisations financed by the budget;
    - property of state enterprises and other economic units of the state vested in corporations.

The SPA has the authority to deal with the property vested in it as follows:

- the SPA will advise on the project of the conversion of a state enterprise into a corporation and put forward proposals;
- if agreement is reached between the enterprise undergoing conversion and the SPA on the ways and means of transformation then, within a definite time limit, the conversion must be implemented according to such agreement;
- if the enterprise under conversion disregards the agreement the SPA may treat the agreement as at an end with immediate effect and the conversion may only be implemented pursuant to Act XIII of 1989;
- if the proposed conversion appears to be contrary to the interests of society on the face of it or might be damaging to the national economy the SPA shall prohibit the proposed conversion;
- the enterprise may appeal to the court for a revision of the resolution within 30 days from the service of the resolution by the SPA.

Management and use of state assets vested in the SPA

Business assets of the state may be managed by any domestic or foreign corporation, partnerships or by private entrepreneurs provided they enter into a management agreement with the SPA first having won the tender published.

Tenders are invited by the SPA and must be inserted in two national daily papers.

The term of the management agreement may not exceed 10 years. The agreement may take the form of contracting, leasing, managing or portfolio management and is governed by the Hungarian Civil Code. Compliance with the obligations contained in the management agreement of state property must be secured by mortgage, lien, deposit, guarantee or some other appropriate security.

Hungary's act on securities and the stock exchange (Act VI of 1990)

The act came into force in February 1990.

The act provides for the setting up of the Securities Supervisory Board, as a government agency, which attends to the issuing to the public and the brokerage of securities and the supervising of the operation of the stock exchange.

Brokers need to be licensed by the board which, provided the conditions of the act are met, will grant a licence either to a company with limited liability or a joint stock company in which only registered shares are held. The following are the conditions needed to be met before a licence can be issued.

In the case of issuing houses and stock jobbers:

- paid up capital of not less than Ft 50m;
- issuing to be the sole object of the company;
- the necessary technical facilities are secured;
- manager with the required qualifications to be in charge of the operation;
- the rules of conducting the business having been approved by the board.

In the case of stockbrokers:

- the paid up capital of a joint stock company not less than Ft 10m and for a company with limited liability of not less than Ft 5m;
- broking is the sole object of the company;
- the necessary technical facilities are secured;
- manager with the required qualifications is in charge of the operation;
- rules of conducting the business having been approved by the board.

A company holding directly or indirectly more than 10 per cent of the equity in a brokerage or vice versa will not be licensed as a broker. No broker will trade in securities of its own issue or in the securities of a company in which it holds directly or indirectly more than 10 per cent of the equity.

The permission of the board given in conjunction with the Hungarian National

Bank is required for the international issue of securities (this is defined as trading in Hungary in securities issued abroad and trading in Hungary in securities issued in foreign currency units).

The board's approval is required for the constitution of any rules of operation of the stock exchange and also to any amendments.

The board will continuously supervise the working of the stock exchange including the issuing of and trading in securities with a view to establishing that they are in compliance with law and with the constitution and the rules of operation of the stock exchange and that the interest of the investors at large are not endangered. Various measures are available to the board to enforce compliance including the imposition of a 'supervisory fine' in some cases.

Public issues

The public issue of bonds and debentures is allowed if the issuer had:

- been in business for at least one year;
- published the prospectus in the form and with the content specified in the act;
- commissioned an issuing house to act (except that a bank may itself issue its own bonds and debentures).

The public issue of shares requires the advertising of a prospectus in the manner and with the content specified in the act. If the public issue of the shares is aimed at increasing the stock capital of a company (pursuant to Section 303 (1) of the Company Act (Act VI of 1988)), then the issuer is additionally required to show that it has been in business for at least one whole year.

The issuer is required up to the date of redemption — so long as its commitments enshrined in the security exist — to publish a report on its business and its financial position at least once every year. The issuer shall in cases as provided by the act publish occasional reports as well as dealing with changes in its business likely to affect the value of the securities or their income.

Trading in securities

When accepting instructions to sell or to buy securities the broker will inform the principal about the official quotation, the market situation and any other significant facts that might have a bearing on the matter in hand. The broker will not refuse instructions in respect of listed securities.

The stock exchange

The stock exchange has its own corporate personality. Business corporations licensed for brokerage are entitled to set up a stock exchange if they secure the compliance with all the statutory requirements. Companies registered in

Hungary are eligible for membership if they meet the statutory requirements. The number of members of the stock exchange is unlimited.

The internal operation of the stock exchange is conducted through:

- general meeting (consisting of all the stock exchange members);
- the stock exchange council (this is the executive body);
- supervisory board, an ethical committee or board and various other non-obligatory committees of experts;
- the secretariat (headed by the managing director).

Any surplus by which takings exceed the expenses will be applied towards the development of the commercial and information services of the stock exchange. Free capital at the disposal of the stock exchange for a limited period will be invested in government securities. The stock exchange is liable for its obligations only with its own assets; the members are not liable for the commitments of the stock exchange.

Subject to the agreement between the parties the disputes between them, particularly between brokers or between issuers and brokers, may be dealt with by the Arbitration Court organised at the stock exchange.

In some cases the head of the secretariat may suspend dealings in a given security for not more than three days. For a suspension in excess of three days a resolution of the Securities Supervisory Board is required.

The council of the stock exchange or the board may suspend dealings in general or at a particular stock exchange in various securities for an unspecified period of time.

To limit insider dealing, those who have confidential (insider) information are prohibited from dealing personally or by proxy in or in connection with the securities in question.

To protect investors, those who have bought or subscribed to a security on a prospectus that later was amended and reissued may within 15 days from the revised publication withdraw from the deal if the change tends adversely to affect the value of the security.

The liability of the issuer and of the broker for losses to the holder of a security due to misleading information is joint and several.

Chapter 5

POLAND

Poland intends to privatise 80 per cent of its state-run economy within the next five years. Privatisation is the government's economic priority. In three years beginning in 1991, the Privatisation Ministry hopes that over 50 per cent of existing state property will be transferred into private hands.

Privatisation is taking place in difficult circumstances. The slump in output was deeper in 1990-91 than expected by the government and exacerbated by the fact that exports to Soviet markets were decimated by USSR domestic difficulties and the collapse of Comecon trading arrangements. Domestic savings are limited and the country's finance and banking infrastructure is rudimentary.

Privatisation

It became clear in 1991 that the relatively leisurely pace of privatisation in 1990 — which closely followed the British style — was too slow, too cumbersome and poorly understood by most Polish citizens. In the first year of privatisation, only 80 per cent of shares in a single company were allowed to go to a foreign owner, with 20 per cent reserved for the work-force.

Large-scale privatisation

Announcements of companies up for bid are published in *Rzeczpospolita*, a Polish daily newspaper. If the company is large, announcements also appear in foreign daily newspapers such as *The Financial Times*, *Wall Street Journal Europe* and the *International Herald Tribune*.

The companies scheduled for privatisation in 1991 included the offering for public subscription in the spring of seven companies: ZPO Wolczanka (clothing, mainly shirts); Otmet Krapkowice (shoes); ZPT Brzeg (margarine, oil and other related products); APO Bytom (clothing, mainly suits); Swarzedzkie Fabryki Mebli (high quality furniture); and Huta Irean (artistic glass). In the event, only five were actually offered for public subscription.

The Privatisation Ministry also prepared a few enterprises to be privatised through trade sales or private placement. These included: Morska Stocznia Remontowa Swinoujscie (ship repair yard); Krakbud (contracting company); Huta Olawa (metal processing plant); Milfor (production of chemical-resistant food containers); Zipo (computer software); and Techma Krakow (contracting company).

Groups of enterprises are being reviewed in several sectors. These include the following industries: pulp and paper; packaging; meat; paint; cement and woodworking.

Valuation and prospectus

Each enterprise to be privatised will be subject to an independent valuation conducted (together) by local and foreign consulting companies. Each potential buyer will receive the prospectus, which will contain relevant financial data and the strategy for the company's development. The ending of each subscription will be followed by the share allocation and the distribution of the deposit certificates.

Large companies can be sold on private offers to a single or group of foreign investors.

In the small- and medium-sized enterprise category, there are around 2,500 industrial enterprises and around 3,000 construction, trade, transport and tourist enterprises.

Capital privatisation

For the small- and medium-sized companies, it is possible to use the capital privatisation method. As in the case of large companies, the smaller enterprises will be converted into joint stock companies, where equity is 100 per cent state-owned. Then the shares are offered to investors (single persons, local and foreign private companies). The employees of these enterprises will also have the right to buy the shares on a preferential basis.

The share sale will be conducted on the basis of a public offer or as a result of the negotiations, started after the public invitation was presented.

Management and employee buy-outs

Management and employee buy-outs will be possible and cheap credit lines will be opened at the National Bank of Poland, probably funded on the basis of the budget debt conversion.

Privatisation by liquidation will probably be the most commonly used method.

Selling enterprises

There are three possible ways for an enterprise or parts of it to be sold: sale; apportionment to the newly established company; leasing or renting of the newly established company to the company's employees.

Any investors — domestic and foreign — are entitled to buy enterprises or parts of them, although leasing will be used mainly by domestic investors.

The apportioning of the liquidated enterprise's equity to the new company is considered to be one of the best ways of establishing joint stock companies. To do this, some shares are held by the Treasury, and some by local or foreign private investors. The Treasury share is sold to citizens through a public offer. This method is suggested for privatisation of small enterprises, mainly in the services sector. It will probably not be used for privatising small- and medium-sized enterprises, especially ones which might need modern technologies and new (foreign) markets.

Privatisation methods

A lack of capital resources in Poland means another method will be needed to privatise the 500 largest enterprises — through the sale of shares on a preferential basis to employees; the distribution of free privatisation bonds (vouchers); and the share allocation to pension funds and to financial brokerage institutions.

Value of bonds

The value of the planned privatisation bonds issued should not be higher than 30 per cent of the share value of the large enterprises subject to mass privatisation. The nominal value of the privatisation bond will not be lower than Zloty 1m. (The zloty is the Polish national currency.)

Allocation of shares

Twenty per cent of the shares will be allocated through ZUS (Social Insurance Institution). The shares held by the state Treasury will be administered by the combined investment funds and sold. At the same time many institutions supporting the privatisation processes and the creation of the capital market will be established. The Warsaw Stock Exchange began its activities in July 1991.

Sales completed

Out of 8,443 state-owned enterprises, 17 had been sold by the end of August 1991. Another 556 were put into private hands through 'liquidation'—a process closest to a leveraged management or workers' buy-out, with the financing (credit) coming from the state. One hundred and eighty-seven companies were transformed by mid-1991 into 100 per cent state-owned limited companies, the first step towards privatisation.

Privatisation by sector

As part of Poland's plan to speed up privatisation, 34 sectors of industry were selected for analysis and restructuring. In phase one the adviser compiles an analysis of the sector with a rough overview of the individual companies. In phase two the adviser works on the actual strategy for privatisation which includes choosing between trade sales, IPOs, auction or management and employee buy-outs. At all stages the advisers report directly to the Privatisation Ministry,

According to the Privatisation Ministry, the initial analysis of projects will last between three and four months. Sectors selected and advisers appointed include: refineries and pipeline (Maison Lazard), ball bearings (Kleinwort Benson); power engineering (Samuel Montagu), machine tools (Company Assistance), surgical equipment (Bankers Trust), passenger cars (Credit Suisse First Boston), trucks and commercial vehicles (Maison Lazard), car components (BZW and Coopers and Lybrand), bicycles (Arthur Andersen), polymer synthetics (Bankers Trust), paint and coatings (DRT Poland, part of Touche Ross), toiletries and detergents (Bain), packing (A D Little), rubber and tyres (LEK), cement (International Finance Corporation), glass (IPG-Price Waterhouse), pulp and paper (Hambros), shoes (Company Assistance), meat processing (Ernst & Young), sugar refining (KPMG), potato processing (Ernst & Young), fruit and vegetables (Creditanstalt of Austria), breweries (Sankt Anna Bank), edible oil (Creditanstalt), tobacco (Morgan Grenfell), construction (Boston Consulting Group). LEK, A D Little, Ernst and Young and KPMG have been appointed only for the first stage of the process.

Advisers are currently being appointed to cover electronics and confectionery. Areas in which advisers are to be appointed include processed foods, railway rolling stock, shipbuilding, electrical engineering, pharmaceuticals and furniture.

Voucher privatisation

It was crucial for political reasons to 'share-enfranchise' the population, with the help of vouchers entitling people to free shares. Government plans for large-scale privatisation through share vouchers distributed free to the population were announced in June 1991. A team from S G Warburg, the merchant bank, was responsible for the plan.

The names of the 400 factories to be included in the country's large-scale privatisation through share vouchers were released in 1991. The list, prepared by Nicom Consulting, drew from a list of over 900 companies which were originally considered for the scheme. One hundred and thirty-two factories on the original list of 919 had their workers, self-management councils refuse to agree to join the scheme. A further 266 were in the throes of privatisation when the list was being drawn up and asked not to be included. Thirty had strikes and were not selected. The 400 accounted for 12 per cent of employment and 25 per cent of state industrial output. But the programme experienced delays. The original list of 400 was cut back in the autumn of 1991 to 204 and then to 111 in 1992 and a new programme drawn up for enterprises taken off the list.

Under the mass privatisation scheme, 60 per cent of the shares in the 400 are to be handed over to between five and 20 foreign-managed investment funds. Twenty-seven million adult Poles will receive shares in each fund. They will be allowed to sell these shares after mid-1993. First dividends are scheduled to be paid in the spring of 1993 at which time shares will become marketable.

The 60 per cent held in trust will be made up of two components: 33 per cent of the shares of any one enterprise will be allocated to a single fund, with 27 per cent spread among other funds.

The state will retain 30 per cent of shares and workers will receive 10 per cent free. Meanwhile, the fund managers will be free to manage, as well as sell and buy shares, in their portfolio.

Case study: Swarzedz privatisation

The International Finance Corporation (IFC), an affiliate of the World Bank, promotes private sector business development. It has taken an active role in privatisation programmes throughout Eastern Europe. In Poland it gave management advice to Swarzedzkie Fabryki Mebli (SFM), one of Poland's most modern furniture factories.

Since summer 1991, the plant had in place an IFC chief financial officer for a few months following its privatisation. In June 1991, SFM was privatised through Poland's first fully underwritten public offering. Of the company's 2.5m shares, 1.9m shares were offered for sale, comprising 1.4m existing shares owned by the Treasury and 500,000 shares newly issued by the company. At an issue price of Zloty 50,000 ($4.44) per share, the offering raised Zloty 95bn ($8.43m), valuing the company at Zloty 125bn ($11.09m).

SFM's remaining 600,000 shares not included in the public offering are accounted for as follows:

- under the 1990 Privatisation Law, 400,000 shares were offered to SFM employees on preferential terms (half price with a deferred payment option);

- 100,000 shares were kept by the state to settle claims of former owners;
- 75,000 shares were paid to IFC as part compensation for its advisory services;
- 18,750 shares are held by the broker selected as 'specialist' for the trading of SFM's shares on the Warsaw stock exchange;
- 6,250 shares were paid to the banks involved in the share distribution system (these shares were then awarded to individual employees of the banks as part of an incentive scheme to make the system work smoothly).

The public offering was divided into two components: a small investor tranche of 900,000 shares for investors making purchases of less than 10,000 shares; and a large investor tranche of 1m shares for investors applying for more than 10,000 shares.

Foreign investors were able to participate in both tranches. The Foreign Investment Law allows foreigners to own up to 10 per cent of a Polish company without approval. For SFM approval was obtained in advance for this limit to be increased to 40 per cent. As a result of the offering, foreign investors now own 24 per cent of SFM (including IFC's 3 per cent holding).

The small investor tranche was sold on a 'first-come first-served' basis through a nationwide network of 200 commercial bank branches, co-ordinated by the Warsaw-based Bank PEKAO SA. The shares in this tranche sold out on the first day of the two-week offering period (20 May 1991). This was considerably quicker than expected, especially given the experience of the first five public offerings in Poland. Of the five, all of which were of similar size to SFM's small investor tranche, only one was fully subscribed after its initial three-week offering period.

SFM was the first offering in post-communist Eastern Europe to use a 'first-come first-served' system of share distribution, a system which is also relatively unusual elsewhere in the world. IFC designed this type of system because of the inefficiencies which were perceived in the first batch of five offerings in Poland and because of the peculiar quality of Polish Convertible Treasury bonds, which make a typical 'subscription plus allotment' system cumbersome to administer. As a result of the success of the SFM offering, the ministry decided to continue using this system for future offerings.

The large investor tranche was sold using a traditional 'subscription plus allotment' mechanism, with the Poznan-based Bank Staropolski acting as receiving agent. For the first time in Poland's privatisation programme, investors were able to subscribe for shares in foreign currency (US dollars). Applications for 1.117m shares were received from six domestic and seven foreign investors, indicating an 11.7 per cent over-subscription. Eventually, 483,000 shares were allotted to large domestic investors and 517,000 to large foreign investors. The Polish insurance company, Warta, is the largest new shareholder with 345,000 shares (13.8 per cent of the company). Of the foreign investors, one is SFM's German sales agent and the remaining six are London-based investment funds or nominee companies, including East Europe Development Fund.

In addition there were aspects of the SFM transaction which represent important steps forward for Poland's privatisation programme. These included the first:

- public offering in Poland to contain a primary capital increase at the same time as a sale of the government's shareholding, thus providing proceeds for the company as well as for the Treasury;
- Polish public offering to be fully underwritten (by four domestic banks in this case);
- example of a Polish company undergoing a financial restructuring (including assumption of debts) prior to its privatisation;
- time a Polish public offering has been split into separate components for large and small investors, thus avoiding the main drawback of public offerings in post-communist economies, namely the risk that a widely dispersed shareholding structure would have little impact on management;
- time that foreign institutional investors (as opposed to active investors) have taken significant stakes in a Polish company being privatised.

IFC's role in the SFM privatisation included:

- legal transformation of SFM from a state-owned enterprise into a joint-stock company;
- company appraisal;
- design of a restructuring plan for SFM, including organisational, operational and financial components;
- implementation of the financial restructuring, involving the first use of Article 22 of the 1990 Privatisation Law, allowing assumption of a company's debts by the Privatisation Ministry prior to privatisation;
- valuation of SFM;
- design of a privatisation strategy for SFM;
- design of a share distribution system;
- preparation of the offering documentation, including the Prospectus;
- identification of and presentations to potential investors;
- managing SFM's stock exchange listing.

SFM's shares were listed on the Warsaw stock exchange on 25 June 1991.

Another privatisation approach

The Polish Privatisation Ministry tried a new approach to selling off state assets quickly and effectively in the autumn of 1991. Advertisements were placed in the national and international business press offering a substantial minority interest in the cosmetics company Pollena-Bydgoszcz and up to 80 per cent of shares in POL-BAF, a starch and potato granulate manufacturer near Lodz. In addition, 51 per cent of the Polam-Pila light bulb producing enterprise was sold to Philips. Eighty per cent of the FAMPA paper machinery producer was sold to Beloit of the US.

These privatisations marked a significant departure from earlier practice and signalled to Western companies that it is possible to buy existing Polish business quickly, with no bureaucratic delay — and with a controlling share.

Privatisation funding

The Privatisation Ministry established in 1991 a foundation designed to raise funds to finance privatisations. The foundation is headed by Krzysztof Bandyka, formerly with Swiss Bank Corporation. This foundation is the Ministry's second one. The first, headed by Henryk Sterniczuk, now concentrates on funding the training of managers.

Information on privatisation

Privatisation Ministry opened a centre for information and negotiations at the Marriott Hotel in Warsaw in the autumn of 1991. The centre helps domestic and foreign investors and provides information about privatisation in Poland. The centre is financed by the World Bank and the Polish Ministries of Privatisation and Foreign Trade. The centre is on the third floor of the Marriott Business Centre and is open from 8am to 9pm. Heading the centre is Andrzej Voigt (Fax: Warsaw 213 361). The ministry has also published two books, available in English. They are *A Guide to Foreign Investment in Poland* and *An Information Guide to the Ministry of Privatisation.*

Stock exchange

Although a milestone in the reconstruction of a market economy was crossed in April 1991 when the Warsaw stock exchange reopened after a gap of almost 50 years, its significance was symbolic. Some stock was traded in the exchange's first session but more glasses of champagne than shares changed hands. Less than 300 shares were traded on the first of the weekly Tuesday sessions.

Foreign investment law

Poland adopted a new foreign investment law in June 1991. The Foreign Investment Law (DzU 41, Item 325 of 1989 amended) was amended by the law on companies with foreign participation (14 June 1991). The law came into effect around mid-July 1991.

The aim of the law is to make investment conditions more attractive and to streamline the permit and registration procedures.

Few restrictions remain. Activities which still require permission from the Privatisation Ministry include management of sea harbours and airports; sales of real estate; non-licensed defence industry; wholesale distribution of imported consumer goods; legal services and contribution in kind by state legal persons (except Treasury-owned companies) of organised parts of its assets. The permission is given by the Ministry, which took over this function from the Foreign Investment Agency from mid-October 1991.

Permits

Application for a permit must be made in the Polish language. A decision should be reached within two months. When no permit is needed, to incorporate in Poland a company needs notarised articles of association registered with the local courts.

To obtain a Privatisation Ministry permit, the following documents are needed: shareholders' names and addresses; name and seat of the new company; description of activities of the company; type and value of contributions to the capital; valuation of contribution in kind; legal position of future shareholders; and financing or banking references of future shareholders. The Ministry will issue a permit within two months from the date the application and relevant documentation is lodged with it.

Setting up a company

Companies may be set up either as limited liability or joint stock companies. Companies are regulated by the Commercial Code of 1934, unless a new law stipulates otherwise.

Foreign physical persons, legal persons and non-legal entities of physical and legal persons abroad can form a company. In Poland, physical and legal persons, state enterprises and the Treasury can set up a company.

Repatriation of dividends

The law provides for the full transfer of dividends and capital abroad in hard currency. The foreign partner may repatriate up to 100 per cent of its share of the profits of the company after taxes.

Contribution to start-up capital

The foreign company's contribution to the start-up capital may be in Polish currency, obtained by selling convertible currency to the National Bank of Poland or in kind. The minimum investment of $50,000 is abolished.

Contribution to the capital of a company can be in the form of cash in zloty after conversion at local banks; in kind, provided this is imported or purchased using zloty after conversion at local banks; dividends on shareholdings in Poland; sales of shareholdings in Poland; and money received from the liquidation of a company.

Tax holidays

Tax holidays are abolished, but the Finance Ministry may exempt a company from income tax if the foreign company's contribution exceeds Ecu 2m and if the company is based in an area of high structural unemployment or ensures the introduction of new technology or where the company is exporting at least 20 per cent of its sales turnover. The exemption may be sought until 31 December 1993.

Companies which set up joint ventures under previous legislation may continue to enjoy their tax holidays until such reliefs and exemptions expire. However, they may waive the tax holiday in order to obtain the right to repatriate up to 100 per cent of locally earned profits, rather than 15 per cent as under previous legislation.

Liquidation and taxation

If a company is dissolved during the tax exemption period or within three years after the expiration of the tax exemption, then the tax has to be paid. Investments into capital or acquisition of shares in excess of Ecu 2m will give the investor a tax benefit equal to the investment. This is granted by the Finance Ministry after submission through the Privatisation Ministry of a special application. To get such a benefit, the company should be set up in a region of high unemployment or introduce modern technologies or export goods and services in excess of 20 per cent of total sales.

Corporate income tax is 40 per cent. The income tax for foreigners employed in companies is 20 per cent. The tax on dividends is 30 per cent. From April 1992, value added tax (VAT) is to be introduced, replacing turnover tax.

Foreign Investment Agency

The Foreign Investment Agency ceased to exist in October 1991. Its controlling function was taken over by the Privatisation Ministry. The State Foreign Investment Agency was set up to deal with promotion of Poland as a foreign investment market.

Banking reform

The Polish domestic banking system began the decentralisation process in

January 1989 when several new commercial banks were set up with branches all over the country. At the same time, the interest rate policy was partially relaxed, leaving banks free to set their lending and deposit rates within the limits established by the National Bank. This has brought some competition and consumer choice to the banking sector. However, quality of banking services remains poor compared with Western standards.

Privatisation of banks

The Finance Ministry has outlined its privatisation programme for the banking sector. In the autumn of 1991, two of the nine existing Polish commercial banks — Bank Slaski w Katowicach and Wielkopolski Bank Kredytowy w Poznaniu — began the initial phase of their privatisation. The book value of Bank Slaski has been estimated at around $140m. The bank has 40 branches and employs 3,000 people. Wielkopolski Bank Kredytowy has an estimated book value of $100m with 44 branch offices employing around 2,700 people. It has a representative office in Berlin.

The World Bank is supporting the programme and providing a $200m credit line to be used for the development of financial institutions. Of this, $150m is to be used for the restructuring of banks, the preparation of the proper legal framework and the development of the financial market. The remaining $50m has been allocated for the modernisation of the banks' equipment and partly for speeding up of the privatisation process.

In May 1991 the Council of Ministers decided to transform Poland's nine commercial banks created in January 1989 into joint stock companies and bring the status of these banks closer to that of Western financial institutions.

The profitability of Polish banks in 1990 was extremely high. This chiefly resulted from a lack of competition in the banking sector. Growing competition is expected to decrease the profitability of banks in 1991.

The main privatisation issue in the case of the banking sector is to find a good strategic investor who will buy an important or minority holding in each bank and take over the responsibility for the bank's further development. Priority will be given to foreign investors.

Under the privatisation plan for the first two banks, about 45 per cent of the shares will be reserved for domestic investors — both institutional and private persons. A public sale based on the subscription will be organised. An indeterminate part of the shares in both banks are to be kept at the disposal of the Polish Treasury and some shares will be sold to the banks' employees. The Polish Treasury will sell shares to strategic investors with priority being given to foreign investors.

Employees have the right to purchase shares of privatised companies at 50 per cent of the share price. The volume of the shares sold in this way is limited.

Foreign banks in Poland

Poland is keen to attract foreign banks. The Finance Ministry and National Bank both see the role of foreign banks in Poland as enabling the expansion of Poland's economic relations with other countries; facilitating the creation of a financial infrastructure for the inflow of other foreign capital; promoting competition in the banking sector; spreading modern banking management; improving banking staff expertise and expanding imports of modern banking techniques.

Activities of banks in Poland are regulated by the following laws:

- Banking Law of 31 January 1989 (Journal of Laws 4, item 21) amended 28 December 1989 (Journal of Laws 74, item 439);
- Act on the National Bank of Poland of 31 January 1989 (Journal of Laws 4, Item 22) amended 28 December 1989 (Journal of Laws 74, item 439).

Provisions of other laws which also apply to banking include:

- Commercial Code of 27 June 1934 (Journal of Laws 57, item 502);
- Foreign Exchange Control Law of 15 February 1989 (Journal of Laws 6, item 33) amended 28 December 1989 (Journal of Laws 75, item 441).

The banking law permits the following forms of involvement by foreigners:

- investment by foreigners (taking 100 per cent or smaller) in new or existing banks constituted as joint stock companies;
- opening branches or representative offices by foreign banks.

Under the bank law a bank must be established by at least three legal persons or 10 'natural persons'. Permission to set up an incorporated bank is given by the president of the National Bank in agreement with the Finance Minister.

Management of banks

The chairman of the bank's board of management is appointed after consultation with the president of the National Bank and founders of a bank can determine its statutes as long as they agree with existing Polish legal provisions.

Permission to set up a bank is given when it can be demonstrated that the capital is available for investment; premises and technical facilities necessary to carry out the activities are available and managerial positions have been entrusted to people with a satisfactory professional background.

The posts of president (or chairman), vice-president(s) and other members of the bank's management board are considered to be 'managerial' positions. At least one member of the board of management should be a Polish citizen.

Opening a branch

In order to open a branch or representative office in Poland it is necessary to obtain a permit issued by the Finance Minster in agreement with the National Bank president. A representative office cannot perform banking operations which under the banking law are reserved for incorporated banks or branches.

The requirements for capital include:

- a minimum capital in a convertible currency brought in by foreign persons must total $6m or its equivalent in another convertible currency;
- the amount in Polish currency contributed by domestic persons is not strictly determined.

Bank employees

Banks can employ Polish citizens and foreigners, provided the foreigners are employed under the relevant Polish regulations. Banks are obliged to perform banking operations under law and may accept foreign exchange deposits from domestic persons on terms agreed in contracts concluded with these persons and taking into consideration all relevant regulations, in particular the act on the National Bank (Article 40) and the Foreign Exchange Control Law (Article 24).

In Poland banks may maintain foreign currency assets abroad up to the level of non-capital liabilities sourced abroad in foreign currency. This does not mean that the foreign-sourced liabilities are to be maintained in foreign currency or that matching of maturities is specified.

Foreign exchange reserves

Banks must maintain foreign exchange reserves at a level determined by the National Bank president in agreement with the Finance Minister.

These banks can perform credit and deposit operations in zloty and in other currencies based on conditions which do not differ from those applied by domestic banks. The Treasury is not responsible for the bank's liabilities with respect to deposits from domestic persons, including savings deposits. However, the Treasury can grant a guarantee or a warranty for such liabilities.

Foreign banks must maintain, as do all domestic banks, an obligatory zloty reserve with the National Bank. This is currently set at 15 per cent of total deposits and is not remunerated.

Taxation of banks

Foreign banks are required to pay taxes the same as domestic banks. Foreign banks should conform to inter-bank and other settlement practices in the Polish market, prepare their accounts in line with Polish practices and regulations and prepare and submit to the National Bank information and data the same as domestic banks.

Correspondence with Polish state offices must be conducted in the Polish language. Monitoring by the Polish financial authorities will encompass foreign banks and the National Bank will be responsible for banking supervision.

Capital adequacy

In the area of capital adequacy, new banks are required to maintain capital at a level not lower than 8 per cent of weighted risk exposure. Polish regulation in this area is to be strengthened and will eventually conform to Bank for International Settlement and European Community norms and methodologies.

Foreign banks may maintain their capital, including accruals, in foreign currencies on account with the National Bank. Capital deposited with the National Bank will be paid at the market rate in the relevant currency for interest rates agreed. Capital revalued in zloty due to foreign exchange movements will not incur tax. Losses will not be deductible.

Remittances abroad

The remittance in foreign currency of at least 30 per cent of profits is permitted. Larger percentages can be negotiated bilaterally. Regulations in this area will be subject to overall conditions applying from time to time to foreign investors in Poland.

Banks may acquire property freely from private individuals. State land and real estate can be acquired on long-term lease (up to 99 years) or in certain circumstances purchased with the permission of the Interior Minister. Joint stock banks formed with Polish shareholders may have real estate contributed as the Polish shareholder's subscription.

Reserve policy

Reserve policy is an area which is currently being addressed by the Finance Ministry for the whole of the banking system. In the interim, banks are permitted to create general reserves of 1 per cent of the total amount of all extended credits per year up to a limit of 5 per cent a year and specific provisions when required. All of these are deductible for tax purposes under specific authority granted to each bank by the Finance Minister.

Twinning

Five Western banks agreed a twinning arrangement with five Polish banks in 1991. The idea is to encourage the flow of Western banking know-how to Poland. The scheme was set up under the auspices of the International Finance Corporation (IFC), an affiliate of the World Bank, and forms part of a wider programme of support from the World Bank to help modernise Polish banking.

The IFC also helped set up a banking joint venture between three Western banks — Amsterdam-Rotterdam Bank, Banca Commerciale Italiana and Crédit Lyonnais — and two Polish banks, Bank for Export Promotion and Greater Poland Credit Bank of Poznan. This venture, International Bank in Poland (IBP), aims to provide wholesale banking and financial corporate services to enterprises operating in Poland. The IBP will use short- and medium-term deposits from the inter-bank market and from corporate clients to provide trade finance and medium-term loans to its customers.

National Bank of Poland

The National Bank is the central bank, regulating the circulation of currency, fixing foreign exchange rates and supervising the foreign currency transactions of the banking institutions.

Foreign Trade Bank

The Bank Handlowy w Warszawie (Foreign Trade Bank), handles the financing of foreign trade and extends foreign currency credits to Polish enterprises. The Bank Handlowy also issues, accepts and endorses commercial paper denominated in foreign currencies, issues bonds and deals in international money and capital markets. The Bank Handlowy has several branches in Western Europe and is a correspondent of some 2,000 banks world-wide.

Bank PEKAO SA

The Bank PEKAO SA conducts retail banking operations in foreign currencies. It handles foreign commercial and financial operations of the private sector and maintains foreign exchange saving accounts of individuals. The Bank PEKAO SA has several branches abroad (such as in the US, France, Germany and Israel).

Export Development Bank

In 1987 the Bank Rozwoju Eksportu, the Export Development Bank, began operations. It was set up in order to provide financial resources to manufacturing enterprises which are interested in restructuring their production to expand export sales.

Export Credit Bank

Poland's state-owned export credit guarantee unit, Korporacja Ubezpieczen Kredytow Ekspor-towych (KUKE), began operations in 1991. KUKE is owned by the Finance and Foreign Trade Ministries, the National Bank of Poland, Bank Handlowy, Export Development Bank and Bank Turystyki. Other shareholders include three state sector foreign trade companies — Metalexport, Varimex and Polimex Cekop — and Warta, one of the state insurance companies.

Insurance law

Poland's insurance law encapsulates requirements in respect of the conduct of insurance business. Supervision is similar to the system of insurance authorisation and prudential supervision used in the European Community. The new law was promulgated on 28 July 1990 and has been amended by further regulations covering specific aspects of the insurance market.

The carrying on of direct and indirect insurance business by all companies, including companies with the participation of foreign capital, requires the approval of the Finance Minister. Under the law, an insurer may conduct insurance business only in the legal form of a joint stock company or a mutual society. Shares of the joint stock company must be registered ones.

Insurance rates

Under the law an insurer has the freedom to set premium rates. For certain types of businesses which are of importance to the population — this excludes commercial business — insurers must draw up standard general terms of insurance. These terms have to be presented to the Finance Ministry for approval.

Insurance terms

The general terms of insurance, tariffs and insurance premiums are set by an insurer and do not need confirmation from any authority. The insurance contract may include additional or different clauses and terms from those provided in the standard general terms of insurance or under the general terms of insurance.

Under the law there are three classes of compulsory insurance:

- motor third party liability;
- fire insurance for farm buildings;
- farmers' civil liability.

An insurer offering compulsory insurance may not refuse to issue such an insurance. The general terms of compulsory insurance need the approval of the Finance Minister. Premium rates are to be set by insurers.

An insurer may use the services of authorised insurance or reinsurance brokers. An insurer may also use the services of other financial intermediaries or agents which need no authorisation from the authorities.

An insurer is prohibited from carrying on any activities which are not connected with or related to purposes other than the insurance business.

The law prohibits insurers to carry on both life and non-life business.

Equity for insurers

An insurer must have equity capital equivalent to the company's solvency margin. One-third of the solvency margin represents the minimum guarantee capital. The amount of minimum guarantee capital is determined by further regulation. The amount envisaged will be between the equivalent of Ecu 200,000 and Ecu 1.4m, depending on the class of insurance business to be undertaken.

Insurance funds

An insurer must establish reserve capital and technical reserves. Technical reserves are intended to cover current and future obligations resulting from the insurance business and will consist of reserves to cover unpaid insurance claims and payments premium reserve for unexpired risks, premium reserve in the life insurance category calculated on the basis of actuarial sums, the capitalised value of pensions and others provided by statute.

An insurance guarantee fund will be set up to settle claims on obligatory third party liability insurance where the person responsible is either unidentifiable or uninsured. The fund will be financed by insurers conducting compulsory insurance business.

A production fund will also be set up to settle claims in the case of an insurer's insolvency, to the value of 100 per cent of life policies, 90 per cent of compulsory and 50 per cent of other policies. There will be two separate accounts: one for life insurance and the other for non-life. The fund will be financed by a levy on the insurance industry.

If an insurer's equity capital is lower than the required solvency margin or guarantee capital, he will be obliged to submit to the Finance Minister an appropriate financial plan to redress that balance. In such circumstances, the Finance Minister may impose limits on the activities of an insurer concerned.

Investment by insurers

According to the law an insurer should invest his funds taking into consideration the type and structure of insurance activities in such a way as to achieve the highest level of security and reliability as well as liquidity of funds. An insurer must inform the Finance Minister of the purchase of stocks in a company which exceed 10 per cent of the value of the nominal funding capital of that company and of investments in companies dependent on an insurer or in companies on which an insurer is dependent.

In such cases the Finance Minister may prohibit or restrict the acquisition of those investments by an insurer.

Insurance funds must be invested in approved assets in Poland, such assets to comprise government financial instruments, shares in Polish companies, mortgage loans, non-agricultural real estate or shares traded on the stock exchange (provided the shares held in any one company are not greater than 10 per cent of the nominal funding capital of that company), in Polish shares not listed on the stock exchange, in shares in Polish companies with limited liability, time deposits, loans secured by life insurance policies or other investments approved by the Finance Minister. Because of the principle of matching foreign exchange risks, investment abroad may also be permitted.

The total amount of shares listed on the stock exchange and unlisted shares may not exceed 30 per cent of the insurance fund or 15 per cent for unquoted shares alone. Investment in real estate may not exceed 25 per cent. These limits do not apply to life insurance tied into investment funds.

Foreign insurers in Poland

Foreign insurers may conduct business in Poland, but only through a joint stock company. Such a company must be set up as a joint venture or be 100 per cent owned by the foreign investors. Permission for foreign insurers to establish branches in Poland will be granted after 1 January 1993.

Reinsurance in Poland

In Poland the main principles of reinsurance abroad will be defined by the Finance Minister. The ministry will consider the suitability of the reinsurance arrangements with foreign companies. The Finance Ministry will not normally allow more than 20 per cent of the liabilities of an applicant company to be reinsured with companies in the group to which it belongs, more than 10 per cent of liabilities to be reinsured with any other company or more than 25 per cent of liabilities to be reinsured in any one country other than Poland.

The Finance Minister will define the provision of the amount which a foreign investor may transfer abroad without exchange control. It is expected that full freedom of the dividend transfer will eventually be allowed.

Authorisation of insurance business

Applications for authorisation to conduct insurance business in Poland should include: the name and address of the applicant, details of the actual and territorial scope of the insurance activities proposed, details of the proposed share capital and funding capital, the estimated costs of the administration of the business and those organising a network of representatives and details of the qualifications of the proposed directors and managers and the actuary concerned in the case of life insurance.

Liquidation of insurance companies

The Finance Minister must be informed of any intention to liquidate the company and of the identity of the liquidator. The minister may authorise liquidation of the company in the case of any failure to act legally or within the confines of the company's funding statutes, or if the minimal guarantee capital is allowed to fall below the level stipulated, or if the company is operating at a loss and making no provision for covering its losses, or if it is not meeting claims or meeting them only after excessive delays.

The Finance Minister must be immediately informed if a company cannot service its debts. An insurer may declare bankruptcy only with the consent of the Finance Minister.

Act on trading in securities and trust funds (22 March 1991)

Chapter I: General provisions

ARTICLE 1

Public trading in securities is the offering for sale or the acquisition or transfer of proprietary rights in securities issued in series, these being made by means of an offer or invitation to negotiate through the media or mass communication or otherwise, where the offer or invitation to negotiate is addressed to more than 300 persons or to an unspecified addressee.

Public trading in securities will be conducted exclusively through the intermediary of entities operating brokerage firms, unless otherwise provided by statute.

ARTICLE 2

Wherever used in this act, the following expressions will have the respective meanings:

- security means a document intended to certify or certifying the existence of a certain property right, expressed in such wording and such manner as to be capable of constituting a separate object of public trading;
- issuer means a person — including a corporate or other entity — issuing a security in his own name;
- securities issued in series means securities representing property rights, divided into equal units, the number of these units being determined in advance;
- primary pubic trading means the offering by the issuer of the acquisition of proprietary rights in securities issued in series or the acquisition of such rights;
- secondary public trading means the offering by persons other than the issuer of proprietary rights in securities issued in series or the actual sale of such rights where the securities have been admitted for public trading or where the offering is of a public character;
- stock exchange means the combination of persons, equipment and technical facilities organised to ensure that in the process of juxtaposing offers to sell and acquire securities all market participants have the same access in the same time to market information and that they can dispose of and acquire rights on the same terms;
- trust fund means a financially separate joint estate of participants managed by a trust fund corporation, this estate having a varying value and a fixed economic object;
- mutual investment means the acquisition and disposal of securities in the interest and on the joint account of participants in trust funds;
- dominant entity means in relation to any entity another entity which commands a majority of votes in management bodies of that entity, including a situation where this arises through agreement with other authorised persons; or is authorised to appoint or recall a majority of members of managing bodies of that entity; or where more than half of the members of managing bodies of that entity are at the same time directors or executives of the entity in question or an entity linked to the entity in question by a relation of dependence.

ARTICLE 3

The provisions of this act do not apply to public primary trading in securities issued by the state Treasury or the National Bank of Poland or securities involving monetary obligations guaranteed by these institutions; transactions in bills of exchange, promissory notes and cheques; public trading in short-term securities with maturities shorter than a year from the issue date.

ARTICLE 4

The issue of securities by a dependent entity will be deemed to have been made by the dominant entity.

In ascertaining the relation of dependence, consideration is given to the voting rights or rights to appoint or recall directors exercisable through the intermediary of another dependent entity or through a person acting on behalf of the authorised person or of the intermediary entity.

ARTICLE 5

In the course of public trading in securities, there will be issued registered deposit receipts confirming the deposit of securities identified in the particulars of the deposit receipt. The issuer of the deposit receipt may be a bank or another institution authorised by statute.

The particulars of the deposit receipt would include

- the name and address of the issuer of the deposit receipt;
- the amount of deposited securities;
- the class and series of the security and the issue date;
- the name and address of the issuer;
- the nominal value of the security;
- the name and address of the owner of the security;
- information on restrictions on the transfer of rights attached to the securities and encumbrances on these rights;
- the date and venue of the issue of the deposit receipt.

The issuer of the entity selling securities by way of flotation will ensure that the entity referred to above will issue a registered deposit receipt to each owner of securities.

The person identified in the deposit receipt will be authorised to exercise all rights attached to the securities specified in the deposit receipt.

The transfer of rights attached to deposited securities, effected through public trading in securities will take place on the conclusion of a contract.

Chapter II: Securities commission

ARTICLE 6

The Securities Commission will be set up as a central body of government administration responsible for public trading in securities.

Supervision over the commission will be performed by the chairman of the Council of Ministers, the Prime Minister of Poland.

ARTICLE 7
The tasks for the commission include:

- overseeing the observance of rules of fair trade and competition in the field of public trading in securities;
- designing, organising and undertaking measures to ensure the efficient operation of the securities market and the protection of investors;
- co-operation with government administrative bodies, the National Bank, securities market institutions and participants in public trading in securities in designing state economic policy with a view to promoting the development of the securities market;
- disseminating knowledge of the principles governing the operation of the securities market;
- undertaking other measures provided for by law.

The Council of Ministers may lay down the detailed terms of reference for the commission.

ARTICLE 8
The commission will consists of a chairman, two vice-chairmen and six members.

The chairman will be appointed and removed by the Prime Minister at the joint request of the Finance Minister and president of the National Bank on consulting the relevant Sejm (parliament) commissions.

The vice-chairmen will be appointed and removed by the Prime Minister at the request of the chairman of the commission.

The commission will comprise representatives of the Finance Minister, Privatisation Ministry, the president of the National Bank, the president of the Anti-Monopoly Office, nominated by them. One member of the commission will be nominated by the Broker Council from among broker association members and one member will be nominated by the stock exchange.

ARTICLE 9
The chairman of the commission will represent the commission and direct its proceedings.

The chairman will make regulations in cases indicated in this act.

The commission will publish the Securities Commission Records according to principles laid down in separate regulations.

ARTICLE 10
The commission and the chairman of the commission will perform their duties the the help of the office of the Securities Commission.

ARTICLE 11
The organisation of the commission and of the securities office will be specified in the charter confirmed by the Prime Minister.

ARTICLE 12
The provisions of the Code of Administrative Procedure will apply to proceedings before the commission, unless provided otherwise by statute.

ARTICLE 13
In civil law cases within the field of public trading in securities, the powers of the public prosecutor arising out of the relevant provisions of the Code of Civil Procedure will also be vested in the chairman of the commission.

Chapter III: Brokerage activity

ARTICLE 14
A natural person may be entered into the register of brokers if he:

- has full capacity to perform legal actions;
- enjoys full public rights;
- has not been sentenced for crimes in respect of property, documents, economic offences, forgery of money, securities or official stamps or fiscal offences;
- has passed an examination before the examination commission for securities brokers.

The Register of brokers will be kept by the commission.

Entry into the register of brokers will be made at the request of the applicant.

The register of brokers, the suspension of a brokerage licence and the removal from the register of brokers will be published in the Securities Commission Records.

ARTICLE 15
The chairman of the commission will:

- appoint the examination commission for brokers and oversee its activities;
- specify the curriculum and the procedures for broker examinations and examinations for advisers referred to in Article 33;
- specify the amount of examination charges for candidates for brokers and the remuneration of members of the examination commission.

ARTICLE 16
A broker will be struck off the register

- at his own request;

- having failed to conduct brokerage activity for five successive years;
- on total or partial incapacitation;
- on being legally sentenced for a crime or offence referred to in Article 14;
- on death.

A broker may be struck off the register or have his licence suspended for a period of between three and six months where he fails through his own fault to use reasonable care in the discharge of brokerage duties or violates the law in connection with the discharge of his duties or violates the professional code of conduct.

The ruling on striking a broker off the register or suspending his licence will be made by the commission after hearing interested persons, or on the latter's own initiative, or at the request of the disciplinary committees (Article 37).

ARTICLE 17

The broker, while conducting brokerage activity, will observe the law and the principles of fair trade, taking special care of the rightful interests of the orders.

The broker will observe professional secrecy in respect of all information which he has obtained in the course of conducting brokerage operations.

ARTICLE 18

The entity operating a brokerage firm may be a natural person, a legal (juridical) person, or an entity without personality-at-law.

The operation of a brokerage firm will be subject to a permit from the commission.

The application to obtain a permit will contain:

- the name and address of the entity operating the firm;
- principal data on the persons responsible for establishing and managing the activity to be permitted;
- the names of partners and the pattern of capital participation where the firm is run by a corporation;
- where relevant, the description of the relation of dependence on or domination over other entities;
- the requested extent of the permit;
- the amount of own resources and credits earmarked for the establishment of the activity to be permitted;
- a statement confirming the clear record, in relation to the crimes and offences referred to in Article 14 on the part of the persons managing the brokerage firm;
- presentation of the organisational aspect of planned activity and especially information on the available premises and telecommunications equipment;
- the list of persons referred to below.

The commission will determine the minimum value of own resources and the maximum level of credit referred to above.

The entity operating a brokerage firm will be required to employ persons with broker licences for the conduct of brokerage operations and to employ persons (Article 33) for operations involving advice on public trading in securities.

The entity operating a brokerage firm must not at the same time conduct economic activity in another field through the firm.

ARTICLE 19
The permit will specify:

- the name and address of the entity operating the brokerage firm;
- the permitted extent and forms of brokerage activity;
- the required amount of the firm's own funds and the limit on the ratio of credits to own funds;
- the required ratio of own funds to turnover;
- the deadline by which the entity operating the brokerage firm should start operations;
- other conditions which the brokerage firm must meet in the course of its activities.

ARTICLE 20
The commission may refuse to issue permits where the application for the permit fails to meet conditions (Article 18) or where the data presented in the application indicate that the entity concerned does not guarantee proper conduct of brokerage activity.

ARTICLE 21
Activities of the broker acting in the capacity of a firm includes:

- offering securities within public trading arrangements;
- acquisition or sale of securities in accordance with legal principles (Article 22);
- management to the order of other parties of their portfolios of securities;
- professional advice in securities trading;
- keeping securities in custody to order of the authorised person.

ARTICLE 22
The entity operating a brokerage firm assumes the obligation to the orderer to sell or purchase securities in its own name by that orderer's account.

The entity operating a brokerage firm will be responsible to the orderer for the payment of the price by the acquirer of securities.

The entity operating a brokerage firm, while acting in the capacity of the firm, may acquire securities in its own name and on its own account for the purpose of subsequent resale, to the extent specified in the permit for brokerage activity.

ARTICLE 23
The shares issued by a joint stock corporation operating a brokerage firm may only take the reform of shares registered in the name of designated parties.

The corporation operating a brokerage firm will notify the commission of the names of persons exercising over 5 per cent of the voting rights at general meetings.

Each subsequent change in the block of shares held by the shareholders (as above) which exceeds 2 per cent of the voting rights will also be notified to the commission.

ARTICLE 24
Brokerage activities may be undertaken by a bank, subject to the issue of a permit by the commission.

The permit is obtained if the bank's operations in the field of public trading in securities is separated organisationally and financially within the bank.

Provisions of Articles 18 and 23 do not apply to banks (as above).

ARTICLE 25
The commission may issue decisions on suspension or revocation of permits.

The commission may revoke a permit where the entity operating the brokerage firm:

- violates the law;
- fails to meet the conditions specified in the permit or transgresses the limits of the permit;
- fails to observe the principles of fair trade or does injury to the interests of the orderer.

Where it is necessary to protect public interest in specific cases (as above), the commission may suspend the permit for a period not longer than one month, taking in that time a decision on revocation or confirmation of the permit.

Such a decision (as above) will be made after a hearing is held.

ARTICLE 26
With a view to checking whether the activities of the entity operating a brokerage firm comply with the terms of the permit, an authorised representative of the commission will be empowered to enter the premises of the entity and its business and to inspect books, documents and other sources of information.

ARTICLE 27
The permit will expire:

- on the death of the person who has established a sole proprietorship;

- where the liquidation of a brokerage firm has commenced;
- where bankruptcy of a brokerage firm has been adjudicated.

ARTICLE 28

A foreign entity intending to undertake broker activity in Poland is required to obtain a permit under rules laid out in this act.

The provisions above do not override the provisions of other acts governing the assumption and conduct of economic activity by foreign parties in Poland and economic activity involving the participation of such parties.

ARTICLE 29

Shares must not be held in more than one corporation conducting brokerage activity. Private individuals or legal persons may not be partners in more than one brokerage firm at the same time.

The provisions above do not apply to the state Treasury.

ARTICLE 30

The entity operating a brokerage firm must not render services involving trading in securities issued by an entity to which it is linked by a relation of domination or dependence.

The provisions above also apply to securities issued by the entity operating a brokerage firm, where the latter trades in securities on its own account.

ARTICLE 31

The entity operating a brokerage firm will notify the commission of any changes in the data contained in the application for a permit to conduct brokerage activity and also of changes in employment of brokers and persons referred to in Article 33, the opening or closure of a branch or the acquisition of over 5 per cent of the voting rights in any other corporation.

ARTICLE 32

The chairman of the commission can specify detailed procedures for the conduct of transactions and settlements by brokerage firms and for the recording of such transactions.

The chairman of the commission may lay down the principles governing the setting up of the brokerage commission.

The Finance Minister, acting in co-operation with the chairman of the commission, may specify the detailed conditions to be met by brokerage firms regarding accounting standards.

ARTICLE 33

The conduct of advisory activity in public trading in securities will require a separate permit, to be granted by the commission under the principles governing the granting of permits for the operation of a brokerage firm.

An investment adviser will be entered in the register of brokers.

The chairman of the commission will specify advisers in order to obtain a permit concerning the qualification to conduct financial analyses connected with securities trading.

Chapter IV: Brokers association

ARTICLE 34
The Brokers Association will be established as a self-governing body of brokers.

Membership in the association will be obligatory and will take effect on entry into the register of brokers.

ARTICLE 35
The Brokers Association will have personality-at-law.

ARTICLE 36
The association will:

- represent brokers and protect their professional interests;
- co-operate with the commission and other state bodies in drafting and enforcing law in the field of public securities trading;
- be responsible for professional upgrading of brokers;
- promote trading customs and the principles of a brokers' code of conduct;
- monitor the discharge of professional duties by brokers and especially adjucate on matters concerning the brokers' code of conduct;
- perform other tasks provided for by law.

ARTICLE 37
The governing bodies of the association will be the convention, the council, the audit committee and the disciplinary committee.

ARTICLE 38
The term of office on the association's governing bodies will be two years.

Elections to the governing bodies of the association will be universal, direct, equal, by secret ballot and with an unlimited number of candidates.

ARTICLE 39
To the extent not regulated by statute, the appointment procedure, powers, organisational structure and operating mode of the association and the manner whereby statements of will are made on behalf of the association will be specified in the charter of the association as approved by the commission.

ARTICLE 40
Supervision of the association will be performed by the commission.

The commission may:

- suspend the resolutions of the association's governing bodies for up to 14 days where these manifestly violate the law or the association's charter;
- appeal to the Voivodship Court against resolutions of the association's governing bodies, where these resolutions violate the law or the association's charter or where they have been adopted in contradiction of the law or the provisions of the charter;
- ask a governing body of the association to consider a particular issue, the body being obliged to adopt a resolution on that issue within a month.

In cases (as above) the Voivodship Court will either overrule the appeal or annul the appealed resolution, sending the matter back for further consideration by the relevant body of the association and setting the guidelines for such consideration, the court's ruling being binding on the association.

The association will notify the commission of the sessions of its governing bodies.

ARTICLE 41
Brokers will be accountable to the disciplinary committee for actions which:

- involve lack of reasonable care through a fault of the broker in the discharge of brokerage duties imposed by law or by contract;
- contravene the professional code of conduct.

ARTICLE 42
The disciplinary penalties will include: warning, reprimand, fine and a ban on performances of elected functions in the association for a period of up to two years.

The fine may by up to three times the broker's recently received remuneration. The revenue from fines will be spent on charity, as specified in a resolution of the Brokers Council.

The disciplinary committees will notify the commission of the disciplinary penalty administered to a broker. The commission will enter a notice of the penalty in the broker's files.

The disciplinary committee (as in Article 41), may ask the commission to strike a broker from the register or suspend his brokerage licence.

The absence of a ruling by the commission on striking a broker off the list or suspending his licence does not prevent the imposition of a disciplinary penalty by the disciplinary committee.

ARTICLE 43
The functions of a prosecutor in proceedings before the disciplinary committee will be performed by the discipliner.

The disciplinary proceedings will be instituted at the request of the discipliner.

The defendant in disciplinary proceedings may use the services of a defence counsel from among the brokers.

ARTICLE 44
Rulings of the disciplinary committee can be appealed to the commission within 14 days of the ruling having been served in writing and with substantiation.

ARTICLE 45
The disciplinary proceedings may not be instituted:

- a year or more after the misconduct;
- six months or more after the misconduct has come to the attention of the discipliner.

Where the misconduct shows features of a criminal offence, the prescribed disciplinary limitation will come into force no earlier than provided for in the statute of limitation in criminal law.

The running of the disciplinary limitation period will be interrupted by any related action of the discipliner.

ARTICLE 46
The notice of punishment will be deleted ex officio after three years from the:

- moment the ruling on warning, reprimand or fine assumes final validity;
- end of the period of suspension of the brokerage licence.

ARTICLE 47
Members of the disciplinary committee, as far as their rulings are concerned, are subject only to the law.

ARTICLE 48
The Brokers Convention will specify the detailed procedures for disciplinary proceedings.

Chapter V: Public flotation

ARTICLE 49
The public flotation of securities will be subject to a permit from the commission.

ARTICLE 50
In order to obtain a permit for public flotation of securities, the issuer or the entity publicly floating the securities will be required to file an application with the commission which will contain:

- the name and address of the issuer;
- principal data on the issue and in particular the class of the security issued, the volume and value of the issue and the expected date of the issue;
- the designation of the entity operating a brokerage firm and floating the securities.

The application must be accompanied by the prospectus and with, respectively, a copy of the charter and the resolution or statement on the issue made by the relevant managing body of the issuer.

The commission will grant the permit referred to in Article 49 within two months of filing an application.

The person referred to above, on obtaining the permit from the commission, will deposit all securities of a given issue with a single bank or another institution authorised to accept such deposits.

The Council of Ministers will specify the detailed conditions to be met by the prospectus.

ARTICLE 51

On obtaining the permit for public flotation of securities, it is required that it be published in two national daily papers as specified by the commission, with the data enabling investors to assess the financial condition, the profits and losses and the economic prospects of the enterprises and also the character of the rights attached to the securities.

ARTICLE 52

The issuer or the entity floating the securities will be required to notify the commission of any substantial change in the data presented in the prospectus and also will be required to supply periodical information to the extent and at dates specified by the commission.

The commission may request the person referred to above to publish within seven days a supplement to the information contained in the prospectus.

Where the conditions referred to above are not met, the commission may issue a decision revoking the permit for public flotation of securities.

Contracts concluded prior to the moment the decision referred to above becomes final will be considered as valid.

ARTICLE 53

The records of publicly floated securities will be kept by the commission, in accordance with the principles and procedures laid down by ordinance of the chairman of the commission.

Chapter VI: Secondary public trading in securities

ARTICLE 54

Secondary public trading in securities will take place on stock exchanges operated by joint stock corporations.

The Council of Ministers may lay down the forms of secondary public trading in securities outside the stock exchange to be conducted through the intermediary of entities operating brokerage firms in accordance with the principles specified in Article 57.

The provisions above do not apply to the:

- transfer of proprietary rights in securities directly between natural persons;
- transfer of proprietary rights in securities between a dominant entity and a dependent entity, unless the transfer of rights takes place according to the procedure referred to in Article 1 without the intermediary of that entity operating a brokerage firm.

The commission may permit secondary trading in indicated securities for a specified period by entities conducting brokerage activity, subject to the requirements referred to in Article 57.

ARTICLE 55

Shares in corporations operating stock exchanges may only be acquired by entities operating brokerage firms by the state Treasury and by banks.

The corporation operating a stock exchange will be required to issue such amounts of shares as to make their acquisition possible for the entities referred to above.

ARTICLE 56

Shares in the stock of the corporation operating a stock exchange may only be in registered form.

Shares held by a shareholder who has discontinued brokerage activity will be redeemed.

ARTICLE 57

The stock exchange will ensure:

- the concentration of the supply of and demand for securities admitted for stock exchange trading in order to obtain their market prices;
- a secure and efficient course of transactions and settlements;
- dissemination of uniform information enabling the assessment of the current value of the securities admitted for stock exchange trading.

ARTICLE 58
The operation of a stock exchange will be subject to a permit. The permit will be issued by the Prime Minister at the request of the commission.

In order to obtain a permit, a corporation intending to operate a stock exchange will file application with the commission. This application will contain the following information:

- the name and the domicile of the corporation;
- persons responsible for the establishment and the management of the stock exchange;
- the expected amount of own funds and credits earmarked for the establishment of the stock exchange and the manner of financing the operations of the stock exchange;
- commitments from at least 10 entities operating brokerage firms to conduct operations on the stock exchange in question;
- the amount and structure of the capital of the corporation intending to operate a stock exchange;
- the amount and structure of the capital of the corporation intending to operate a stock exchange;
- the expected seat of the stock exchange and the technical equipment enabling stock exchange operations and especially the equipment guaranteeing communication with the National Depository (referred to in Article 71).

The application should be accompanied by the charter of the corporation, draft by-laws and a feasibility study (economic, financial analysis) for the operation of the stock exchange by the corporation.

ARTICLE 59
The charter of the corporation intending to operate a stock exchange will contain the following:

- the conditions of which securities may be admitted for trading on the stock exchange;
- the manner and procedure for settlement of disputes concerning the course of stock exchange transactions;
- the name of the body adopting the by-laws of the stock exchange.

ARTICLE 60
The by-laws of the stock exchange will specify the:

- types of transactions effected on the stock exchange;
- procedure for trading in securities on the stock exchange;
- conditions and procedure for the quotation and suspension and discontinuation of quotation of securities on the stock exchange;
- opening days and hours of stock exchange sessions;
- right to be present on the stock exchange and the attached conditions;

- manner of setting and publishing the quotations;
- manner of classifying securities quoted on the stock exchange;
- amount of the regular annual charge for use of stock exchange equipment;
- amount of transaction charges and manner of calculation;
- system of recording and settlement of stock exchange transactions.

ARTICLE 61

Any changes in the charter or by-laws of the stock exchange to changes in the data provided in the application (Article 58) are subject to approval by the commission.

ARTICLE 62

Where a stock exchange fails to observe the law, the commission may ask the Prime Minister to revoke the permit to operate the stock exchange.

ARTICLE 63

The corporation operating a stock exchange must not be oriented to profit. The shareholders will exercise any right to participate in annual profit.

The object of the corporation will only be to operate the stock exchange.

ARTICLE 64

Parties to stock exchange transactions may only be shareholders of a corporation (Article 55), operating a brokerage firm.

Stock exchange transactions concluded by persons other than those referred to above will be null and void.

Collusions to increase or lower the price of securities artificially is unlawful.

ARTICLE 65

A joint fund for insurance against civil liability on account of stock exchange transactions, formed from contributions by shareholders, will be established by the corporation operating a stock exchange.

The procedure governing the level of contributions to the fund and the disposal of fund resources will be laid down by the general meeting of the corporation operating a stock exchange.

ARTICLE 66

The corporation operating a stock exchange will appoint a supervisory board (board of directors), to be known as the stock exchange board.

The board will consist of the chairman and between 10 and 14 members, half of whom will be appointed from among non-shareholders, namely from among issuers, acquirers of securities, representatives of chambers of commerce and industry and financial institutions.

ARTICLE 67

The board at the request of the management committee, will adopt the by-laws of the stock exchange, to be approved by the general meeting. The by-laws will be drawn up with regard to Article 60.

ARTICLE 68
In order to operate the stock exchange in Warsaw a single shareholder corporation of the state Treasury will be established.

The provisions of Article 58 and 63 do not apply to the Warsaw stock exchange.

ARTICLE 69
A security admitted for trading on one stock exchange may be traded on another stock exchange subject to approval by the commission.

A refusal to register securities for stock exchange trading may take place no earlier than two years from the day this act takes effect.

ARTICLE 70
The entity operating a stock exchange will have the duty and the exclusive right to include the words stock exchange in its business name.

ARTICLE 71
The admission of securities for stock exchange trading will be contingent on their being deposited with the National Deposit of Securities.

The National Deposit of Securities will be operated by the corporation (Article 68).

The corporation may transfer its rights related to the operation of the National Deposit of Securities to other entities possessing personality-at-law, subject to the consent of the Prime Minister.

The corporation will in particular have the following operational tasks for the operation of the National Deposit of Securities:

- keeping and registering the securities admitted for stock exchange trading;
- keeping the registry of deposit accounts for entities authorised to deposit securities with it;
- registering the changes in deposit accounts, arising out of transactions between authorised entities;
- supervising the conformity of the volume of issue with the amount of securities in circulation;
- servicing deposit accounts to meet the issuer's obligations to the owners of securities.

The Council of Ministers will define the principles governing the operations of the National Deposit of Securities.

Chapter VII: Substantial share acquisitions

ARTICLE 72

Whoever becomes the holder of a corporation's shares admitted for public trading in amounts entitling him, respectively, to 10 per cent, 20 per cent, 33 per cent, 50 per cent, 66 per cent, 75 per cent or more of the votes at the general meeting will be required to notify this to the commission, the Anti-Monopoly Office and the corporation in question within seven days.

The acquisition or possession of shares by a dependent entity will be regarded as the acquisition or possession by the dominant entity.

The corporation within a month of a regular general meeting or the notification referred to above will publish in two national daily newspapers the names of the shareholders possessing 10 per cent or more of the shares referred to above.

ARTICLE 73

Whoever intends by a single transaction or a series of repeated transactions to acquire shares of a single corporation so to become within 12 months the holder of shares ensuring 33 per cent or more of the votes at general meetings, may do this only by means of public invitation to apply to sell or exchange shares (to be known as the invitation).

The intention to acquire or possess shares on the part of a dependent entity will be regarded as the intention to acquire or possess on the part of the dominant entity.

The intention to make the invitation must be notified to the commission and to the stock exchange where the shares which are the subject of the intended transactions are quoted.

The notification will contain:

- the name and address of the person intending to announce the invitation;
- the designation of the securities which are the subject of the invitation;
- the amount of shares which the inviting entity intends to acquire and information on the size of the block of shares which the inviting entity intends to obtain;
- the planned date of the announcement of the invitation and the deadline for the application to sell or exchange shares;
- the price he intends to pay, the concept of price also encompassing the value of things or rights which the inviting entity intends to offer in exchange for shares;
- permits from the relevant bodies for the acquisition of shares, where required by separate regulations.

The notification will be accompanied by a receipt from a bank or another institution confirming that the inviting entity has deposited a surety equalling at least 50 per cent of the value of the intended transaction.

ARTICLE 74
The commission, within seven days of notification, on consulting the Anti-Monopoly Office, may forbid the publication of an invitation, where the provisions of this act or the Monopolistic Practices Act have been violated, where an important interest of the national economy has been jeopardised, or where the price offered in the invitation is lower by 10 per cent than the average market price in the last three months prior to the publication of the invitation.

ARTICLE 75
Where the provisions of this act have been violated by the inviting entity, the commission may order a withdrawal of the invitation prior to the deadline for applications to sell or exchange shares. Applications effected will be annulled.

ARTICLE 76
The inviting entity may be represented only by an entity operating a brokerage firm.

ARTICLE 77
The announcement of invitation will be made publicly on the stock exchange and in two national daily newspapers.

The announcement will contain the information referred to in Article 73 and will specify the name of the brokerage firm representing the inviting entity.

ARTICLE 78
On announcement of invitation, the stock exchange will discontinue any transactions in the shares referred to in the invitation. Any transactions involving these shares effected after that moment will be invalid ex lege. Where such transactions are allowed in public trading outside the stock exchange, this will also apply to such transactions.

ARTICLE 79
The deadline for applications to sell or exchange shares must not be shorter than 25 days.

Prior to the expiry of the deadline referred to above, the inviting person may change the terms of the invitation. In such case, however, subject to prior notification and the absence of reservations from the commission, he will prolong the deadline referred to above to ensure that there are no less than 15 days between the announcement of the changes in terms and the new deadline.

The invitation may be withdrawn only in cases provided for in this act or in a ruling of the commission.

ARTICLE 80
Prior to the expiry of the deadline referred to in Article 79, other invitations referring to the shares in question may be announced. However, the price

indicated in such invitations must not be lower than 105 per cent of the price indicated in an earlier invitation.

Where another invitation is announced, the person who has announced an earlier invitation may uphold or withdraw it, or announce another invitation.

ARTICLE 81

The person responding to the invitation will, through the intermediary of an entity operating a brokerage firm, apply to sell or exchange shares in an open register run for that purpose by the stock exchange on which the shares are quoted.

The person responding to the invitation may specify the price demanded for the shares.

The person who has applied to sell or exchange shares may demand annulment of his application by notifying the entity operating a brokerage firm which has been retained to make entries in the register.

On notification, referred to above, the response to the invitation will become null and void, unless the notification has been made after the deadline indicated in the invitation. Where there are doubts, the notification will be regarded as having been made prior to the deadline.

ARTICLE 82

The disclosure to anyone of information concerning the names of the applicants and the amounts of shares and prices demanded by the latter will be illegal.

ARTICLE 83

A person responding to the invitation will deposit with the entity operating a brokerage firm the shares intended for sale or exchange or present a receipt confirming the deposit of the shares elsewhere.

ARTICLE 84

On the expiry of the deadline indicated in the invitation, the stock exchange will compile a list of applications specifying the amount of shares and the proposed prices, while not naming the applicants. The list will be presented to the inviting entity.

The inviting entity will acquire all shares presented for sale or exchange at the price offered in the invitation.

Where the amount of shares presented exceeds the amount declared in the invitation, the acquisition will be effected in a manner as proportional as possible to the amounts of shares offered by each applicant, ignoring fractional amounts.

ARTICLE 85

The corporation whose shares are indicated in the invitation must not take any action prior to the expiry of the deadline for subscription to sell or exchange shares which would prevent or thwart the attainment of the objective referred to in Article 73.

ARTICLE 86
Any person who acquires shares and who does not adhere to the requirements of Article 72 or who acquires shares without fulfilling the condition set forth in Article 73, cannot exercise the voting rights attached to those shares.

ARTICLE 87
Whoever has become the holder of shares of a single corporation representing over 50 per cent of the votes available to be cast at the general meeting will, prior to executing any powers arising out of the voting rights, announce an invitation to subscribe for sale or exchange the remaining shares of the said corporation.

The price offered in the invitation must not be lower than the highest prices paid by the entity in question for the shares within the preceding 12 months or in the absence of such a price being the average market price for the last 30 days prior to the invitation being announced. The concept of price will be taken to include the value of things or rights which the inviting person intends to provide in return for the shares.

ARTICLE 88
The provisions of this chapter do not apply to the acquisition of shares from the state Treasury, subject to the provisions of Article 72.

Chapter VIII: Trust funds

ARTICLE 89
The object of the trust funds (known as funds) is the mutual investment of money in securities.

The provisions of this chapter apply to funds with a variable number of participants and non-transferable participation units.

The funds may be managed only by trust fund corporations (referred to as corporations), supervised by the commission.

ARTICLE 90
Corporations will be established exclusively in the form of joint stock corporation domiciled in territory of Poland. A legal person may be a single partner incorporator of such corporation.

Corporations referred to above will have the duty and exclusive right to include the words trust fund corporation in their names.

To the extent not regulated in this act, the corporations referred to above will be governed by the provisions of the Commercial Code.

ARTICLE 91

The business of the corporation will be exclusively the rendering of services which consists of the investment of entrusted capital, accumulated in one or more of specially established funds of different purposes and in the management of these funds.

The corporation must not be involved in the management of funds the assets of which are different from those referred to in Article 102.

ARTICLE 92

The nominal share capital of the corporation will be not less than Zl. 1bn contributed entirely in cash.

The securities issued by the corporation may only be registered securities. The corporation must not transform these securities into bearer securities.

The debt of the corporation may not exceed 10 per cent of its capital. The concept of debt does not include the value of the managed funds.

ARTICLE 93

The incorporator of the corporation may not be a member of the management committee and may not own over 10 per cent of its share capital.

The corporation may not use fund assets for the acquisition of securities issued by a member of the management committee or by an entity linked with the latter by relation of domination or dependence.

ARTICLE 94

Members of the supervisory board are appointed and dismissed in general meeting with the agreement of the commission.

ARTICLE 95

The corporation will publish in two national daily newspapers at least once a year a separate report on the condition of each fund.

The commission may make the approval of the charter of the corporation or changes to it contingent on including provisions requesting the publication of these reports more frequently than once a year.

The provisions above do not infringe on the obligation to publish balance sheets and other data on the condition of joint stock corporations.

ARTICLE 96

The Finance Minister may determine the detailed accounting standards to be observed by the corporation.

ARTICLE 97

The charter of the corporation, the by-laws of a fund and the selection of the trustee bank referred to in Article 112 are subject to joint approval by the commission. The commission will also approve any change in the charter, the by-laws or bank selection.

ARTICLE 98
Where a corporation fails to observe the provisions of this act, the commission may request the dissolution of the corporation.

ARTICLE 99
The corporation will dispose of the funds in its own name, but on the joint account of the participants in the fund.

ARTICLE 100
The corporation must not invest assets in securities issued by itself.

ARTICLE 101
The corporation will be operated in the best interests of the participants in the funds.

The objective and operating mode of the fund and especially the sale and purchase of participations, the calculation of net asset values and the principles governing the publication of information on the condition of the fund, will be specified in the by-laws, to be adopted by the general meeting of shareholders and approved by the commission.

The by-laws will be published in two national daily newspapers.

ARTICLE 102
The assets of the fund may only comprise proprietary rights in securities.

The assets of the fund must not be transferred to funds designed for different purposes.

The purposes for which a fund was established cannot be changed.

ARTICLE 103
The corporation will provide the participant in the fund with a written certificate of participation. The certificate should contain the:

- date of the certificate;
- name of the fund;
- amount of purchased units of participation.

The participation unit referred to above represents a title to participate in the income of the trust fund in accordance with the by-laws of the fund.

The issue of the certificate is subject to registration by the corporation.

The units of participation are not transferable and do not bear interest.

ARTICLE 104
In return for the redemption of participation units, the corporation will pay an

amount equalling a corresponding portion of the fund's net assets on the day of presentation.

The payment will be effected at dates specified by the corporation, not less frequently than once a month.

ARTICLE 105
The corporation will sell participation units with no limitation at the price reflecting the fund's net asset value on the day of sale, in proportion to the total amount of the existing units of participation in the fund.

ARTICLE 106
When disposing of and redeeming units of participation, the corporation may levy a charge in accordance with the principles laid down in the charter.

ARTICLE 107
At least 90 per cent of the value of the fund assets may only be invested in securities admitted for public trading or in securities issued by the state Treasury or the National Bank.

Up to 10 per cent of the value of fund assets may be invested in other securities provided that the price of these securities can be determined at a frequency not lower than necessary for the calculation of the net value of the assets of the fund.

ARTICLE 108
No more than 5 per cent of the value of fund assets may be invested in securities of a single issue.

ARTICLE 109
Any income from the invested capital, net of the statutory remuneration of the corporation, will be added to the value of the fund.

The charter of the corporation and by-laws of the fund may vest the corporation with the right to deduct other costs.

ARTICLE 110
The corporation will publish the information on the condition of the funds at least once a month.

ARTICLE 111
Prior to liquidation of the fund, the corporation will notify the commission, publish the intention of liquidation in two national daily newspapers and specify the deadline, not shorter than six weeks, for the redemption of participation units.

Within two weeks of the end of the deadline, the corporation will distribute, in return for the redeemed participation units, an amount at least proportional to the amount obtained from the sale of fund assets, but not lower than the value of fund assets on the day the intention to liquidate the fund was published.

ARTICLE 112

The corporation will entrust the assets of the fund to a trustee bank for custody.

The trustee bank will be required to:

- ensure safe custody of the assets of the fund;
- ensure that the disposal of and redemption of fund participation units complies with the law and with the by-laws of the fund;
- calculate the net asset value of the fund under the law and by-laws of the fund;
- execute the orders of the corporation, unless these contravene the law or by-laws of the fund;
- ensure that in transactions involving assets of the fund, the amounts due are paid within periods defined in the by-laws;
- ensure that the income of the fund is reported in accordance with the law and the by-laws of the fund.

The contract on entrusting fund assets to a bank may also provide for other obligations on the part of the trustee bank.

ARTICLE 113

The trustee bank must not be an incorporator of the corporation or the buyer of securities issued by the trust. It may not undertake the management of the corporation.

The corporation must not use the resources of the fund for the purchase of securities issued by the bank referred to above or by an entity linked to the bank by a relation of domination or dependence.

Chapter IX: Civil liability and criminal responsibility

ARTICLE 114

The issuer will be liable for damage caused to anyone as a result of a defect in a security or untrue or dishonest information contained in the documents required by law unless he and the person he is responsible for prove to be blameless.

The liability referred to above will also be borne by the entity publicly floating the securities.

The liability referred to above cannot be limited or excluded in advance.

ARTICLE 115

The issuer of a deposit receipt will be liable for damage caused to anyone as a result of a defect in the deposit receipt or of its having been used by an unauthorised person, unless the damage has been the exclusive fault of the injured party or a third party for whom the maker is not liable.

Where the issuer has acted to the order of another party, their liability will be joint and several.

ARTICLE 116

Where the data contained in the prospectus or other information on the issue influencing the value or price of the security are changed, the acquirer of securities in primary public trading may withdraw from the contract unless he has acted in bad faith.

The right to withdraw from the contract will expire a month after announcement of the changes to be made under law or by a decision of the commission.

ARTICLE 117

Whoever publicly floats securities not admitted for public trading will be liable to imprisonment of up to two years, restriction of personal liberty or a fine.

ARTICLE 118

Whoever provides in the prospectus untrue or incomplete data on the financial condition of the issuer or the person floating the securities will be liable to imprisonment of between six months and five years.

ARTICLE 119

Any broker disclosing the information covered by an obligation of professional confidence will be liable to imprisonment of up to three years.

Whoever uses insider information while trading in securities will be liable to imprisonment of between six months and five years.

Insider information, within the meaning of this act, is information which has not been made public but which after publication could substantially influence the value or the price of a security.

ARTICLE 120

Whoever operates in the field of public trading in securities without the required permit will be liable to restriction of personal liberty or a fine.

ARTICLE 121

Whoever conducts operations referred to in Chapter 8 without confirmation required by law, will be liable to imprisonment of up to two years, restriction of personal liberty or a fine.

ARTICLE 122

Whoever fails to make the notification referred to in Article 72 or fails to fulfil the duty referred to in Articles 73, 85 and 86 or discloses the information referred to in Article 82 will be liable to restriction of personal liberty up to three months or a fine.

Whoever holds shares or becomes a partner in more than one corporation or partnership conducting brokerage activity in contravention of the prohibition referred to in Article 29, will be liable to restriction of personal liberty of up to three months or a fine.

Whoever commits the act referred to above while acting for a legal person will be liable to the same penalty.

Chapter X: Amendments to other legislation

ARTICLE 123
Amendments will be made in the Presidential Ordinance of 27 June 1934 introducing the Commercial Code.

ARTICLES 124 AND 125
In the Income Act of 16 December 1972, changes will be made.

ARTICLE 126
In the Corporate Income Tax Act of 31 January 1989, changes will be made.

ARTICLE 127
In the Foreign Exchange Act of 15 February 1989 changes will be made.

Chapter XI: Interim and closing provisions

ARTICLE 128
Within two months of this act taking effect, the Privatisation Minister, acting in co-operation with the Finance Minister, will establish on behalf of the state Treasury the corporation referred to in Article 68.

The state Treasury will dispose of shares in the corporation referred to above at the request of the entities operating brokerage firms and at the request of banks.

The members of the first stock exchange board will be appointed by the Privatisation Minister, acting in co-operation with the Finance Minister.

The first management committee of the corporation referred to above will comprise the chairman and two officers appointed by the Privatisation Minister for a period of three years.

ARTICLE 129
The first convention of brokers will be convened by the commission within six months of entry of 50 brokers into the list.

ARTICLE 130
The provisions of this act will be extended to cover the securities publicly traded on the day this act takes effect within six months of this act taking effect. By that time, the issuers of these securities will be required to meet the conditions referred to in Articles 49, 50 and 51.

The condition referred to in Article 50 will be regarded as met where at least three-fourths of the securities referred to above are placed in deposit.

ARTICLE 131
Entities publicly trading in securities on the day this act takes effect may conduct this activity without meeting the conditions referred to in Chapter III for three months of this act taking effect.

ARTICLE 132
This act takes effect on the day of promulgation.

Law on the Insurance Business in Poland (Law of 28 July 1990)

Chapter I: General provisions

ARTICLE 1
This law stipulates the general provisions and principles of undertaking and carrying on the insurance business against loss or damage and insurance of persons.

ARTICLE 2
Direct and indirect (reinsurance) insurance business may be carried on only with the approval of the Finance Minister.

ARTICLE 3
Insurance will be compulsory or voluntary. Insurance protection will be based on contracts concluded between the insurer and the insured.

ARTICLE 4
Compulsory insurances are:

- third party motor insurance of owners of motor vehicles against damages resulting from the movement of these vehicles;
- insurance of farm buildings against fire and other hazards;
- third party insurance of farmers;
- other insurance provided for by laws in force or international conventions ratified by Poland.

ARTICLE 5
The Finance Minister will issue an ordinance setting out the general conditions of compulsory insurances. This ordinance will determine when the insurance contract has to be concluded, the basic scope of responsibility of the insurer, the minimum guaranteed sum insured, the rights and obligations of the insured and the insurer resulting from the insurance contract. The ordinance will also

establish the basic system of tariffs which will make tariffs dependent on the duration of the non-claim period and making sure that the tariffs of various insurers are comparable.

The insurers may also include in their tariffs other elements relevant to their loss burden.

The level of insurance premiums will be set by the insurer.

The Finance Minister will determine the way to confirm the fulfilment of the duty to get insurance.

The insurer offering compulsory insurance cannot refuse such an insurance.

ARTICLE 6

Insurers are under an obligation to draw up standard general insurance terms. Insurers will present these general insurance terms to the Finance Minister for approval.

The Finance Minister will set the rules for drawing up and publishing the standard general insurance terms.

General insurance terms and tariffs, with the exception of insurances mentioned in Article 4, and insurance premiums, will be set by the insurer. General insurance terms may differ from standard general insurance terms.

General insurance terms will stipulate what is the object of insurance and its scope, how the insurance contracts are to be concluded, the scope and duration of cover provided by the insurer, the rights and obligations of the contracting parties and how damage will be assessed and indemnity payments made.

General insurance terms should provide the insured with a possibility of terminating the contract within 30 days (natural persons) or seven days (legal persons) if the contract was made for more than six months. Termination of the contract by the insured does not free him from obligation to pay premiums for the period of coverage provided by the insurer.

The period during which termination is not possible, as provided for in the contract, must not exceed two years.

The insurer is under an obligation to offer insurance according to the standard general insurance terms. The insurer may offer insurance according to the general insurance terms.

ARTICLE 7

The insurance contract may include additional or different stipulations from those provided for by the standard general insurance terms or by the general insurance terms.

The insurer is under an obligation to indicate to the insured the differences between the standard general insurance terms and the general insurance terms issued by the insurer.

ARTICLE 8
The indemnity payment resulting from insurance against loss or damage cannot exceed the loss or damage suffered unless the contract stipulates otherwise.

If the same risk is covered by two or more insurance contracts, the indemnity payment is made up to the actual value of the loss or damage suffered within the insured sums in each contract and taking into consideration the indemnity payments (if any) made under other insurance contracts.

This does not apply in the case of life and disability insurance.

Those entitled to indemnity resulting from an accident covered by the third party insurance may make claims directly to the insurer.

If the loss or damage is covered by insurance specified in Article 4 and/or in the case specified in Article 51, the insured may make claims directly to the Insurance Guarantee Fund.

ARTICLE 9
The insurer cannot divulge any information relating to the insurance contracts made by the insured. This does not apply to requests by the courts of law, the prosecutor's office or a third party who is the beneficiary under the terms of the insurance contract.

ARTICLE 10
The insurer cannot directly be involved in any other business apart from insurance and related business.

ARTICLE 11
The insurer may carry on insurance business only as a joint stock company or a mutual society.

Shares of the joint stock company can only be nominal ones.

The provisions of the Commercial Code apply to all aspects of the insurance joint stock company which are not covered by this law.

Chapter II: Mutual society

ARTICLE 12
A society which insures its members on a mutual basis becomes, upon being granted permission to operate an insurance business, a mutual society.

The society becomes a legal person upon being entered into the register of mutual societies.

The register of societies is held by the district court for Warsaw Praga.

The register is open for inspection.

The Justice Minister will issue an ordinance setting out procedural rules regarding the register, what information should be entered into it, how it should be kept and detailed regulations specifying how it can be inspected.

ARTICLE 13
The statutes of the mutual society will be invalid unless made in a notarial form.

ARTICLE 14
The statutes should state the name and the registered office of the society. The name should make it clear that it is a mutual society.

The statutes should specify its managing and supervisory structure.

ARTICLE 15
The statutes should specify the operational territory of the society and types of insurance offered.

If the society is to carry on the reinsurance business this should be mentioned in the statutes.

ARTICLE 16
The statutes should stipulate the rules of becoming and ceasing to be a member. Membership must be made dependent upon entering into an insurance contract. Unless the contract stipulates otherwise, membership is terminated on expiry of the insurance contract.

ARTICLE 17
The statutes will set the level of the guarantee capital.

The statutes should provide for the creation of the reserve capital (Article 427 of the Commercial Code). The provisions regarding the yearly net profit and joint stock capital respectively apply to balance surplus and guarantee capital.

The statutes will stipulate what members should contribute to the society. The payment of benefits received by a member from the society does not relieve him from the obligation of paying dues.

The statutes must make it clear if the society may reduce the benefits paid to its members under the terms of their insurance contracts. It is, however, not allowed to reduce these benefits if the statutes provide for unlimited supplementary payments by its members of their unlimited contributions in making up for the losses sustained.

The members of the society will not be responsible for its obligations.

ARTICLE 18
The statutes of the society will stipulate how the balance surplus should be used and what to do if a loss has been made.

ARTICLE 19
The members' contributions to the society and the benefits paid by the society to its members will be the same if the circumstances are the same.

If a society offers several classes of insurance, the statutes should stipulate that additional payments by members to offset losses sustained and repayment of premiums by the society to its members are calculated on the basis of closing balances made separately for each class of insurance.

ARTICLE 20
The rules for convening the annual general meeting and those regarding admission of members to participate in it will be provided for in the statutes.

ARTICLE 21
Articles 390, 392-96, 401-03, 405-07, 411-17 of the Commercial Code apply to the annual general meeting of the society with the following amendments:

- the term joint stock company is replaced by mutual society and the term stockholders is replaced by members of the society authorised to participate in the annual general meeting;
- the rights of minority stockholders, provided for in these articles will apply to minority members and authorised to participate in the annual general meeting as defined by the statutes;
- the provisions relating to shares apply to the titles of participation in the annual general meeting.

ARTICLE 22
Articles 366, 367 and 368-75 of the Commercial Code apply to the board of the society. The terms joint stock company and stockholders are replaced by society and members of the society.

ARTICLE 23
Articles 377, 378, 379, 380, 382-86 and 387 of the Commercial Code apply to the supervisory body of the society. The terms joint stock company and stockholders are replaced by society and members of the society.

ARTICLE 24
The statutes may be changed by the annual general meeting by a majority of at least three-quarters of those voting.

The meeting may empower the supervisory body of the society to make editorial changes in its resolutions or changes requested by the Finance Minister before granting permission to change the statutes.

Changes to the statutes may not affect rights resulting from the existing insurance contracts.

ARTICLE 25
The statutes of the society should contain provisions relating to advertising by the society.

ARTICLE 26
The statutes of the society should contain provisions regarding the winding up of the society and the appointment of liquidators, their number and their powers.

Resolutions concerning the dissolution of the society or its merger with another society require a majority of three-quarters of those voting.

ARTICLE 27
A society which has a limited scope of activity because it has a small membership or a small number of insurance contracts because the sums insured or its territorial area are small may be recognised by the Finance Minister as a small mutual society.

Such recognition by the Finance Minister must be entered into the register.

Articles 17 and 21-23 will not apply to small mutual societies.

ARTICLE 28
The general insurance terms may be incorporated into the statutes of the society.

ARTICLE 29
The general insurance terms of the society will be adopted by the annual general meeting.

The meeting of the society may empower the society's supervisory body of the society to make editorial changes to its resolution on general insurance terms.

The statutes of the society may empower the supervisory body of the society to make editorial changes to the general insurance terms, provided that such changes will be presented for approval to the next annual general meeting.

Chapter III: Principles of starting up and carrying on insurance business

ARTICLE 30
The Finance Minister will grant a licence to start an insurance business at the request of the interested party.

An application to the Finance Minister requesting a licence to start an insurance business should specify the:

- name, registered office, territorial coverage and scope of the activity of the insurer;
- share of guarantee capital at the disposal of the insurer;
- estimated costs of organising the insurer's administration and its network of

agents; the insurer has to prove that it has a special organisation fund for this purpose at its disposal;

- organisational form of its activity;
- qualifications of people proposed for managerial posts as well as the actuary if the insurer offers life assurance.

ARTICLE 31

The application for a licence should be accompanied by a business plan proving that the insurer has funds equivalent to the minimum of the guarantee capital referred to in Article 46.

The business plan should include:

- the statutes of the insurer, indicating whether or not the insurer is involved in reinsurance business;
- the general insurance terms;
- a programme of reinsurance;
- financial projections of the first three years of operation specifying projected costs, burden of losses, income from premiums and the financial situation of the insurer.

ARTICLE 32

A licence will be granted for carrying on the insurance business in one or more classes of insurance mentioned in the Annex to this law.

Any changes in the scope of the business or territorial coverage will also require permission.

ARTICLE 33

A licence cannot be granted if the persons who are to become managers do not have relevant educational qualifications or professional experience.

A licence cannot be granted for carrying on simultaneously life assurance business and the remaining forms of insurance of persons or against loss or damage.

The granting of a licence is dependent upon the employment by the insurer of an expert in insurance mathematics, finances and statistics (an actuary).

The actuary has to calculate the technical and insurance reserves according to the business plan.

ARTICLE 34

The insurer may use the services of an insurance intermediary offered both by natural and legal persons.

The insurer may use the services of insurance or reinsurance brokers including insurance intermediaries. The brokerage may be undertaken by natural or legal bodies subject to a licence being granted by the Finance Minister.

The Finance Minister will specify criteria relating to natural and legal bodies applying for a licence to start up a brokerage business, as well as the scope of such activity and the procedure for granting licences mentioned above.

ARTICLE 35

The Finance Minister may revoke a licence to operate an insurance business in one or more insurance categories if the insurer:

- ceases to fulfil the conditions required for holding a licence;
- breaks the law;
- has not, within the time specified, drawn up a financial or short-term payment plan (Article 48).

ARTICLE 36

If the licence is withdrawn, the insurer cannot conclude any new insurance contracts and cannot extend existing contracts and the insured sum cannot be increased. The Finance Minister may restrict the financial freedom of the insurer or appoint a receiver.

The terms of receivership and its duration will be determined by the Finance Minister.

A decision to withdraw a licence with respect to the whole operation of the mutual society is tantamount to the liquidation of the society.

ARTICLE 37

A Polish subject, as defined by the Polish currency law, may only enter into an insurance contract with the insurer operating under a licence granted according to this law.

A foreign subject carrying on a business in Poland may insure the business only with an insurer as defined above.

The Finance Minister may specify circumstances when insurance contracts may be concluded with insurers other than those mentioned above.

Chapter IV

Conditions governing the starting up and carrying on the business of insurance by companies in which there is a foreign financial interest or in which foreign insurers have an interest.

ARTICLE 38

A licence by the Finance Ministry is required to start up and carry on insurance business by companies in which there is a foreign financial interest or in which foreign insurers have an interest.

ARTICLE 39

A licence to carry on insurance business by a company with foreign capital may be granted if the:

- company complies with conditions which Polish insurers are required to satisfy;
- contribution by the foreign partner amounts to at least one half of the minimum guarantee capital required.

The above does not apply if the foreign partner buys the shares of the company which already carries on insurance.

ARTICLE 40

Insurance funds created by virtue of insurance contracts concluded in Poland as well as own resources will be invested in Poland and may not be transferred abroad (Chapter VI).

ARTICLE 41

A foreign insurer may carry on insurance business in Poland only through its principal agent whose registered office or residence is in Poland.

The appointment of the principal agent must be entered in the commercial register.

A principal agent must maintain books relating to its business in Poland, in Polish and publish a balance sheet and a profit and loss account in Polish and make them available to any insured person on request.

A principal agent is under obligation to keep documents relating to its operation at its registered office in Poland.

ARTICLE 42

The Finance Minister will grant a licence for carrying on insurance business (Article 41) at the request of the interested foreign insurer.

Any changes in the scope of activity or territorial coverage will require a permission by the Finance Minister.

In order to obtain a licence, an insurer must submit to the Finance Minister:

- an application containing the particulars (Article 30) and the business plan (Article 31);
- a certificate issued by the supervisory body in the country where the foreign insurer has its registered office stating that the said insurer is authorised to carry on the insurance business and the certificate should specify the classes of insurance covered;
- a balance and profit and loss account for the last three years of operation;
- proof of having own resources equivalent to at least 50 per cent of the guarantee capital (Article 46);

- proof that Polish insurers may carry on the insurance business in the country of origin of the foreign insurer;
- details of the qualifications of the person who is to become the principal agent.

The foreign insurer is under an obligation to have own resources equivalent to the solvency margin (Article 45). The margin will be calculated taking into account the performance of the principal agent. The minimum guarantee capital of the foreign insurer may not be lower than 50 per cent of the minimum guarantee capital (Article 46).

The foreign insurer is under an obligation to pay a deposit against future obligations of the insurer. The deposit will be equivalent to 25 per cent of the minimum guarantee capital (Article 46) and will be considered as part of own resources.

The own resources of the foreign insurer (as above) will be invested in Poland.

The foreign insurer is under an obligation to create the technical and insurance reserves (Article 49) against obligations resulting from insurance business and invested in Poland (as provided for in Chapter VI).

A licence may be granted if conditions (Articles 39 and 41) are met and the deposit (as above) is paid.

The Finance Minister may withdraw the licence to carry on insurance business by a foreign insurer if:

- the foreign insurer has ceased to be authorised to carry on the insurance business in the country where it has its registered office and in cases specified in Article 35;
- state interest so requires.

A licence may not be granted to the foreign insurer simultaneously offering life assurance and other types of insurance.

ARTICLE 43
When granting a licence to a company with foreign capital or a foreign insurer to do insurance business, the Finance Minister will specify the portion of the profits which may be repatriated without a currency permit and that portion cannot be lower than 15 per cent of profits paid to the foreign body.

ARTICLE 44
The laws and regulations regarding the employment and social security of foreign persons employed in companies with foreign capital apply respectively in all matters relating to the employment contracts with foreign insurers (Article 39) and social security of persons being foreign persons in the meaning of the Currency Law.

Chapter V: Finance of the insurer and insurance funds

ARTICLE 45
The insurer is under an obligation to have own resources equivalent to the solvency margin.

One-third of the solvency margin constitutes the guarantee capital.

ARTICLE 46
The Finance Minster will issue an ordinance which will determine:

- which resources are own resources;
- what the solvency margin is and how it should be calculated;
- minimal amount of the guarantee capital for every type of insurance and for reinsurance.

Together with the yearly balance the insurer will submit to the Finance Minister a calculation of the solvency margin and a proof of own resources amounting to the solvency margin.

ARTICLE 47
The insurer is under obligation to have its yearly balance and profit and loss account verified by an independent accountant or another appropriate body.

ARTICLE 48
If the insurer's own resources are lower than the solvency margin required, he is under an obligation, at the request of the Finance Minister to submit an appropriate financial plan to redress that balance.

If the insurer's own resources are lower than the guarantee capital required, the insurer is under an obligation to submit to the Finance Minister for approval a short-term solvency plan aimed at increasing own resources.

The Finance Minister may, as outlined above, place a time limit on the activities of the insurer, including the investments of resources.

ARTICLE 49
The insurer will create:

- a reserve capital;
- technical and insurance reserves.

In addition to those mentioned above, the insurer may create other funds and special reserves.

The funds and reserves (as above) will be called the insurance fund.

The funds and reserves (as above) and payments to the funds (Articles 51 and 57) will be regarded as costs.

ARTICLE 50
Technical and insurance reserves are intended to cover current and future obligations resulting from insurance activities.

Technical and insurance reserves consist of:

- reserves to cover unpaid insurance claims and payments;
- reserves of premiums for unemployed risks;
- reserve of premiums in the life assurance category calculated on the basis of insurance mathematics;
- the capitalised value of pensions;
- other technical and insurance reserves as provided for in the statutes.

The reserves (as above) will be increased by the income received from their investment.

ARTICLE 51
An Insurance Guarantee Fund will be set up.

The fund is to be used to pay claims arising from the compulsory insurance (Article 4) for:

- bodily injuries if the perpetrator cannot be identified;
- material damage and personal injuries if the perpetrator did not have compulsory insurance.

ARTICLE 52
The fund will have legal personality. Its registered office will be in Warsaw.

ARTICLE 53
The income of the Insurance Guarantee Fund will comprise:

- payments from the insurers carrying on business (Article 4) as a percentage of premiums collected, such percentage being set by the Finance Minister;
- income from resources of the fund invested (Articles 61-64).

ARTICLE 54
The Insurance Guarantee Fund will be run by a board.

The board will consists of representative of insurers carrying on compulsory insurance business (Article 4).

ARTICLE 55
The Finance Minister, in consultation with the Insurance Chamber will determine the procedure for appointing the board of the Insurance Guarantee Fund and its organisation.

ARTICLE 56
The operational costs of the Insurance Guarantee Fund will be covered from its income.

Income of the Insurance Guarantee Fund will not be subject to income tax.

ARTICLE 57
The Finance Minister, in consultation with the Insurance Chamber, will create the Insured Persons Protection Fund and determine its organisational structure, its method of operation and the percentage of premiums to be paid to the fund by the insurers.

The insurers are under an obligation to contribute to the Insured Persons Protection Fund, one for the category of life assurance and one for other types of insurance of persons and insurance against loss and damage. The Insured Persons Protection Fund will pay claims when an insurer becomes insolvent as follows: 100 per cent in the case of life assurance; 90 per cent in the case of compulsory insurance; 50 per cent in the case of other types of insurance.

Contributions to the Insured Persons Protection Fund will be made in case the insurer becomes insolvent.

The board of the Insured Persons Protection Fund will be elected by all insurers operating in Poland.

ARTICLE 58
The Finance Minister will issue an ordinance laying down the rules governing insurance accountancy and financial reporting by insurers and those governing reinsurance of risks for foreign insurers.

ARTICLE 59
The financial result is the difference between the insurer's income and the costs with allowances made for losses and windfall profits.

The Finance Minister will issue an ordinance which will determine the rules for calculating the financial result.

Income is subject to income tax applicable to legal bodies as provided for in separate regulations.

Chapter VI: Investments

ARTICLE 60
The insurer may invest resources.

ARTICLE 61
The insurer should invest its resources, taking into consideration category and structure of its insurances, in such a way as to achieve both the highest level of security and reliability as well as liquidity of funds.

The insurer has to inform the Finance Minister about:

- the purchases of shares of a company if they represent over 10 per cent of the nominal value of the guarantee capital of the company;
- investments in companies dependent on the insurer or if the insurer is dependent on them.

ARTICLE 62
The Finance Minister may (Article 61) forbid purchases by the insurer of shares in a company or restrict it if this may harm the finances of the insurer.

The provisions above also apply in cases when a member of the board or supervisory board of the insurer is a member of the board of the company mentioned above or is a significant shareholder or significantly influences the policy of the board of the company.

ARTICLE 63
Subject to provisions above, the insurer invests its insurance fund exclusively in Poland as:

- paper issued or guaranteed by the state promissory notes or Treasury notes and credits extended to the state or guaranteed by the state;
- bonds of local companies;
- mortgages;
- real estate with the exception of farms;
- listed securities, provided the share of the insurer does not exceed 10 per cent of the nominal value of the stock of the company;
- local unlisted securities and shares in local companies established as stipulated by the Commercial Law provided that these companies will be submitting in the future a yearly balance, a profit and loss account prepared according to the rules applicable to joint stock companies;
- term banking deposits;
- loans secured by own life insurance contracts;
- other investments indicated by the Finance Minister.

Insurance funds generated by insurance contracts in foreign currencies are invested in these currencies.

The Finance Minister may generally authorise insurers to invest insurance funds abroad and determine applicable procedure.

ARTICLE 64
Investments in listed securities cannot exceed 30 per cent of the insurance fund and investment in unlisted securities cannot exceed 15 per cent of the fund.

Investments in real estate cannot exceed 25 per cent of the insurance fund.

Restrictions do not apply to life assurance if they are related to the investment fund.

Chapter VII: Merger of insurers, transfer of insurance contracts, voluntary and forced liquidation

ARTICLE 65

The Finance Minister may allow insurers to merge. The insurers have to prove that after merging they will have own resources amounting to the required solvency margin.

ARTICLE 66

The insurer may arrange with another insurer for the transfer of all or some of its insurance contracts (portfolio transfer). Such an agreement requires authorisation by the Finance Minister.

The insurer taking over the insurance portfolio has to prove that after the transfer is made he will have own resources amounting to the solvency margin required.

The insured have to be informed beforehand by the insurer about his intention to take over the insurance contracts. The insured have the right to dissent. The dissenting insured have the right to give notice of termination of contract within three months after approval has been given.

ARTICLE 67

The liquidation of an insurer can be voluntary or forced.

ARTICLE 68

The insurer has to inform the Finance Minister immediately of any reasons for liquidation and notify him of the composition of the liquidating body.

The Finance Minister may appoint a liquidator ex officio.

ARTICLE 69

The liquidators are under an obligation to submit progressive reports on the liquidation as determined by the Finance Minister.

ARTICLE 70

Articles 445, 446, 448, 449-51, 452-54, 457, 459 and 460 of the Commercial Code apply to mutual societies, with the exception of small mutual societies and the joint stock company and stockholders are being replaced by the mutual society and its members.

The liquidator informs the Finance Minister immediately of the liquidation of the small mutual society.

ARTICLE 71

The resources of the insurance funds are destined to pay insurance claims. Other obligations of the insurer may be paid out of the insurance funds only after all insurance claims have been paid.

ARTICLE 72
The Finance Minister may order a compulsory liquidation if the:

- insurer breaks the law or is inconsistent with the operational plan;
- the annual general meeting does not adopt a resolution making up for the balance losses or if such a resolution is adopted but the loss is not covered within the specified period;
- insurer does not execute the adopted short-term solvency plan within the specified period and the amount of the guarantee capital is lower than the minimal guarantee capital required;
- insurer does not pay claims or pays them late or partially.

ARTICLE 73
In the case of forced liquidation, a liquidator is appointed by the Finance Minister.

ARTICLE 74
If the liquidation of the insurer is decided or ordered, it is not permitted to conclude new insurance contracts, extend existing ones or increase the insured sums.

Chapter VIII: Bankruptcy

ARTICLE 75
The provisions of the Bankruptcy Law apply to the bankruptcy of insurers with exceptions provided in this law.

ARTICLE 76
If the insurer stops paying its debts or its assets are not sufficient to cover its liabilities, he has to report it to the Finance Minister.

The insurer may be declared bankrupt only with the consent of the Finance Minister.

The Finance Minister may request that the insurer be declared bankrupt.

ARTICLE 77
In the category of insurances against loss or damage or insurance of persons, priority is given to claims resulting from compulsory insurance first, and then claims from insurance of persons.

ARTICLE 78
In bankruptcy proceedings of an insurer doing life assurance, the interests of the insured and beneficiaries are represented by the curator appointed by the court.

The curator undertakes all actions necessary to protect claims of persons (as above).

ARTICLE 79
The curator (Article 78) is authorised to transfer the insurances in virtue of a contract.

ARTICLE 80
If the transfer of insurances (Article 78) is not made within four months after the bankruptcy was declared, the insurance contracts become null and void.

ARTICLE 81
If the insurer is declared bankrupt, the insurance contracts with the exception of life insurance, become null and void within a month after the bankruptcy was declared.

Chapter IX: Insurance supervision

ARTICLE 82
The Finance Minister supervises the operation of insurers.

ARTICLE 83
Subject to provisions of Article 9, the Finance Minister may at any time inspect finances of the insurer.

The Finance Minister may request from the insurers explanations and information on the insurer and its finances and may order the insurer to submit the requested data.

ARTICLE 84
Up to 50 per cent of the costs of supervision are borne by the insurers in proportion to the premiums collected.

ARTICLE 85
The decisions of the Finance Minister in matters covered by this law may be appealed by the insurers to the supreme administration court as provided for in the Code of the Administrative Procedure.

Chapter X: Representation of insurers

ARTICLE 86
Insurers may form an association, the Chamber of Insurance.

ARTICLE 87
The statutes of the Chamber of Insurance define its detailed tasks and principles or operation, its organs and the procedure of their election, the scope of operation and the rules governing its finances.

ARTICLE 88
The Chamber of Insurance is a legal body.

ARTICLE 89
The principal tasks of the Chamber of Insurance include:

- giving opinions on draft legislation on insurance matters;
- initiating actions by the Finance Minister (Article 48);
- representing economic interests of the members of the chamber and undertaking actions aimed at protecting those interests;
- fulfilling other tasks resulting from specific laws and regulations.

ARTICLE 90
The Chamber of Insurance is financed by the insurers.

Chapter XI: Final provisions

ARTICLE 91
Any person who is carrying on insurance business without a proper permission or contract to its provisions is subject to imprisonment or a fine.

ARTICLE 92
A person or legal body who declines to get an insurance contract (Article 4) is under an obligation to make a payment amounting to triple the yearly premium.

The Council of Ministers will determine which organs are authorised to verify the compliance with the obligation (Article 4) and will establish procedures for setting and collecting such payments.

Income from these payments constitute income of the Insurance Guarantee Fund.

Making payments as above does not relieve anyone from the obligation to conclude an insurance contract (Article 4).

ARTICLE 93
The Treasury will participate until 31 December 1991 in the expenses of the Insurance Guarantee Fund if they are greater than income of that fund.

ARTICLE 94
Any disputes arising out of the insurance contracts are dealt with by the courts with territorial competence with regard to the seat of the insured unless the insurance contract or the general insurance terms stipulate otherwise.

The provisions above do not apply to foreign bodies.

ARTICLE 95
Insurers who were carrying insurance business before the entry into force of this law will continue this activity if until:

- 30 June 1991 they meet the conditions mentioned in Article 33;

- 30 September 1991 they show proofs of having own means amounting to the required guarantee capital;
- 31 December 1991 they meet conditions mentioned in Article 11.

The insurers (as above) who at the time of entry into force of this law do not meet conditions set out in Article 46 and whose own resources are lower than the minimum guarantee capital, are under an obligation to submit to the Finance Minister before 31 March 1991 a proof that they have own resources amounting to the minimal guarantee capital and a short-term solvency plan.

Creation of a new insurer effected according to Article 33 by an insurer who was carrying on insurance business before the entry into force of this law requires permission of the Finance Minister.

Liquidation of insurers who ceased to be authorised to carry on insurance business before the entry into force of this law is performed according to the existing laws and regulations.

ARTICLE 96

The co-operatives carrying on insurance business under the law of 20 September 1984 on Insurance of Persons and against Losses and Damages (Journal of Laws 45, item 242 and Journal of Laws of 1989, 30, item 160), in virtue of this law on 31 December 1990 are obliged to transform into joint stock companies.

The transformation of a co-operative into a joint stock company requires a resolution of the general meting of its members adopted by an absolute majority of votes in accordance with the procedure specified in its statutes. It also requires adoption of the statutes of the joint stock company.

The shareholders' fund is being transformed into the company stock which is being allocated to the members of the co-operative as decided by the general meeting and the statutes of the company.

ARTICLE 97

Polish National Insurance is being transformed into a joint stock company owned by the Treasury.

The Finance Minister will issue the ordinance which will set the rules of transforming Polish National Insurance and the procedure of taking over the obligations resulting from the existing insurance contracts.

Until Polish National Insurance is transformed, but no later than 31 December 1991, it continues to operate according to the existing laws and regulations and subject to the relevant provisions of this law.

ARTICLE 98

Subject to provisions above, this law rescinds the Law of 20 September 1984 on Insurance of Persons and against Losses and Damages.

The following remain in force:

- provisions of Articles 24 and 71-72;
- provisions of Article 6 until 30 September 1990;
- provisions of Article 6 until 31 December 1991.

ARTICLE 99
This law enters into force on the day of its publication, but Articles 42 and 43 enter into force on 1 January 1993.

Law on the Minister of Ownership Changes (Privatisation Minister) in Poland (enacted 1 August 1990)

ARTICLE 1
The office of the minister of ownership changes (Privatisation Ministry) is established under this law.

ARTICLE 2
The Privatisation Minister will implement the state's policy on ownership changes and will:

- prepare guidelines on state policy on the privatisation of state-owned enterprises;
- prepare, in collaboration with the Foreign Trade Minister, guidelines on state policy on capital co-operation with foreign partners;
- carry out tasks specified in regulations on the privatisation of state-owned enterprises;
- make analysis of the state of ownership changes;
- co-operate with trade unions, associations, chambers of commerce and other civil organisations and with bodies of state administration and local government in the formation and development of private enterprises;
- initiate personnel training and further education in privatisation activity, capital markets and development of private enterprises and publicise experiences and information in these areas;
- perform other tasks arising out of other laws.

The tasks of the Privatisation Minister will not infringe the powers of others under separate laws.

The Minister, in co-operation with the Finance Minister and the president of the National Bank of Poland, will undertake measures leading to the formation of institutions for a securities market.

ARTICLE 3
The Privatisation Minister may contract legal or natural persons to undertake specified civil law and factual activities within the Minister's terms of reference.

ARTICLE 4
The Council of Ministers, by decree, will specify the detailed terms of reference of the Privatisation Minister.

The council will issue the statutes of the Privatisation Ministry and issue a list of organisational units to be responsible to the minister. The statutes may provide for the establishment of regional offices of the ministry and specify their terms of reference.

ARTICLE 5
The Privatisation Board (Ownership Changes Board) will be set up as the advisory board of the Council of Ministers on matters concerning the privatisation of state enterprises.

The board will present opinions on:

- draft proposals on matters referred to in Article 2 of the Privatisation of State Enterprises Act;
- the transformation of a state-owned enterprise into a company on the basis of the Privatisation of State Enterprises Act;
- requests for gratuitous transfer of shares held by the Treasury in a company established as a result of the transformation of a state-owned enterprise;
- requests to permit exceptions to normal procedures for the sale of shares under the Privatisation Act;
- drafts of the decisions referred to in the Privatisation Act and on drafts of decrees to be issued on the basis of the Act;
- especially complex issues related to privatisation, at the request of the Privatisation Minister.

The president, vice-president and seven members of the board will be appointed by the Prime Minister, after consulting the appropriate parliamentary commission. The Prime Minister, after consulting the appropriate parliamentary commission, may replace the president, vice-president or a board member or the whole board.

The by-laws of the board will be adopted by the Council of Ministers.

ARTICLE 6
The following amendments will be made in Article 4 of the Joint Ventures Act (23 December 1988):

- paragraph one, after 'Prime Minister' insert 'at the request of the Ministry of Ownership Changes';
- in paragraph two, replace 'the Prime Minister' with 'the Minister of Ownership Changes';
- in paragraph three, replace 'Minister for International Economic Co-operation' with 'Minister of Ownership Changes'.

ARTICLE 7
This act takes effect on the day of its promulgation.

Poland's act on the privatisation of state-owned enterprises (enacted 1 August 1990)

Chapter I: General provisions

ARTICLE 1
The privatisation of a state-owned enterprise is based on offering to third parties, shares or stocks of a company evolving from the transformation of state-owned enterprises and owned exclusively by the Treasury or offering to third parties the assets of a state-owned enterprise or the sale of the enterprise. A state-owned enterprise can be transformed into a company or liquidated on the basis of this act.

ARTICLE 2
On a motion of the Council of Ministers, parliament will determine annually the general directions of privatisation and specify the use of resources obtained from privatisation activity. Parliamentary decisions are made in accordance with the enactment of the yearly budget act.

The Council of Ministers, by decree, will specify those state-owned enterprises which are particularly significant to the national economy and whose privatisation requires the approval of the council.

ARTICLE 3
The regulations specified in this act concerning the articles of incorporation, shares supervisory council, equity (share) capital and general meetings (of a joint stock company) apply equally to the contract, original capital and the meeting of shareholders of a limited liability company.

ARTICLE 4
Wherever this act refers to foreign parties it means natural persons domiciled abroad; legal persons having their own registered seat abroad; or partnership of natural persons or legal persons, not possessing legal personality.

Disposing of shares is understood to mean the sale of shares, disposal of the rights to shares, their use as collateral or lease of them.

An integrated part of the assets of a state-owned enterprise means a set of tangible and intangible assets which can constitute a separate enterprise, specifically a plant, shop or a service establishment.

Chapter II: Transformation of a state-owned enterprise into a company

ARTICLE 5

The Privatisation Minister may transform a state-owned enterprise into a company provided that the:

- joint request of its executive director and the employee council is submitted after obtaining the opinion of the general assembly of the employees (delegates) and the opinion of its founding body, or;
- the request of the founding body is submitted with the consent of the executive director and the employee council after obtaining the opinion of the general assembly of employees (delegates).

The request referred to above should include specifically: a financial and economic analysis of the enterprise to be transformed; a draft of the company's founding deed as required by the Commercial Code; and a proposal for preferential treatment for employees of the company to acquire shares in that company from the Treasury.

The Privatisation Minister can refuse the transformation of a state-owned enterprise into a company due to the financial or economic condition of the enterprise or important national interest.

A refusal to transform a state-owned enterprise into a company must be made known within three months from the date of submission of the request and, apart from the grounds, include a list of conditions upon the fulfilment of which the transformation of the enterprise will be permitted or the time-period in which the issue of transformation will be reconsidered.

Objections to the refusal should proceed in accordance with Article 61 of the Act of 25 September 1981 on state-owned enterprises.

ARTICLE 6

The Prime Minister, on the motion of the Privatisation Minister, can order the transformation of a state-owned enterprise into a company. In this case the regulations of Article 5 do not apply.

A motion (as above) should be presented after obtaining the opinion of the executive director and employee council of the state-owned enterprise and the founding body. If no opinion is expressed within a month, it is assumed that there are no objections.

The Privatisation Minister will be in charge of the activities leading to privatisation.

ARTICLE 7

The Commercial Code will apply, unless this act provides otherwise, to companies emerging from the transformation of a state-owned enterprise.

ARTICLE 8

A company emerging from the transformation will remain a company owned exclusively by the Treasury until the shares are disposed of to third parties.

A transformed company will assume all the rights and duties of the transformed enterprise.

All rights and responsibilities deriving from administrative decisions are transferred to the transformed company.

ARTICLE 9

By virtue of this act, employees of a transformed enterprise become the employees of a company (with the exception mentioned below).

The employment relationship of those employed by nomination cease from the day of the enterprise's removal from the register of state-owned enterprises. This is deemed a withdrawal of nomination. Re-employment of such persons by the company will occur on terms agreed by both parties.

The executive director of a transformed state-owned enterprise is not entitled to the compensation described in the Act on State-Owned Enterprises, if the director remains employed as a member of the board of directors of the company resulting from the transformation of the state-owned enterprise.

The company will be responsible for obligations arising from the terms of employment which existed prior to the transformation of the enterprise.

ARTICLE 10

The articles of incorporation of a company emerging from the transformation will be settled by the Privatisation Minister acting on behalf of the Treasury.

ARTICLE 11

The closing annual balance sheet of a state-owned enterprise will constitute the opening balance sheet of a company, the founding fund and the enterprise fund becoming the initial capital of the company. The company's articles will specify which part of the initial capital constitutes equity capital and which reserve capital.

ARTICLE 12

Immediately after a company's articles are adopted, the board of the company will apply for the company to be entered into the commercial register.

After a company is entered in the commercial register, the state-owned enterprise is automatically removed from the state-owned enterprise register.

ARTICLE 13

Articles 14-16 apply to companies resulting from the transformation of state-owned enterprises, provided the Treasury holds all the shares.

ARTICLE 14
Up to the moment that the shares are disposed of to third parties, companies are bound by the regulations of the general rules of accounting in state-owned enterprises, taking into consideration the Commercial Code.

The Finance Minister, by an executive order, can determine for companies specific accounting rules which observe the Commercial Code.

ARTICLE 15
The company's management must publish an audited annual balance sheet and a profit and loss account in a daily printed newspaper, within a period of two weeks from the date of verification.

The publication should contain the name of the institution or person who audited the balance sheet.

ARTICLE 16
A company that came into existence in accordance with this act can be a sole founder of a joint stock company.

ARTICLE 17
A supervisory council will be set up in a company which evolved from the transformation of a state-owned enterprise. The employees of the company are entitled to elect one-third of the members of the council.

The regulations of the company's articles on the election of the members of the council by the employees cannot be repealed or amended while more than half of the shares remain in the hands of the Treasury, unless consent is given by a majority of those members of the council who are elected by the employees.

A company's employees elected to the council enjoy the same legal protection of their terms of employment as members of the employee council in state-owned enterprises.

Election of the members of the council conducted by the voting of separate groups (Article 379 of the Commercial Code) apply only to that part of the council which is not elected by the employees.

Chapter III: Disposing of shares to third parties

ARTICLE 18
Transferring and encumbering shares belonging to the Treasury in companies which have emerged from the transformation of state-owned enterprises. Subscribing for the shares in such companies, provided the Treasury remains the sole shareholder, are regulated by the Commercial Code (unless the present act specifies otherwise).

Gratuitous transfer of shares requires the consent of the Council of Ministers.

ARTICLE 19
The Privatisation Minister decides whether shares owned by the Treasury will be offered to other parties. Shares should be disposed of within two years from the date of recording the company in the commercial register, unless the Council of Ministers provides for a longer period.

Offering shares to foreign parties requires the approval of the president of the Foreign Investment Agency if the par value of these shares exceeds 10 per cent of the share capital or where these are privilege shares.

The regulations above apply when disposing of shares to legal persons, with a registered seat in Poland, controlled directly or indirectly by a foreign party.

The Privatisation Minister is authorised to decide whether to increase the share capital of a company owned exclusively by the Treasury through an issue of new shares. The regulations of this article apply to the extent relevant to the acquisition of shares by a foreign party.

ARTICLE 20
Before offering shares to third parties, the Privatisation Minister will order an economic and financial study for the purpose of asset valuation and establishing whether the implementation of organisational, economic or technical changes is required.

The Privatisation Minister can grant an exemption from an economic and financial study, as above, if the company was valued before its transformation and the disposal of shares is to occur directly afterwards.

The Privatisation Minister will order an analysis in order to determine the legal status of a company's assets, with specific consideration to claims on those assets by third parties.

The Privatisation Minister, by an executive order, will determine the rules and the methods of preparing such an analysis and the qualifications required by the persons preparing such a report.

ARTICLE 21
The Privatisation Minister can make it a condition that company shares are only offered to third parties after the implementation of changes (Article 20).

ARTICLE 22
Before offering shares to third parties, the Privatisation Minister, with the approval of the Finance Minister on behalf of the Treasury, can take over part or all of the company's debt.

The Privatisation Minister will announce the intention to take over the company's debts in the same manner as that required for making company announcements. He will call creditors to present their reservations no later than two months from the day of issuing such an announcement.

Those creditors, who within the period of time specified above do not state their agreement for the debt take-over, must be satisfied or secured prior to the company's debt take-over. The statement on the take-over of the company's debt is made by the Privatisation Minister as if making a company announcement.

ARTICLE 23

Subject to exceptions specified in Article 24, shares belonging to the Treasury will be sold on:

- an auction basis;
- a public offer basis;
- a negotiated basis after a public invitation.

In specific cases the Council of Ministers, on a motion of the Privatisation Minister, can permit Treasury shares to be sold in a different manner to those specified above.

Selling Treasury shares in ways other than those specified above, or without the permission required above, is void.

The Privatisation Minister in agreement with the Finance Minister, will specify by executive order the financing principles of the offer of Treasury shares in companies resulting from the transformation of state-owned enterprises.

ARTICLE 24

Employees of a state-owned enterprise transformed into a company are entitled to buy up to 20 per cent of the total amount of shares of the company held by the Treasury on a preferential basis. Employees retain the right to buy and acquire more shares on generally available terms.

Offering shares to employees on a preferential basis will take place no later than two months from the time that the shares are offered on general terms.

Employees' rights to buy shares on preferential terms expire within one year from the moment of opening the sale of shares to employees.

Shares sold on a preferential basis to employees will be sold at a 50 per cent discount compared to the price set for natural persons, who are Polish citizens, offered on the first day of sale. This price is not subject to change during the period discussed above.

The total value of discounts given to the employees of an enterprise which was transformed into a company must not exceed the product of the average pay per employee in the state enterprise in the 12-month period prior to the registration of the new company in the commercial register and the number of employees purchasing shares.

The number of shares sold on a preferential basis to individual groups of employees and the conditions and deadlines for payment will be specified by the company's articles, as under Article 5.

Agricultural producers who are permanently connected with a company either through contracts of co-operation or of deliveries of agricultural produce may purchase shares in that company on the same preferential basis prescribed for employees.

The Council of Ministers will specify the types of companies in which shares may be purchased under the conditions above.

ARTICLE 25
Parliament, on a motion of the Council of Minsters, will pass a resolution regarding the issue and value of privatisation coupons which can be used to pay for acquiring:

- shares issued as a result of the transformation of a state-owned enterprise;
- title to participation in financial institutions (mutual investment funds) which will have at their disposal shares created as a result of the transformation of state-owned enterprises;
- enterprises or integrated parts of the assets of state-owned enterprises (Article 37).

The privatisation coupons issued as above will be distributed free in equal amounts to all citizens of Poland resident in the country.

The Council of Ministers will determine by decree the expiry date of particular issues of coupons, their form and distribution rules and the rules for making use of such coupons, rules limiting and under certain conditions prohibiting, the transfer of coupons.

ARTICLE 26
The Council of Ministers by decree may also decide that certain issues of coupons (Article 25) be available on credit terms.

ARTICLE 27
On the basis of separate legal provision, payment for the purchase of shares from the Treasury can also be effected in securities.

The Council of Ministers will at the request of the Privatisation Minister specify by decree the required form of payment for shares acquired from the Treasury.

The Privatisation Minister upon the approval of the Finance Minister can allow Polish citizens to pay for shares by instalments.

ARTICLE 28
The Privatisation Minister will entrust shares to a bank or another financial institution according to rules specified in a contract, if the rights to these shares have not been acquired within a period of three months from the end of the time that they were to be offered (Article 19).

A bank or another financial institution, according to the contract, can exercise the rights deriving from ownership of the transferred shares. All revenues earned are transferred to the Treasury.

ARTICLE 29

State legal persons cannot, without the prior consent of the Finance Minister, purchase shares belonging to the Treasury.

ARTICLE 30

The regulations of the present chapter apply also to the transfer of rights and acquisition of shares in a company in which the sole shareholder is a company exclusively owned by the Treasury.

ARTICLE 31

The provisions of Article 41 of the Act on Economic Activity with the Participation of Foreign Investors (23 December 1988) do not apply to the area regulated by this chapter.

ARTICLE 32

In case of an increase in the share capital of a company created as a result of the transformation of a state-owned enterprise, the contribution of a foreign party to share capital will be in accordance with the conditions specified in Article 16 of the Act on Economic Activity with the Participation of Foreign Investors (23 December 1988). To the extent relevant, this provision applies to payment for shares.

ARTICLE 33

Net income from shares belonging to foreign parties, which were acquired according to the rules in Article 32 can be repatriated according to the rules in Articles 19, 20 and 29 of the Act on Economic Activity with the Participation of Foreign Investors (23 December 1988).

Despite the non-fulfilment of the conditions specified in Article 32, the Finance Minister, at the request of the Privatisation Minister, can consent, in accordance with the principles specified above, to the transfer abroad of income from shares acquired or bought by foreign parties.

ARTICLE 34

Proceeds obtained from the sale or redemption of shares and the amount of liabilities due to a foreign party in the case of the liquidation of a company can be transferred abroad after tax without foreign exchange permission.

The Finance Minister, by an executive order, will specify the rules for transferring amounts of Polish currency obtained as above. These amounts will be wholly transferred abroad within a period not longer than five years from the day of obtaining them, unless an international agreement to which Poland is a party specifies otherwise.

ARTICLE 35

Any contribution in kind to the share capital by foreign parties will not be subject to import custom duty or other charges similar in effect to such duty.

ARTICLE 36

The regulations specified in Articles 31-35 apply to companies of which the sole founder is another company exclusively owned by the Treasury and also to the contributions, payment for shares, taxation and transfer abroad by a foreign party of income and proceeds obtained from the sale or redemption of shares or amounts due to the foreign party in the case of liquidation of such companies.

Chapter IV: Privatisation of state-owned enterprise by means of asset liquidation

ARTICLE 37

A founding body, after obtaining the consent of the Privatisation Minister, may rule that a state-owned enterprise be wound up in order to:

- sell its assets or integrated parts of the enterprise's assets;
- use the enterprise's assets or integrated parts of the assets as a contribution to a company;
- allow the enterprise's assets or integrated parts of its assets to be let, upon payment, for a specified time.

The decision to wind up and liquidate is made by the founding body on its own initiative or at the request of the employee council of the enterprise.

The employee council and the executive director of the enterprise have the right to challenge the decision referred to above (Article 61 of the act specified in Article 5).

ARTICLE 38

Liquidation in order to allow an enterprise's assets to be let, upon payment, as discussed in Article 37, may take place if:

- a motion to liquidate and to allow the assets to be let, upon payment, is adopted by the employee council after obtaining the opinion of the general assembly of the employees (delegates);
- the permission to let these assets is for the benefit of a company;
- a majority of the employees of the liquidated enterprise join the company;
- only natural persons are partners in this company, unless the Privatisation Minister determines otherwise;
- the amount of share capital or the equity capital of the company will not be less than 20 per cent of the joint value of the founding fund and the fund of the liquidated enterprise.

Winding up against payment, use of assets, may occur regardless of the conditions prescribed above, if the company which ought to fulfil these conditions is not created within two months from the day of the employee council's decision on winding up or on the approval of the general assembly of employees (delegates).

ARTICLE 39

The letting of assets against payment will be based on a contract concluded in the name of the Treasury by the founding body.

In the contract referred to above the parties can determine that, after a certain period of time, the user has the right to purchase those assets which he is using. In determining the purchase price, the value of all rentals or other dues paid by the user to date will be taken into account.

The Finance Minister will prescribe the principles for determining amounts due for the use of Treasury assets in cases referred to above.

ARTICLE 40

Where a state-owned enterprise is wound up on the basis of the regulations of the Act on State-Owned Enterprises, a founding body in the name of the Treasury can:

- contribute to a company the assets remaining after the liquidation of an enterprise or a part of it;
- sell the assets remaining after the liquidation of an enterprise or a part of it.

ARTICLE 41

When selling assets of a liquidated enterprise or integrated parts of it, or allowing them, on payment, to be let, the founding body will apply the regulations specified in Articles 23, 25 and 39 as it is relevant.

ARTICLE 42

The regulations of Chapters II and III of this act apply to the extent relevant to companies exclusively owned by the Treasury created on the basis of Articles 37 and 40 and also to the disposing of shares in such companies.

ARTICLE 43

The rules for the sale of an enterprise apply to the extent relevant to the sale of an integrated part of the assets of a state-owned enterprise.

Chapter V: Specific, temporary and final regulations

ARTICLE 44

For notarial deeds connected with the transformation of a state-owned enterprise into a company, the Notary Office will charge a fixed fee. The Justice Minister will determine by executive order the level of fee payable to public notaries.

ARTICLE 45
The provisions of this act apply as relevant to the privatisation of municipal enterprises, subject to the provisions below.

The powers of the Privatisation Minister and the founding body will be exercised in respect of municipal enterprises by the municipal council or the council of the association of municipalities.

The municipality or the association may on the basis of an agreement with the Privatisation Minister transfer the conduct of all activities associated with privatising a municipal enterprise to the minister. The conclusion of the agreement requires a resolution of the municipal representatives or the representatives of the association.

ARTICLE 46
The Finance Minister in the interest of the national economy at the request of the Privatisation Minister may exempt a company from income tax and tax on wage increases for a period of three years from the date a foreign party acquires shares belonging to the Treasury or acquires shares issued by a company owned exclusively by the Treasury.

In the event of declaring the liquidation of a company during a period of income tax exemption or within three years from the end of this period, the company is obliged to pay the tax for the whole period of exemption. In this case the tax obligations arise at the moment of the liquidation of the company.

ARTICLE 47
The Council of Ministers, within a period of two months from the act coming into force will present to parliament the motion mentioned in Article 2 for the year 1990.

ARTICLE 48
The following changes are introduced to the Decree Law on the President of Poland (27 June 1934), the Commercial Code (57, item 502, 1946; 57, item 321, 1950; 34, item 312, 1964; 16, item 94, 1989; 13, item 95, 1988; 41, item 326):

- in Article 207 after 'company employees' add 'having a position of general accountant, legal adviser, plant manager or other direct subordinate to the board members';
- in Article 378 after 'company employees' add 'having a position of general accountant, legal adviser, plant manager or other direct subordinate to board members'.

ARTICLE 49
The following changes are introduced to the Act on State-Owned Enterprises (25 September 1981: 1987, number 35, item 201):

- Article 25.3 is to read: 'Article 25.3 The order to liquidate a state-owned enterprise on the basis of the State-Owned Enterprises Act will be issued in agreement with the Privatisation Minister';

- Article 29 is repealed;
- Article 30, paragraph 1, 'and the procedures for liquidating a state-owned enterprise in order to establish a company' delete;
- in paragraph two after 'after the liquidation of a state-owned enterprise' add 'and also a liquidation on the basis of the Act on Privatisation of State-Owned Enterprises';
- in Article 46 after 'founding body' insert 'according to the Act of (date) on the Privatisation of State-Owned Enterprises'.

Uncompleted liquidation proceedings that started under the State-Owned Enterprises Act will be continued under this act.

ARTICLE 50
The following changes are introduced to the Act of 28 December 1989 dealing with detailed principles for dissolving employees' terms of employment for reasons related to the employer and dealing with amendments to some laws (4, item 19, and 10, item 59, 1990):

- Article 8, paragraph three will read: '3 Severance payments are not payable to employees who: (1) are entitled to obtain a single termination payment on retirement or disability retirement; (2) at the date of dissolving the terms of employment, accepted an offer to be employed in a firm that has taken over all or part of the asset of the firm employing them to date or in a firm created as a result of such a take-over; (3) after dissolving the terms of employment, start to undertake economic activity on their own account or as part of a company or co-operative related to the take-over of specified movable or immovable assets of the employer organisation; this applies also to to an employee who at the moment of dissolving the contract of employment is a partner/shareholder in a company or a member of a co-operative, executing such a take-over.'

ARTICLE 51
This act takes effects on the day of its promulgation.

Chapter 6

ROMANIA

Romania's reform progress suffered from political instability and a lack of help from western financial and government institutions. Following the overthrow of the communist regime, the National Salvation Front-formed government was unable to convince the West that the changes taking place in the country were aimed at dismantling a centrally planned economy and introducing a market one. A series of political set-backs, including serious riots in the capital Bucharest, led to the fall of the Petre Roman Government in autumn 1991. While the perception of Romania's reform progress from outside the country was stunted, in reality the country had achieved some significant advancements. Privatisation, although delayed because of political in-fighting, began by the end of 1991, with the passage of the privatisation law in early autumn 1991. Economic reforms were far-reaching, including the liberalisation of prices and foreign trade. By November 1991, the government introduced internal convertibility and was hoping that the West would finally recognise that the country's reform efforts were real and far-reaching.

Banking reform

Romania's banking reform began with the dismantling of the previous system which, despite the existence of four specialised banks, was in fact a mono-bank system dominated by the National Bank. From 1 December 1990, the National Bank assumed traditional central bank functions and almost all its commercial credit and deposit operations were transferred to the newly established Romanian Commercial Bank.

At the same time, the specialised banks were transformed into state-owned commercial banks. Three new private commercial banks were also established and several applications and licences are under consideration by the National Bank. All the new banks were set up as shareholding companies.

There now exists in Romania a two-tier banking system consisting of the National Bank as a central bank with the independent commercial banks below, free to operate anywhere in the country and with whom they wish.

Legal framework

The legal framework for prudential supervision in Romania is based on a new central bank and banking law. The Law on Banking Activity and the Status-Law of National Bank of Romania aim to protect the interest of the creditors and maintain a stable banking system. All domestic banks and branches of foreign banks in Romania are subject to supervision by the National Bank. The system of bank supervision allows for both on-site and off-site controls. The regulation and supervision department of the National Bank has drafted prudential regulations and is empowered to conduct regular surveillance of the banks, relying on analysis of bank reports and inspections. The department comprises a regulation division, central risk office and supervision division.

Banks are defined by law as those juridical persons which have as a principal business the activity of collecting funds from the public through deposits or non-negotiable instruments payable on demand or on short notice as well as granting credits. Banks are established in Romania as juridical persons under the law for commercial companies. They cannot be established in the form of societies with limited liability. The establishment, operation and liquidation of branches of banks that are foreign juridical persons are governed by the law on commercial companies, following the recognition of these banks as foreign juridical persons under Romanian law. Subsidiaries of foreign banks in Romania are formed under the law on the operation of agencies of foreign companies and foreign economic organisations.

Licensing

A licence from the National Bank is needed for a bank to conduct business. Under the banking law, the National Bank established the documentation that must be presented on application for a licence and the conditions under which a licence is granted. The National Bank also established the conditions under which a licence will be revoked or withdrawn. The National Bank will keep a register of all banking licences issued and in force and this register will be open to the public.

In the case of merger, dissolution, liquidation or bankruptcy, the provisions of the law on commercial companies will apply and special provisions and express instructions of the National Bank. The merger of two or more banking companies must receive a new licence from the National Bank.

Participation of a bank in a company or enterprise whose activity has no connection with banking cannot exceed 20 per cent of the capital of the company or enterprise, unless the National Bank says otherwise.

In order to protect the rights of depositors, the law provides for setting up of funds for the insurance of money deposits held by banks for the benefit of physical persons.

In order to supervise Romanian banks operating abroad, the National Bank will co-operate with the supervisory authorities of the respective foreign country. Information concerning foreign banks operating in Romania may be given to the banking supervision authorities of the country of origin, but only on the basis of reciprocity.

The prudential supervision of banks is in its infancy in Romania. The National Bank regulation and supervision department is developing a comprehensive off-site monitoring system based on a set of prudential regulations regarding capital adequacy, liquidity, loans to large customers, investment limits and other matters. The National Bank is being helped in this by a team of experts from the Netherlands Bank under an International Monetary Fund technical assistance. On-site supervision and examination of asset quality have not yet been developed.

Implementation of prudential supervision has been complicated by structural factors, and by many inadequacies of the legal and administrative infrastructure for banking. Laws on bankruptcy, treatment of collateral, mortgagees and other regulations are needed. Standards on accounting regulations and a system of independent auditing needs to be developed. A large proportion of non-performing loans in the total assets of Romanian banks has made it difficult to implement prudential rules until the banks are recapitalised. The problem of 'old' housing credit portfolio consisting of credits at low, fixed interest rates also needs to be solved.

National Bank

The National Bank is a purely central bank, having given up all other commercial interests. It has functions similar to all other European central banks, issuing and controlling the legal tender and exercising the control and supervision of all banking activities. The bank is headed by a governor and participates every month at the Bank for International Settlements (BIS) meetings in Basle. Domestically the bank has an extensive network throughout the country. It controls official exchange rates.

Commercial Bank of Romania

Taking up all of the National Bank's commercial business is Commercial Bank of Romania. The bank represents competition to the long-established Romanian Bank for Foreign Trade. The capital of Commercial Bank is around Lei 12bn paid up capital of Lei 7bn. The bank has a full licence to operate in all banking activities.

Agricultural Bank

Agricultural Bank is a specialised bank working with the agricultural companies, farms and individuals and extending credits in this area. Although it existed for the last 30 years, it has been reorganised as a public limited company. Capital stands at Lei 9bn (30 per cent paid up, divided in 1.2m shares of Lei 5,000 each).

The bank has a full licence for all domestic banking operations and is also allowed to carry out international transactions. The main problem for the bank — and a point valid for all new commercial banks in Romania — is how to build up an international correspondent banking network.

Romanian Bank for Development

The Romanian Bank for Development, the former Investment Bank of Romania, will follow many of the activities of the old bank. It has worked in the past with the International Monetary Fund and World Bank in dispersing loans and is expected to do so in future. Apart from this function, it will deal with financing important projects in Romanian industry, and has developed recently a department dealing with credit facilities to small, private enterprises.

Romanian Savings Bank

CEC, the Romanian Savings Bank, is also a state bank and is the only savings bank in the country. It has an extensive network in every town and village in Romania. The bank needs to modernise methods and equipment as well as training staff. It does not have any international ambitions at the moment.

Romanian Bank for Foreign Trade

Romanian Bank for Foreign Trade is the most important internationally known Romanian bank. It was established in 1968 and has an international network of over 3,000 correspondent banks. The bank has an initial capital of Lei 7bn of which $110m is held in dollars. The bank has subsidiaries in London, Paris, Frankfurt, Milan and Cairo and has opened a full branch in New York, replacing the representative office which it has run from there since 1979.

The bank will in time be privatised, with the state retaining a 20 to 30 per cent holding and the rest sold to private investors. All the international loans, banking and financial transactions Romania has been involved in over the years have been conducted through this bank. Coopers & Lybrand has been asked to deal with the privatisation of the bank.

There are plans to set up an export credit guarantee bank in Romania and create at least one other private bank with foreign participation. Foreign banks are also showing interest in setting up in Bucharest.

Foreign banks

There are some foreign banks in Romania. Manufacturers Hanover Trust has a full branch, established in 1974, dealing with commercial banking in Romania, the Balkans and the Middle East. It has been very successful from its first year of operation and has grown into one of the most profitable branches of the US bank abroad.

Société Générale of France was established in Bucharest in 1981. Frankfurt Bucharest Bank and MISR Romanian Bank are branches of Romanian joint venture banks in Frankfurt and Cairo respectively. The two banks, set up in 1981 have an important share in Romanian exports abroad. They deal in all aspects of international banking. Banque Franco Roumaine Paris opened a branch in Bucharest in 1991.

Private banks

Private banks in Romania are represented by Mindbank, Bank Co-op (created in 1990) as the first co-operative banks in Romania. They offer export credit facilities.

Commercial Bank Ion Tiriac is Romania's first private bank in the full sense of the title. Shareholders include Ion Tiriac, a former Romanian tennis player, plus Boris Becker, Guillermo Villas and Henri Leconte and unspecified German interests. The bank deals mainly in granting credits for small, private enterprises and in property business.

Foreign exchange market

The following Romanian banks have been authorised to participate in the inter-bank foreign exchange market: Romanian Commercial Bank, Romanian Foreign Trade Bank, Romanian Investment Bank, Agrobank, Tiriac Bank, Mindbank, Bankcoop, Dacia Felix Bank (Cluj), Romanian Savings Bank.

Internal convertibility

In November 1991, Romania introduced internal convertibility. The new foreign exchange regime is managed by a float with interventions by the National Bank to smooth fluctuations in the exchange rate of the national currency. The currency was initially devalued, with support from the International Monetary Fund (IMF) and World Bank for the move. At the same time as internal convertibility was introduced, the exchange rate for the leu was unified. This was a consequence of further trade liberalisation and of pressure from the IMF to scrap the dual exchange rate system which favoured inefficient companies.

Under internal convertibility state companies will surrender to authorised banks 100 per cent of their foreign exchange receipts from export of goods and services at the exchange rate of the day. Companies with mixed capital (state and private) will surrender only part of their foreign exchange holdings, corresponding to the share of the state in the company. After 31 December 1991, however, the balance of holdings of foreign exchange will be surrendered at the exchange rate of the day.

Private companies can use their foreign exchange holdings to make payments in foreign currency until 31 December 1991 after which the remaining holdings will be exchanged at the prevailing rate of exchange.

Companies are permitted to buy from authorised banks at the exchange rate of the day foreign currency for imports of goods and services.

Foreign exchange can be obtained at the authorised commercial banks by any economic agents in Romania, irrespective of the form of ownership, but only for international currency account payments. Capital transfers from the country can be done only with prior authorisation of the National Bank. All payments within Romania must be in the national currency, the leu. The use of the leu is allowed only within Romania.

Physical persons may continue to hold foreign exchange in the form of banknotes and coins or in bank deposits. Physical persons are allowed to effect foreign exchange transactions only through foreign exchange offices or exchange desks at commercial banks authorised by the National Bank to do such deals.

Privatisation

The law itself was approved by parliament on 31 July 1991, but a series of political problems delayed the start of the programme. The government embarked on its privatisation programme in the autumn of 1991. The programme is broken down into three major areas. One part is agricultural reform, an ongoing process. The Land Law was passed in 1991, establishing the legal framework for the transfer of agricultural land into private property. Under this, over 8m hectares of agricultural land, representing about 75 per cent of the total agricultural area, is liable to be privatised.

In housing the government plans to sell flats from the state housing fund to present occupants. A special law has been approved by parliament to allow for this. A law was under preparation in late 1991 which would compensate owners of houses and flats that were nationalised in the past.

Privatisation of commercial companies

The privatisation of commercial companies is covered by the Privatisation Law, enacted in August 1991. The law is an operational document which sets out the privatisation strategy to be followed. The specific objectives of privatisation are to create profitable private companies and increase shareholder value, raise funds for restructuring and rehabilitating commercial companies, set an example of commercial and entrepreneurial management practices to be followed by other companies, provide the foundation for an efficient capital market and educate the Romanian public on the operations of capital markets.

Transformation of enterprises

In July 1990, parliament adopted a law transforming all Romanian state-owned enterprises into either joint stock or limited liability companies (commercial companies) to be later privatised or as self-sufficient administrations (regie autonomes), which are to remain under state control. Under this law (number 15), eligible Romanian citizens would receive, free, nominal securities representing in aggregate 30 per cent of the nominal share capital of the newly created commercial companies. To prepare, organise and co-ordinate the 30 per cent transfer programme, as it became known, and the privatisation process in general, the National Agency for Privatisation (NAP) was set up.

Private ownership funds

Under the privatisation law, 30 per cent of the shares of each commercial company is transferred to five private ownership funds (known as POFs). These funds are to be allocated shares of specific commercial companies by the Privatisation Agency. Each of the five funds will issue one certificate of ownership in bearer form to each eligible citizen. As a result, eligible citizens will own an indirect 30 per cent interest in the commercial companies. All citizens living in Romania over the age of 18 on 31 December 1990 were eligible to receive certificates free.

The holders of the certificates can sell or exchange them for shares of commercial companies that are to be privatised within five years from the effective date of the law. They also have the option to convert their certificates at the end of a five-year period into shares of Private Ownership Funds following the reorganisation of these funds into commercial companies mutual funds. The certificates, however, cannot be transferred to non-Romanian natural or legal persons.

The five funds will be organised as joint stock companies governed by Romanian company law. For their first five years of operation, the funds will be covered by specific provisions of the Privatisation Law. During this period they will function as regular joint stock companies but their shareholders — citizens holding certificates of ownership — will not have voting rights or attend annual meetings. All the business of the funds will be managed by a seven-member board of directors for each fund. The board members will be nominated by the government and approved by the Economic Commissions of the National Assembly (parliament) and Senate. The members of the boards of directors will be chosen among persons with commercial, financial, industrial or legal experience.

Management of the private ownership funds

The funds are obliged under the law to manage the shares allocated to them to maximise the value of the certificates of ownership. They can sell shares or buy them. They will also distribute dividends to certificate holders when possible and assure brokerage services for the exchange of issued certificates into shares of commercial companies.

State Ownership Fund

The remaining 70 per cent of state-owned nominal share capital of commercial companies — except the portion of the share capital of companies to be privatised under the early privatisation programme — will be transferred to a State Ownership Fund created under the law as an independent legal entity.

Although the fund will be a public institution, it will function as a commercial company, managed by a 17-member board of directors. The board will consist of five members appointed by the President of Romania, three appointed by the Senate, three by parliament, five chosen among the leading staff of the central public administration and appointed by the Prime Minister and the State Secretary for Privatisation.

The fund will have its own budget and be exempt from profit tax. The main aim will be to reduce ownership interest in commercial companies until they are completely privatised. The fund will be obliged to prepare commercial companies for privatisation by taking steps to increase their efficiency, restructure, rehabilitate and if necessary liquidate companies.

Early privatisation

There are also provisions in the privatisation law which allow for the early privatisation of 30 companies. These 30 companies will be privatised through the sale of shares before the various funds and organisational structures are in place. The privatisation agency will be responsible for selecting the 30 companies, on the basis of recommendations of branch ministries.

Early privatisation may be accomplished by the commercial companies themselves, irrespective of the existence of the funds and is to be encouraged by the publication of a list of assets targeted for sale during the first year following the introduction of the privatisation law. The proceeds from the share sales of early privatisation candidates will be contributed 30 per cent to the private ownership funds and 70 per cent to the state ownership funds. Proceeds from the sale of assets will be retained by the commercial companies.

Share sales

Privatisation through the sale of shares will in general be unrestricted. Shares in commercial companies may be sold to any domestic or foreign person or company by means of a public offering, auction (sale to the highest bidder), direct negotiations (private sale) or a combination of these methods. All sales are subject to approval by the National Privatisation Agency. The agency must respond within 30 days of receiving the proposed conditions of the sale. Conditions for presenting, organising and effecting sales of shares will be provided in regulations to be published in the Official Gazette.

When a purchaser wants to acquire 100 per cent of the shares of a commercial company, the law provides that the state ownership fund will delegate to the private ownership fund the power to negotiate the conditions of the sale.

Asset sales

The law also provides that all asset sales to be effected on the basis of either a public auction (sale to the highest bidder) or a sealed bidding procedure. Regulations on this are to be published in the Official Gazette.

Assets that fall within the scope of the law and must be sold under it are identified as assets that represent units that can be organised and operate independently. Such assets are most likely to be held by commercial companies engaged in commerce or tourism or in the fields of processing, local or service industry.

A list of assets that will be offered for sale within the first 12 months of the law's adoption have been prepared by the National Privatisation Agency and were published by the end of 1991.

Any person or company, domestic or foreign, can purchase assets. Any assets purchased, however, cannot be resold, leased or transferred for at least one year. Any existing leasing contracts or other contracts regarding the use of assets purchased will remain valid for at least two years from the date of the sale.

Public offerings

When shares of a commercial company are sold by public offering, the employees and management of the company have the right during a limited time prior to the public offering, to purchase shares at a discount of at least 10 per cent below the offer price. If there is an auction, their bid will win if their offer is not less than 10 per cent less than the highest bid and if they agree to all other conditions of the offer. As regards negotiated sales, all terms being equal, the sale will be given to the employees or management.

Employee and management buy-outs

For the sale of assets, employees or retired employees together with Romanian citizens who have entered into a leasing or management contract with the commercial company making the sale will be allowed to purchase any assets sold by the commercial company as long as they offer conditions for purchasing equal to those of the other prospective purchasers.

Employees or management that want to purchase shares or assets may receive certain financial help from the state funds, the private ownership funds and commercial companies.

Foreigners participating in the privatisation process, by purchasing shares and assets, will not be required to make any preliminary registration with the Romanian Development Agency. Under the privatisation law, the agency is to issue to foreigners purchasing shares or assets the certificate of investor required of foreign investors under the Foreign Investment Law.

Foreign investment law

Romania's foreign investment law (35/1991) came into effect in April 1991. Of most interest to foreign investors will be provisions guaranteeing the repatriation of profits, including local currency sums converted into hard currency at the official exchange rate representing a portion of the profits or the winding up of the investment.

There are few restraints imposed on foreign investors. They are not allowed to own land or purchase residential buildings not related to the direct investment or to construct such housing. However, foreign investments are allowed in any economic sector.

Incentives

The law is considered quite liberal and includes a number of incentives. Capital equipment brought in by the foreign investor as his participation in a venture is exempted from customs duties. Supplies needed for production purposes are also exempted from customs duties for two years from the date the project is commissioned.

Profit tax is exempted from the date productive operations begin for various economic sectors:

- five years for agriculture, industry and construction;
- three years for the exploration and production of natural resources, communications and transport;
- two years for trade, tourism, banking, insurance and other services.

Tax on profits

Reductions of tax on profit are granted selectively. There is a 50 per cent reduction if profits are reinvested in Romania to upgrade or expand operations or to protect the environment. A 25 per cent reduction on profit tax is given if at least 50 per cent of the necessary raw materials and energy are imported and if at least 50 per cent of the resulting products and services are exported.

The 25 per cent reduction also applies if over 10 per cent of the expenditure goes for research, development and training. It also applies if at least 50 per cent of the capital equipment is obtained from domestic production and if at least 50 per cent of new jobs are created through reinvestment or expansion.

If there is a voluntary liquidation of the foreign investment within a time-span shorter than twice the period for which the foreign investment enjoys the profit tax exemptions, the foreign investor will pay the taxes on profits for the whole duration of the investment out of the liquidation money or out of other rights to which the foreign investment is entitled.

Repatriation of profits

A portion of the annual profits in lei can be transferred abroad through currency exchange conducted by any authorised bank. This is selectively calculated to be between 8 to 15 per cent of the foreign investment contribution in hard currency to the investments in various economic sectors:

- 15 per cent for sectors of national economic importance as laid down by the Romanian Development Agency (see separate article, this section);
- 12 per cent for the exploration and production of natural resources, industry, agriculture, construction, communications, transport and other areas of national importance;
- 10 per cent for finance, banking and insurance;
- 8 per cent for other fields of activity.

Hard currency accounts held by joint ventures and foreign investors can be opened inside Romania or abroad with registered banks. Lei accounts can be opened only with Romanian registered banks. Both joint ventures and foreign investors are free to dispose of their accounts.

Certificates

Under the law the Romanian Development Agency must issue foreign investors with a certificate within 15 days from the application's registration after presentation of the relevant documents. For joint ventures and commercial companies, this includes the contract of association, the statutes, commercial contracts and other legally drafted documents related to the proposed investment.

The agency will reply to the application within 30 days from registration. If the foreign investor does not receive confirmation of the application within this period, the investment is deemed to have been approved and may be implemented.

Summary of the transformation of the Romanian economy

Property rights, land ownership and use: Law 18/2-91, Land Law. The law is limited and applies only to agricultural land.

Financial sector restructuring: Law 19/2-91 on covering losses of state enterprises; Law 33/3-91 on banking activities; Law 34/3-91 statute of National Bank of Romania. A draft law on insurance companies was presented to parliament in autumn 1991 for discussion.

Foreign investment law: Law 35/3-91 on foreign investment.
Developing private enterprise environment: Law 54/1990 on organisation and conduct of economic activities; Law 15/8-90 on the reorganisation of state enterprises; Law 31/11-90 on companies; Council Order 139/5-90 on chambers of commerce and industry.

Privatisation: Law 7-91 on privatisation.

Labour markets: Law 30/11-90 giving rules on hiring employed according to competence; Law 31/2-91 on collective labour contracts; Law 14/2-91 on wage settlement procedures; Law 15/2-91 on duration of labour day and special working conditions.

Land: Law 9/7-90 on provisional prohibition of land trading among living persons.

Competition: Law 12/7-90 on protection against some illicit commercial activities; Law 1/1-91 on preventing unfair competition.

Imports: Decision 1191/11-90 on application of import tariff structure; Decision 1274/12-90 on import tariff reductions and introduction of drawback regime; Decision 6/1-91 on export and import regime. New tariffs have reduced the effective protection and limits the range of tariff rates to between 10 and 30 per cent.

Accounting and auditing: Law 30/3-91 on organisation and function of financial surveillance and the financial guard.

Romania's commercial companies privatisation law

In order to achieve the transfer of state ownership to private ownership, under conditions that ensure the distribution to qualified Romanian citizens of the equivalent of 30 per cent of the nominal share capital of commercial companies, this law, which contains provisions concerning the sale of shares or assets of commercial companies to natural or legal persons, domestic or foreign, has been adopted.

Chapter I: General provisions

ARTICLE 1
This law provides the legal framework to effect the transfer of ownership from the state to the private sector.

In order to achieve this goal, the law sets forth the procedures for the distribution, free of charge, of certificates of ownership to qualified Romanian citizens; methods for the privatisation of commercial companies; the offering for sale of shares of assets of commercial companies to employees; and the participation by natural or legal persons, Romanian or foreign, in the sale and purchase of shares or assets of commercial companies.

ARTICLE 2
The provisions of this law apply to joint stock or limited liability companies organised under Chapter 3 of Law 15/1990 and to commercial companies established under Law 31/1990 by commercial companies of which the Romanian state is the only shareholder. These are hereinafter referred to as commercial companies. Some self-sufficient administrations will also be transformed by the government into commercial companies.

ARTICLE 3
The privatisation of commercial companies will be achieved by the transfer, free of charge, of a portion of state-owned shares and by the sale of the remaining shares following this transfer, under the provisions of this law.

Assets of commercial companies may be transferred by direct sale under the provisions of this law.

The free transfer will be achieved by the distribution of certificates of ownership which are shares in commercial companies of financial nature, named private ownership funds.

The holders of certificates of ownership under this law may sell their certificates; exchange them for shares of any commercial company that is to be privatised any time within a period of not more than five years from the effective date of this law; or convert the certificates at the end of the five-year period into shares of private ownership funds following the reorganisation of the funds into commercial companies (mutual funds).

The administration and sale of shares or social parts owned by the state will be effected by a public institution of commercial and financial character, the state ownership fund.

The protection of certificate holders and of employees and management of commercial companies involved in the privatisation process and conditions for participation by foreign investors is governed by this law.

Chapter II: Establishment and organisation of private ownership funds

ARTICLE 4
Five private ownership funds will be established as joint stock companies. The main principles of the articles of association of each fund will be proposed by the government and approved by parliament.

The articles of association of each fund will specify the rights and obligations of the fund and its organisation and functions.

ARTICLE 5
The funds will initially own, in aggregate, 30 per cent of the nominal share capital of commercial companies, as provided under Chapter 3 of Law 15/1990, except the portion of the share capital of commercial companies to be privatised under Chapter 5 of this law.

The allocation of 30 per cent of the nominal share capital of commercial companies among the five ownership funds will be effected by the National Agency for Privatisation.

ARTICLE 6
The private ownership funds, as shareholders in commercial companies, will have all the rights and liabilities of shareholders under law with respect to the commercial companies.

ARTICLE 7
The main objectives of the private ownership funds are to:

- issue certificates of ownership under this law;
- seek to maximise profits accruing to holders of certificates of ownership;
- examine and develop methods for using the certificates to obtain shares of commercial companies;
- assure brokerage services for the exchange of issued certificates into shares of commercial companies;
- revolve its portfolio of shares and make investment in order to maximise the market value of certificates;

- take action to accelerate the privatisation of commercial companies allocated to each of them, including such action as may involve the sale of shares regardless of whether such shares are held by the state ownership fund and inform the fund of any such action.

ARTICLE 8
Each private ownership fund will be managed by a board of directors consisting of seven members.

The first board of directors and the first auditors of each fund will be nominated by the government, recommended by the Economic Commissions of the National Assembly and Senate and approved, separately by the two chambers of parliament, for a five-year period.

The members of the first board of directors and the first auditors of each fund may be removed by the authorities that elected them.

A person may only be on the board of directors of one fund and may not be simultaneously on the board of directors of a commercial company allocated to that fund.

ARTICLE 9
The board of directors of each private ownership fund will elect from its members a president and a vice-president.

ARTICLE 10
The activities of and the decisions made by the private ownership funds will be based on commercial principles in accordance with each fund's approved articles of association.

ARTICLE 11
Each private ownership fund may use its revenues and profit in the proportion established by its board of directors for:

- dividend distribution to holders of certificates of ownership;
- deposits in interest-bearing accounts;
- to cover all its operational expenses and any other commercial activities within its scope of activities.

ARTICLE 12
The board of directors of each fund will approve its annual report which will be published in the Official Gazette of Romania.

The annual report will include descriptions of any measures taken by the private ownership fund to accelerate the privatisation process.

The results of each fund's activity will be made public.

ARTICLE 13
The board of directors of each private ownership fund will approve its fund's balance sheet and profit and loss account.

ARTICLE 14
The private ownership funds will act as joint stock companies under this law and under Law 31/1990 for a period of five years from the effective date of this law.

After the expiration of this period, the funds will be reorganised into regular joint stock mutual fund companies.

Persons that still own certificates of ownership at the date of the reorganisation of the private ownership funds into joint stock companies will become shareholders in the new companies. The certificates will be transformed into shares in these joint stock companies and the shareholders will determine the manner in which their voting rights will be exercised, either directly, by mandate or by correspondence.

ARTICLE 15
Each private ownership fund will issue under the conditions of this law, free of charge and on an equal basis to all Romanian citizens resident in Romania and aged 18 or older on or before 31 December 1990, certificates of ownership in bearer form with a nominal value determined by the proportion between the capital of each fund and the number of citizens eligible to receive certificates of such a fund.

The certificates represent an undivided interest of Romanian citizens in the private ownership funds.

ARTICLE 16
The list of Romanian citizens eligible to receive certificates will be prepared by the National Agency for Privatisation in collaboration with the county prefectures and the town hall of Bucharest and with the Interior Ministry.

ARTICLE 17
The National Privatisation Agency will distribute the certificates of ownership with the assistance of the local bodies of the public administration.

The distribution of the certificates will be carried out under conditions established by the agency on the announced date and place published in the Official Gazette and made public.

ARTICLE 18
Certificates of ownership not claimed within 180 days of the date announced by the National Privatisation Agency will be forfeited and annulled by the private ownership funds.

ARTICLE 19
Certificates of ownership may be traded on the stock exchange on the terms set

forth in the law concerning the organisation and functions of the stock exchange.

ARTICLE 20

In accordance with procedures established by the board of directors of each private ownership fund, certificates of ownership may be exchanged for shares of commercial companies.

ARTICLE 21

Holders of certificates of ownership will have the right to:

- receive annual dividends which will be paid under the conditions and upon the dates designed by the private ownership funds;
- propose measures for improving each fund's specific activity, to initiate financial reviews to be carried out by the auditors or to ask for the replacement of members of the board of directors, if justified, and provided that any such request is supported by the holders of at least 10,000 certificates;
- purchase shares at a discount of 10 per cent to the public offering price, in an amount up to the market value of the certificates held by a holder, during a period of five years from the effective date of this law, for a limited period prior to the commencement of a public offering of shares of commercial companies by the state ownership fund;
- obtain brokerage services from the private ownership funds for the exchange, under market conditions, of certificates into shares of any commercial company being privatised;
- include any further rights established by law for shareholders.

ARTICLE 22

The certificates of ownership may not be transferred to non-Romanian natural or legal persons.

Chapter III: Establishment and organisation of state ownership fund

ARTICLE 23

The state ownership fund is established as a public establishment of commercial and financial nature.

ARTICLE 24

The state ownership fund will initially own 70 per cent of the nominal share capital of commercial companies organised under Chapter 3 of Law 15/1990, except the portion of the share capital of commercial companies to be privatised under Chapter 5 of this law.

ARTICLE 25

The state ownership fund, as a shareholder in commercial companies, will have all the rights and liabilities of a shareholder under law, with respect to the commercial companies.

In this respect the main obligations of the fund will be to:

- reduce its ownership interest in the share capital of commercial companies until they are completely privatised;
- define minimum performance criteria for commercial companies, including their dividend policy;
- restructure and rehabilitate commercial companies or liquidate non-profitable ones;
- participate in the implementation of measures designed by the private ownership funds to accelerate the privatisation process;
- carry out, together with the private ownership funds, customary tasks required of shareholders at general meetings.

ARTICLE 26
The state ownership fund will conduct its activity and make decisions on the basis of commercial principles.

The fund may use its revenues in the proportion established by the board of directors, for the purposes of:

- deposits in interest-bearing accounts;
- investments in commercial companies necessary to restructure, rehabilitate and increase the profitability of those commercial companies, but without increasing by means of such investments the state's ownership in the commercial companies;
- loans to Romanian natural or legal persons with private capital to facilitate the purchase of shares or assets of commercial companies;
- reducing its ownership interest in the share capital of commercial companies until their complete privatisation;
- defining the minimum performance criteria for commercial companies, including their dividend policy;
- restructuring and rehabilitating commercial companies or liquidating non-profitable ones;
- participating in the implementation of measures designed by the private ownership funds to accelerate the privatisation process;
- carrying out, together with the private ownership funds, customary tasks required of shareholders at general meetings.

ARTICLE 27
The state ownership fund, in the exercise of its obligations, will maintain accounting records in accordance with standards applicable to commercial companies. Any litigation involving its activities will be submitted for settlement to the competent courts and agree, in contracts concluded with

foreign parties, that eventual litigation may be submitted to arbitration in Romania or abroad or to courts.

The state ownership fund will not be granted any immunity from jurisdiction or execution relative to its activities.

ARTICLE 28

Each year the state ownership fund will draw up a privatisation plan for the forthcoming year and a report describing its activities over the last 12 months.

The plan will include proposals for privatisation of at least 10 per cent of the shares initially held.

The plan and report will be submitted to the Government for its information and to parliament for its approval.

The report and financial statements of the fund will be published in the Official Gazette and be made public.

After the expiration of a seven-year period from the beginning of the fund's activity, on the basis of the report submitted to parliament, a decision will be made by parliament on the state ownership fund's activities and as to the continuing administration of the state's remaining participation in commercial companies.

ARTICLE 29

The state ownership fund will cease its activities once the complete privatisation of commercial companies is achieved.

The assets owned by the fund at the time of liquidation will be transferred to the state budget.

The state budget will assume any financial obligations of the fund that remain unsatisfied following its liquidation.

ARTICLE 30

The state ownership fund will be managed by a 17-member board of directors. The board will consist of: five members appointed by the president of Romania and chosen among persons with experience in commercial, financial, legal and industrial matters; three members appointed by the Senate; three members appointed by the National Assembly; five members appointed by the government to represent the leading staff of central public administration; and the State Secretary for Privatisation.

ARTICLE 31

Each member of the board of directors will be appointed for a five-year term and may be re-elected for only one additional term.

Board members may be removed by the authority which appointed them.

The board will elect from its members a president and vice-president.

The State Secretary for Privatisation may not be elected to either one of these functions.

Board meetings will be chaired by the president, or in his absence, by the vice-president.

ARTICLE 32

The auditors of the state ownership fund will be appointed and removed by the two chambers of parliament, based on the proposal of the Economy and Finance Ministry.

ARTICLE 33

The state ownership fund's organisational and functional regulations will be prepared by the board of directors and approved by the government.

ARTICLE 34

The board of directors will require the presence of 12 directors in order for valid actions to be taken and the votes of three-quarters of the directors present for valid decisions to be made.

ARTICLE 35

The board of directors will meet at least once a month.

The board may be convened for special meetings by the president or at the request of at least five of the directors.

The board meetings must be convened by a notice in writing at least five days in advance of the proposed meeting and the notice must contain the agenda.

ARTICLE 36

The president of the board will carry out the board of directors' decision and in this respect he is responsible among other things for:

- executing or approving the state ownership fund's contracts;
- approving financial operations in the name of the state ownership fund;
- appointing and removing management of the state ownership fund;
- engaging and representing the state ownership fund in relationships with natural or legal persons as well as in a court of law;
- presenting annually the privatisation plan, the revenue and expense budget, the activity report and the report concerning the execution of the budget, prepared under Article 28, for the approval of the board of directors

ARTICLE 37

The management of the state ownership fund will be carried out by an executive general manager appointed by the president of the board of directors with the directors' approval.

The board's president may delegate to the executive general manager the right to engage and to represent the state ownership fund in retaions with natural or legal persons as well as in court.

The executive general manager will carry out his actions under the control of the board of director's president.

ARTICLE 38
During the course of its activities, the state ownership fund will be exempt from profit taxes and forbidden to make any payments to the state budget or any local budget from its income.

Chapter IV: Special provisions concerning the general meetings and boards of directors of the commercial companies

ARTICLE 39
The general meeting of the commercial companies' shareholders will be formed by the representatives of the state ownership fund and the private ownership fund to which the commercial company is allocated.

The councils of state representatives will continue their activity and represent the state ownership fund in the first general meeting of the shareholders.

The conditions for the appointment, revocation, dismissal and remuneration of the representatives of state ownership fund in the general meeting of the shareholders will be established by the functional regulations of the state ownership fund.

ARTICLE 40
The general meeting of the shareholders of each commercial company will appoint a board of directors consisting of three to nine persons, of whom one will be the president of the board of directors and the general manager or manager of the commercial company.

Each private ownership fund will have the right to appoint to the board a number of members proportional to the capital it holds in that commercial company.

ARTICLE 41
Provisions of Articles 39 and 40 apply to commercial companies as long as they have as their only shareholders the state ownership fund and one or more private ownership funds.

Chapter V: Early privatisation before the organisation of the funds

ARTICLE 42
The National Privatisation Agency is authorised to initiate the privatisation of some commercial companies by the sale of shares before the organisation of the private ownership funds and state ownership fund.

At the proposal of the state-owned commercial companies and on the basis of recommendations of branch ministries, the agency will select the commercial companies to be privatised. No more than 0.5 per cent of the total number of commercial companies covered by this law will be selected.

ARTICLE 43
Valuation of the social capital of commercial companies and sale of shares before the organisation of the fund will be authorised by the councils of state representatives.

The employees and management of commercial companies will benefit from the rights provided in Article 48 if they participate in the sale of shares prior to the organisation of the funds.

ARTICLE 44
The commercial companies that are to be privatised through the sale of shares before the organisation of the funds may enter into technical assistance contracts with Romanian or foreign companies.

The technical assistance contracts with foreign enterprises must be approved by the National Privatisation Agency.

ARTICLE 45
The proceeds from the sale of shares in the commercial companies sold prior to the organisation of the funds will be deposited in an interest-bearing account at the National Bank.

The sums referred to above will be contributed 70 per cent to the state ownership fund and 30 per cent to the private ownership funds on an equal basis, respectively, at the time of their organisation.

Chapter VI: Sale of shares of commercial companies

ARTICLE 46
Shares in commercial companies owned by the private ownership funds and the state ownership fund may be sold to natural or legal persons, domestic or foreign by means of:

- public offering of shares;
- sale of shares on the basis of an open auction or an auction limited to pre-selected bidders;
- sale of shares through direct negotiation;
- any combination of the above.

ARTICLE 47
The employees or management of a commercial company may participate in purchasing shares through any of the procedures in Article 46.

ARTICLE 48

Shares in commercial companies to be sold by the state ownership fund through a public offering or an auction will be offered for sale to the employees or to the management of the companies on a preferential basis as follows:

- in a public offering of shares, the employees and management will have the right for a limited period to purchase up to 10 per cent of the shares offered for sale at a discount of 10 per cent to the public offering price;
- in a sale of shares through an auction, any employee or management member or a group comprised of such persons will have the right to a preferential purchase of shares in the event that such persons or group of persons offer a price that is at most 10 per cent lower than the highest price offered in the auction and that they respect all the other conditions of the offer.

Shares in commercial companies to be sold by the state ownership fund through direct negotiation will be awarded to the employees or to management of such companies in the event that they offer conditions for purchasing equal to those of other prospective purchasers.

ARTICLE 49

The state ownership fund, under conditions established by its board of directors, will have the right to grant facilities to the employees and to members of management and to retired employees who purchase shares in the companies as follows: credits; deferred payment; payment by instalment; and other facilities, taking into account the specific aspects of the shares and the material conditions of the sale.

ARTICLE 50

The sale of shares by the state ownership fund will be carried out in accordance with the procedures set forth in Article 46.

The sale will be carried out only with the approval of the National Privatisation Agency if by this sale the state ownership fund loses its position as main shareholder in the company.

In order to receive the agency's approval, the state ownership fund is required to present to the agency, prior to the sale, in written form, the main conditions of the sale.

The agency is required to approve or reject the proposed sale within 30 days from the date the conditions are received.

ARTICLE 51

If natural or legal persons, domestic or foreign, wish to purchase 100 per cent of the shares of a commercial company, the state ownership fund will delegate to the private ownership fund to which the company is allocated the power to negotiate on its behalf the conditions of the sale.

ARTICLE 52
The conditions for organising the effecting of the sale of shares and of presenting the proposed sale, and the criteria on the basis of which the National Privatisation Agency will approve or reject the sale, will be established by regulations issued by the agency and approved by the government.

The regulations mentioned above will be published in the Official Gazette.

Chapter VII: Sale of assets of commercial companies

ARTICLE 53
Commercial companies that own assets that represent units that can be organised and function independently, have the right to sell such assets.

ARTICLE 54
The sale of assets (referred to above) will be effected on the basis of a public auction or sealed bidding to the highest bid.

ARTICLE 55
The sale of assets of commercial companies, through a public auction or sealed bidding to the highest bidder, will be effected under the legal provisions and the regulations issued by the National Privatisation Agency and approved by the government.

The regulations mentioned above will be published in the Official Gazette.

ARTICLE 56
The National Privatisation Agency will prepare within three months a list of assets of commercial companies that are to be offered for sale within 12 months of the effective date of this law.

ARTICLE 57
Any natural or legal person, domestic or foreign, will be eligible to participate in any sale of assets pursuant to the provisions of this law.

The persons that purchase assets under this law will not have the right to sell or lease them or to transfer their use in any other way for a one-year period from the date of the conclusion of the contract of sale and purchase.

ARTICLE 58
Public institutions, self-sufficient administrations and commercial companies that have the state as a unique shareholder do not have the right to participate in any sale of assets under Article 53 of this law.

ARTICLE 59
The employees, except members of management but including retired employees, of the commercial companies that sell assets pursuant to the provisions of Article 54 are eligible to participate in any sale of any asset.

The sale will be effected for the benefit of the employees or retired employees as well as to Romanian citizens who have entered into a leasing or management contract with the commercial company making the sale, in the event that they offer conditions for purchasing equal to those of the other prospective purchasers.

ARTICLE 60
The commercial company that is selling, on approval by the National Privatisation Agency, and the private ownership funds and the state ownership fund, under conditions established by their boards of directors and based on commercial principles, may grant facilities to the employees or retired employees in the event that they purchase assets as follows: credits; deferred payment; payment by instalments; and other facilities taking into account the specific aspects of the assets to be sold.

ARTICLE 61
The sale of assets of commercial companies will be considered final at the time of concluding the contract of sale and purchase in accordance with this law.

ARTICLE 62
The proceeds of sales of assets may only be used by the commercial companies for the purposes of new capital investments and repayment of debts incurred in connection with receipt of medium- or long-term credits for capital investment.

Chapter VIII: Tasks of the National Agency for Privatisation

ARTICLE 63
The National Privatisation Agency is the government body responsible for the co-ordination, guidance and control of the privatisation process.

ARTICLE 64
The agency is mainly to:

- submit for government approval the articles of association of each private ownership fund prepared by the agency on the basis of agreed-upon main principles;
- publish in the Official Gazette the methodology to be used for the certificates of ownership distribution;
- prepare the list of Romanian citizens eligible to receive certificates of ownership;
- ensure the distribution of these certificates;
- establish criteria with respect to early privatisation;
- approve the contracts regarding special assistance concluded with foreign consulting firms;
- approve the sale of shares of commercial companies in early privatisation;
- submit for government approval the methodological regulations concerning the sale of shares and assets;

- assist commercial companies involved in the privatisation process;
- control the legality of documents concluded under this law;
- publish periodically an information bulletin;
- fulfil any other tasks provided by law.

In order to achieve its tasks, the National Privatisation Agency is entitled to request data and information from central and local public bodies and from commercial companies.

Central and local public bodies and commercial companies are required to answer the agency's requests within 20 days.

Chapter IX: Sanctions

ARTICLE 65
The following conduct is considered to be in contravention of the regulations on privatisation if it is not an offence according to penal law:

- transfer of certificates of ownership by Romanian citizens as prohibited by Article 22;
- sale or transfer by natural or legal persons, domestic or foreign, of the rights to assets sold by commercial companies before the end of the one-year period from the date of the contract conclusion;
- enter into contracts regarding special assistance with foreign enterprise for early privatisation without the approval of the National Privatisation Agency;
- divulgence by the National Privatisation Agency or commercial company employees or any other representative involved in the privatisation process of any non-public information on the sale of shares or assets of commercial companies.

ARTICLE 66
The contraventions listed in Article 65 are subject to the following sanctions:

- fines from Lei 50,000 to Lei 100,000 for the contraventions referred to in the first three points of Article 65;
- fines from Lei 150,000 to Lei 200,000 for the contravention referred to in the last point in Article 65.

The sanctions may also be applied to legal persons.

ARTICLE 67
The ascertaining of contraventions and applying of sanctions are tasks of the persons authorised by the National Privatisation Agency and by financial control bodies.

ARTICLE 68
The contraventions stipulated above are governed by the provisions of Law 32/1962 on the ascertaining and sanctioning of contraventions.

Chapter X: Final provisions

ARTICLE 69
Members of the board of directors of the private ownership funds and state ownership fund, their employees and employees of the National Privatisation Agency, members of government, officials, deputies and members of parliament involved in the implementation of this law will declare their wealth at the beginning and end of their responsibility or employment.

ARTICLE 70
The private ownership funds and state ownership fund may set up commercial companies for promoting or accelerating the economic restructuring and privatisation of commercial companies.

ARTICLE 71
The private ownership funds and state ownership fund are entitled to enter into contracts with natural or legal persons, domestic or foreign, for special assistance in the area of privatisation and economic restructuring.

ARTICLE 72
Natural and legal persons, domestic or foreign, may participate according to the provisions of this law in the purchase of shares or assets of commercial companies without preliminary registration with the Romanian Development Agency.

In the case of foreign, natural or legal persons, purchase of shares or assets of commercial companies according to this law, the Romanian Development Agency is obliged to issue the certificate of investor referred to in Article 24 of Law 35/1991.

ARTICLE 73
Within six months from the effective date of this law, the government will prepare a draft of the law on the establishment of the stock exchange.

ARTICLE 74
Provisions of this law apply in the case of the sale of shares of limited liability companies.

ARTICLE 75
The social capital of commercial companies which has been allocated pursuant to Article 36 of Law 18/1991 relating to land ownership is excluded from the amount of capital to be distributed to the private ownership funds and state ownership fund.

ARTICLE 76
For the purposes of this law, it is understood that members of management of commercial companies represent the private ownership funds and state ownership fund at the general meetings of shareholders, and are members of boards of directors and members of management committees or persons assimilated to them.

ARTICLE 77
Reparation for goods taken abusively by the state will be settled by a special law.

ARTICLE 78
Branch locations of the private ownership funds and state ownership fund will be set up throughout the country according to the criteria used to allocate commercial companies to each fund.

ARTICLE 79
As of the effective date of this law, Article 23 (paragraphs 2 to 8 of Law 15/1990) and any other legal provisions inconsistent with this law will not be deemed applicable.

Romania's foreign investment law (Law 35, 3 April 1991)

To induce foreign investment in Romania the present law is passed comprising provisions meant to confer foreign investors' guarantees and incentives as well as the complete and unrestrained use of the results of their activity.

Chapter I: General provisions

ARTICLE 1
For purposes of this law the term foreign investment will mean:

- the establishment of new companies, subsidiaries and branches, either having wholly owned foreign capital or by association with Romanian legal or natural persons, with observance of Company Law 31 of 1990;
- participation in the increase of registered capital of an existing company or the acquisition of shares or capital stock belonging to such companies, as well as bonds and other securities;
- concession, lease or administration as provided for by the law, of businesses, public services, production subunits, pertaining to autonomous state enterprises or to regular companies;
- acquisition of ownership rights over movable and immovable property as well as other real estate rights, except for the land ownership rights;
- acquisition of industrial and intellectual property rights;
- acquisition of personal estate rights or other rights related to services having economic value that are associated to an investment;

- purchase of production spaces and other buildings, except for residence buildings not related to the investment, as well as the construction of it;
- participation in agreements for exploration, exploitation and production sharing of natural resources.

ARTICLE 2
Participation of foreign investors in Romania may consist of:

- funds in freely convertible currencies;
- machinery, equipment, means of transport, components, spare parts and other goods;
- services, industrial and intellectual property rights (patents, licences, know-how, trademarks, copyrights), expertise and methods of organisation and management;
- profits lawfully obtained in freely convertible currencies or in lei from business activities carried out in Romania.

ARTICLE 3
The term 'foreign investor' means any natural or legal person residing or having its place of business abroad and which is conducting investment in Romania under any of the forms listed in this law.

ARTICLE 4
Foreign investments may be effected in all sectors of industry, exploration and production of natural resources, agriculture infrastructure and communications, civil and industrial works, scientific research and technology development, trade, transport, tourism, banking and insurance services and other services, provided that they will not infringe the regulations in force meant to protect the environment or affect Romania's national security and defence interests or harm the public order, health and good morals.

Chapter II: Guarantees

ARTICLE 5
Foreign investments in Romania will not be nationalised, expropriated, requisitioned or subjected to other measures of like effects, except in the public interest with observance of the legal procedures set forth by the law and against payment of a compensation equivalent to the affected investment which will be prompt, adequate and effective.

ARTICLE 6
Compensation will be assessed in relation to the market value of the investment on the date of occurrence of one of the acts listed in Article 5.

ARTICLE 7
In case the compensation cannot be ascertained as provided in Article 6, then it

will be determined by the parties on equitable principles, taking into account the capital invested, its appreciation or depreciation and the current returns.

ARTICLE 8
Should such determination of the compensation (Articles 6 and 7) not be satisfactory to the foreign investor's request, it will be established through the courts of law, in accordance with legal provisions.

ARTICLE 9
Foreign investors will enjoy the right to:

- participate in the management and administration of investments, in keeping with the terms of the contracts and by-laws agreed on;
- assign its contractual rights and obligations to other Romanian or foreign investors;
- transfer abroad the profit in freely convertible currency to which they are entitled, as well as the portion of the profits in lei, as set out in Article 16;
- transfer abroad in keeping with the provisions of the contracts concluded, the accounts collected for copyrights, technical assistance, expertise and other services;
- transfer abroad the amounts obtained in freely convertible currencies from total or partial sale of stocks, shares, bonds and other securities or from liquidation of investments;
- transfer abroad in freely convertible currencies in three annual instalments the amounts in lei obtained as a result of winding up the investments;
- transfer abroad in the agreed freely convertible currency the amounts achieved as compensation in the event of one of the acts listed in Article 5.

ARTICLE 10
Foreign investments will for the whole duration of their existence enjoy the legal status set forth in this law.

ARTICLE 11
Foreign investors will enjoy the legal status of this law irrespective of their citizenship or nationality.

Chapter III: Incentives

ARTICLE 12
Imported machinery, equipment, installations, means of transport and any other outfits constituted as participation of the foreign investor are exempt from import custom duties.

ARTICLE 13
Raw materials, supplies and components imported for production purposes are exempt from import customs duties for a period of two years of activity, counted from the date the project is commissioned.

ARTICLE 14

Foreign investments are exempt from payment of tax on profit as follows:

- investments in industry, agriculture and the construction sector for a period of five years from commencing productive operations;
- investments in the exploration and production of natural resources, communications and transport for a period of three years from commencing the respective operations;
- investments in trade, tourism, banking and insurance services and other services for a period of two years from starting operations.

ARTICLE 15

In addition to the exemptions provided for in Article 14, there are reductions of tax on profits granted after the expiration of the initial tax holiday period as follows:

- a 50 per cent reduction of the tax due for the profits reinvested in enterprises set up in Romania with a view to widening and upgrading the technical and material basis, improving the manufacturing technologies or expanding the activity, to obtain additional profits and for the investments aimed at securing the protection of the environment;
- a 25 per cent reduction of the tax due on condition that at least 50 per cent of the necessary raw materials, energy and fuel are provided through imports; at least 50 per cent of the products and services are exports; over 10 per cent of the expenditures are made for scientific research and development of new technologies in Romania and for professional training; at least 50 per cent of the machinery and other equipment necessary for developing existing investments are obtained from domestic production; at least 50 new jobs are created through a new investment or expansion on existing investments.

ARTICLE 16

Foreign investors are entitled to transfer abroad in freely convertible currency, through currency exchanges conducted by the Romanian Bank for Foreign Trade or other authorised banks, a portion of the annual profits in lei equivalent to 8 to 15 per cent of their contribution in cash and in kind in freely convertible currency paid to the registered capital as follows:

- 15 per cent of the paid contribution to the registered capital for investments made in the fields of special importance for the national economy including manufacture of anti-polluting technologies as set out by government decree;
- 12 per cent of the paid contribution to the registered capital for investments made in the fields of exploration and production of natural resources, industry, agriculture, construction sector, communications and transport, other than those provided for above;
- 10 per cent of the paid contribution to the registered capital for investments made in the fields of finance, banking and insurance;

- 8 per cent of the paid contribution to the registered capital for investments made in other fields of activities.

ARTICLE 17
On suggestions prepared by the Romanian Development Agency, fields of special importance for the national economy will be established through government decision. Additional incentives could be granted by law on government proposal for investments effected in the fields mentioned above.

ARTICLE 18
In case voluntary liquidation of foreign investment occurs within a time-span shorter than twice the period for which foreign investors enjoy the exemptions provided for under Article 14, foreign investors will pay the taxes on profits imposed by the law for the whole duration of the investment. The taxes due in accordance with the provisions above will be paid with priority out of the results deriving from the liquidation of the investment or out of the other rights to which the foreign investors are entitled.

Chapter IV: Registration of the applications for foreign investors

ARTICLE 19
Foreign investment in Romania, irrespective of their legal status, will be made on the basis of an application by the foreign investor registered with the Romanian Development Agency.

ARTICLE 20
The Romanian Development Agency will study the reliability of the investor, the field and the legal form of the investment and the amount of the capital to be invested.

ARTICLE 21
The Romanian Development Agency answers applications of foreign investors on the basis of data and information that it has available or that it may obtain on request from the central and local organisation of public administration as well as from autonomous state enterprises and regular companies in the field of activity where the foreign investment will be made.

The ministries and other central and local organisations of public administration will answer within 10 days to the request of the Romanian Development Agency.

ARTICLE 22
The Romanian Development Agency will answer the application of foreign investors within 30 days from their registration.

In the event that no confirmation is received by the foreign investor during the time period set forth, the investment will be deemed to have been approved and may be implemented.

ARTICLE 23
The foreign investors have the right to effect investments under the conditions set forth in Romanian law, either on the basis of the confirmation issued by the Development Agency or on the basis of foreign investor's application in the absence of any response from the agency.

ARTICLE 24
The legal status of foreign investors in Romania is proven by the certificate of investor issued by the Development Agency.

The certificate is issued at the foreign investor's request within 15 days from registering the applications, on presentation of relevant documents including the contract of association and the statutes, the commercial contracts and other legal papers drafted in accordance with the provisions of Romanian law and taking into consideration the legal status of the investment.

The certificate is opposable to the Romanian authorities for the establishment of the foreign investor's rights.

Chapter V: Financial, foreign currency and commercial operations

ARTICLE 25
The collection and payment operations related to the foreign investments will be effected through lei (the Romanian currency) and fully convertible currency accounts open with banks having the place of business in Romania or through freely convertible currency accounts open with banks having the place of business abroad.

Joint ventures and other foreign investors may freely dispose of the balances of their own accounts.

ARTICLE 26
The accounts in freely convertible currency will be fed by the financial contribution of the investors, foreign currency borrowings and by foreign currency revenues.

ARTICLE 27
Joint ventures and other foreign investors may contract credits in lei and in foreign currencies from local financing institutions or loans in freely convertible currencies from foreign banks and financial institutions.

ARTICLE 28
The activity of the joint ventures and of the foreign investors will be carried out on the basis of commercial contracts concluded with the observance of legal provisions and at agreed upon prices in lei and in foreign currency.

ARTICLE 29
Payments in freely convertible currency, including the amounts due to the foreign investor, will be effected only from the balances of the foreign investors or, as the case may be, the joint venture's bank accounts.

ARTICLE 30
The profits in freely convertible currency and in lei due to the foreign investors can be used to make new investments in Romania, to buy Romanian goods and services or can be exchanged in the financial market under existing legal provisions.

Chapter VI: Final provisions

ARTICLE 31
In the event the foreign investments in Romania are made by setting up commercial companies in association with Romanian natural or legal persons, the contribution of the Romanian associates to the registered capital may consist of the right of property or other real rights over land or other immovable necessary estate for the whole duration of the joint venture.

ARTICLE 32
The expatriate personnel necessary to implement the foreign investment will be agreed on by the contracting parties or by the foreign investor, as the case may be. Such personnel will be employed in management and expert jobs only.

ARTICLE 33
The wages of local and expatriate personnel employed by foreign investments will be settled by the agreement of the parties.

ARTICLE 34
The provisions of this law will be applied to the extent that they do not contravene international agreements and arrangements of foreign investments undersigned by Romania.

ARTICLE 35
On coming into effect, Decree 424 of 1972 ruling the establishment and functioning of joint ventures in Romania, Decree Law 96 of 1990 for inducement of foreign investment in Romania and other contrary legal provisions are abrogated.

Regulation on current operations and transfer of capital using foreign currency (Monitorul Official, 13 May 1991)

Based on the provisions of Articles 33 and 62 of Law 32/1991 on the status of the National Bank of Romania, the bank has drawn up the following regulation.

Chapter I: General dispositions

ARTICLE 1
The provisions of this regulation are applied for current operations and transfer of capital using foreign currency as well as for certain operations using lei on, from and for the payment territory of Romania.

ARTICLE 2
As supplement for this regulation, the National Bank of Romania will issue norms for its application.

ARTICLE 3
Payments carried out in Romania will be performed only with the national currency, the Leu (and its subdivision, the Ban) unless otherwise stipulated by law.

ARTICLE 4
The payment territory of Romania coincides with the territory of the Romanian state, with the exception of areas having special custom, fiscal and payment statute, known as custom territory.

ARTICLE 5
This regulation and its norms of application in Romania consider as foreign currency the currency expressed in freely convertible currency which can be used in current economic operations and transfers of capital.

ARTICLE 6
The persons who may perform current operations and transfer of capital using foreign currency are physical persons, Romanian or foreign citizens, with permanent residence or temporarily in Romania as well as agreed juristic persons, defined in this regulation as legal subjects.

Chapter II: The rate of exchange of the Leu

ARTICLE 7
In Romania, temporarily two rates of exchange are operational: the official rate of exchange established by the National Bank of Romania and the rate of exchange of the currency market.

ARTICLE 8
The legal subjects may perform current operations and transfer of capital using the official rate of exchange and the rate of exchange of the currency market.

Chapter III: Possession of available foreign currency

ARTICLE 9
Inside Romania the legal subjects are entitled to obtain income and to possess foreign currency under the laws.

ARTICLE 10
The legal subjects may open and keep foreign currency in banking accounts, in banks situated in Romania, authorised by the National Bank.

ARTICLE 11
Possession and use by agreed juristic persons and by Romanian and foreign citizens having permanent residence in Romania of foreign currency in accounts opened in foreign financial banking institutions is allowed only on the basis of a previous licence issued by the National Bank.

Chapter IV: Current operations and transfer of capital using foreign currency and Leu, constituting the object of this regulation

ARTICLE 12
Amounts in cash possessed in Romania by legal subjects may be transferred to and from Romania only in the legal conditions of this regulation and of its norms of application.

ARTICLE 13
Physical persons may enter Romania with foreign currency in the cash equivalent to $50,000. Any amount in excess of this limit is allowed to enter Romania through banks.

ARTICLE 14
Physical persons residing in Romania may leave Romania possessing foreign currency in the cash equivalent to a maximum of $5,000 without authorisation or special permission.

The amount in cash in excess of $1,000 per person per trip is constituting currency transferred in cash and it can be used only for current transactions of payment for certain assets and services for medical purposes, studies and other reasons which are listed in the norms of this regulation.

The amount in cash in excess of $1,000 must be declared and justified before the Romanian custom authorities by a banking certificate confirming that the respective amount transferred in cash originates from a banking deposit and is serving a current operation.

ARTICLE 15
Direct or indirect banking transfers abroad from the accounts of physical persons residing in Romania and of Romanian juristic persons, should have the

nature of current transactions with the exception of cases stipulated by law and which are the object of a previous licence by the National Bank of Romania, issued on a case-by-case basis.

In this sense, the banks are responsible for the application of the law, of this regulation and of the norms for its application.

The amounts owned by physical persons, as detailed above, in excess of the upper limit of $5,000 in cash, may be transferred abroad only through banks under conditions of this article in order to achieve certain current operations. The banks will not change the limit of these transactions as long as they considered them carried out in good faith, but will keep records, and will control permanently the volume and the nature of these operations, the documents on which they are based, informing the banking supervision authorities of the National Bank whenever irregularities are observed and the case of operations surpassing the amounts detailed in this regulation.

ARTICLE 16

On entering or leaving Romania, physical persons, Romanian and foreign citizens temporarily in Romania, are under obligation to declare to the Romanian customs authorities the amounts of foreign currency they possess which are in excess of the equivalent of $1,000.

Physical persons temporarily in Romania cannot leave Romania with an amount of foreign currency in cash higher than that declared on entering Romania. Any supplement is transferred through banks, as stipulated by law, this regulation and its norm of application.

ARTICLE 17

The transfer of Romanian public securities (state securities) expressed in foreign currency is carried out only if certified by the competent Romanian authorities.

ARTICLE 18

To and from Romania, physical persons having permanent residence or being temporarily in Romania are not allowed to carry cash in excess of Lei 2,500 per person per trip.

ARTICLE 19

The transfer of Romanian public securities expressed in Lei may be carried out only if certified by the competent Romanian authorities.

ARTICLE 20

Currency operations and transfer of capital using foreign currency is performed by legal subjects in a different manner, at the official rate of exchange or at the exchange rate of the currency market, through banks or other juristic persons, including currency exchange agencies authorised by the National Bank of Romania, in conditions of the law, this regulation and the norms for its application as follows:

- a bank may perform currency exchange operations and may participate in currency exchange agencies as stipulated in the licences issued by the National Bank of Romania;
- currency exchange agencies may be set up under Law 31/1990; they are Romanian juridical persons;
- other Romanian juridical persons may request a licence from the National Bank in order to perform currency exchange operations in addition to their basic activity, provided they respect the provisions of law 31/1990, the norms regulating their activity, this regulation and its norms of application.

Chapter V: Surveillance and control of operations with foreign currency and with Leu which are the object of this regulation

ARTICLE 21
The surveillance and control of the activity of foreign currency and lei which are the subject of this regulation are the duty of the National Bank.

To do this the National Bank will collaborate with the banks, ministries, departments and other agencies and government authorities concerned with such operations.

ARTICLE 22
Juridical persons authorised to perform foreign currency operations and transfer of capital with foreign currency and with lei which are the object of this regulation have the obligation to inform the National Bank about their active and passive assets expressed in foreign currency in the order of their exigency as well as movements in the accounts of non-residents and in the balance of active foreign assets, surpassing the equivalent of $100,000 when applying the provisions of Law 33/1991.

The information will be made as stipulated by the National Bank in the norms for the application of this regulation.

ARTICLE 23
Any infringement of this regulation will be punished by the supervising and controlling authorities of the National Bank, commensurate with the gravity of the offences, including the annulment of a licence (as detailed in Chapter IX, Law 33/1991).

If other irregularities are observed in the performance of foreign currency operations and in the transfer of capital, the National Bank authorities will inform the authorised institutions listed in Article 21 so sanctions can be applied.

Chapter VI: Final dispositions

ARTICLE 24
The National Bank of Romania will issue norms for the application of this regulation within 30 days of its publication.

ARTICLE 25
From the date of publication of this regulation, any contrary disposition in this domain is abrogated.

Romanian insurance law (Law 41/1991 on the setting up, the organisations and functioning of a commercial insurance company)

Chapter I: General provisions

ARTICLE 1
In Romania insurance is carried out by insurance companies, insurance and reinsurance companies and reinsurance companies which assume liabilities by accepting risks against payment of certain premiums by the insured and reinsured respectively.

Insurance activity is carried on by intermediary agencies. These conclude or place contracts for the companies or perform other services regarding the issuing and running of contracts.

ARTICLE 2
The setting up of commercial insurance companies with foreign participation in the capital will only be effected by the association with Romanian legal and/or natural persons.

ARTICLE 3
Commercial insurance companies are set up as shareholding or limited companies.

The companies are created and operate according to the law of commercial companies and the law of foreign investments as well as the provisions of this law.

ARTICLE 4
Foreign commercial insurance companies and associations may set up representative offices in accordance with the law and under the following conditions:

- they must have legal status in their country of origin; they must have been involved in insurance activities for at least the last 10 years and not be under any moratorium, in receivership or any similar situation;
- they must deposit in a Romanian bank a cash guarantee equivalent to the minimum paid-up capital stipulated in Article 8 of this law;
- they must obtain the approval of the Office for Supervising Insurance and Reinsurance Activity, within the Finance Ministry.

Representative offices set up in Romania may conclude:

- insurance contracts and reinsurance contracts with foreign legal or natural persons or for assets under their ownership;
- reinsurance contracts with insurance companies;
- insurance-reinsurance companies and Romanian reinsurance companies.

Chapter II: Special provisions on the setting up, organisation and functions

ARTICLE 5
Commercial insurance companies will be registered with the previous approval of the Office for Supervising the Insurance and Reinsurance Activity within the Finance Ministry.

ARTICLE 6
The applications for obtaining this approval must enclose the following documents: a feasibility study describing the scope of the activity and a financial plan; the draft contract of the company and its statute; the declaration regarding the written capital; and the contributions in kind.

Within 15 days from receipt of an unfavourable notice, the applicant may lodge a complaint with the Finance Ministry.

A motivated decision on the latter can be fought in a court of appeal in Bucharest within 15 days of its receipt.

ARTICLE 7
Commercial insurance companies may offer one or several types of insurance and/or reinsurance, in accordance with the provisions of their statutes.

They may offer the following main types of insurance:

- life;
- personal, other than life (accidents);
- motor vehicle;
- marine and transport;
- aviation;
- fire and other property;
- public liability;
- credit and guarantees;
- financial loss;
- agriculture.

ARTICLE 8
The minimum subscribed capital of an insurance company is:

- Lei 25m for insurance companies, insurance and reinsurance companies and reinsurance companies, separate for each kind of insurance and reinsurance from Article 7;

- Lei 1.5m for intermediary agencies.

The paid-up capital may not be lower than 50 per cent of the subscribed capital.

ARTICLE 9
Commercial insurance companies may exercise activities of insurance and reinsurance in lei and in cases where they have obligations to pay in hard currencies, these operations may be exercised in hard currencies.

ARTICLE 10
Insurance companies and insurance and reinsurance companies also offering life insurance have the obligation to hold separate accounts for this kind of insurance, to manage separately the funds relating to the life insurance activity and to make payments out of such funds only for life insurance and to calculate the final results of life insurance separately from other kinds of insurance.

ARTICLE 11
On an annual basis, the amount of potential losses that insurance companies, insurance and reinsurance companies and reinsurance companies endorse by selling premiums or taking risks by reinsurance must not exceed, after deduction of the potential losses that have been reinsured outside the company, five times the amount of the paid-up capital and of the capital reserves of the company.

ARTICLE 12
In order to diminish liabilities undertaken by contracts, the insurance company, the insurance and reinsurance company and the reinsurance company may affect outward reinsurance by ceding certain shares of the assured liabilities to other companies, either reciprocally or unilaterally, in accordance with the common practice.

ARTICLE 13
Insurance companies and insurance and reinsurance companies may conclude agreements concerning co-insurance, pools and other typical forms of co-operation in order to insure or reinsure special risks which cannot be undertaken by a single company.

ARTICLE 14
Intermediary agencies (insurance brokers) cannot conclude insurance contracts for foreign insurance companies with Romanian legal or natural persons or for goods under their ownership.

ARTICLE 15
Commercial insurance companies can associate within national professional unions and may adhere to international organisations of a professional nature.

Chapter III: Reserves, tariffs, placements

ARTICLE 16

Insurance companies, insurance and reinsurance companies and reinsurance companies have the obligation to set up, according to the object of their activity, some premium reserves for life insurance as well as premium and loss reserves for other types of insurance and/or reinsurance.

The premium reserves for life insurances will be set up on the basis of actuarial calculations and will be handled separately.

The premium reserves for the other types of insurance and/or reinsurance are constituted on the basis of the quota of the unexpired risks.

The loss reserves are set up on the basis of estimates of statistical data and of actuarial calculations regarding the payments to be affected in future. These cannot be less than 40 per cent of the difference between premiums cashed and losses paid in respect of insurance and/or reinsurance with validity during the year.

The loss reserves cannot, even if identifiable, be traced by insured or creditors.

Insurance companies, insurance and reinsurance companies and reinsurance companies which perform operations in foreign currencies may set up their reserves in lei and/or foreign currencies.

The amount established for the premium reserve for life insurance as well as for the premium and loss reserves for the other kinds of insurance/reinsurance, will be deducted from the gross income with a view to obtaining profit subject to taxation.

ARTICLE 17

Insurance companies and the insurance and reinsurance companies will establish the terms of the insurance contracts for the facultative insurance, observing the provisions of the law on insurance contracts and premium tariffs for insurance contracts.

In operations of reinsurance, the terms of operations and the amount of the premium will be determined on the basis of negotiated reinsurance contracts according to common practice.

ARTICLE 18

Intermediary agencies (insurance brokers) will set the commissions or fees that will be paid for the service they provide, in accordance with tariffs agreed on the basis of the contracts negotiated with the insurance companies, insurance and reinsurance companies and reinsurance companies.

ARTICLE 19
For the conclusion of the insurance contract or for their issue and running, insurance companies may use insurance agents.

Their remuneration will consist in commissions on the amounts cashed or in fees set according to the tariffs agreed on the basis of negotiated contracts.

ARTICLE 20
Commercial insurance companies may invest in Romania their own funds and those temporarily drawn by the activities carried on in the form of income from interest accrued on cash held/deposited with the banks or savings banks.

These companies may invest the capital, the capital reserves and technical reserves in bonds of fixed or mobile assets or can use them for giving credits to institutions of a bank profile, subject to the observance of a certain cash (liquidity) coefficient, established according to common practice.

Commercial insurance companies with foreign participation and those which perform insurance and reinsurance operations in foreign currencies may make the investments in lei and/or in foreign currencies.

Chapter IV: Balance sheet

ARTICLE 21
The financial year begins on 1 January and ends on 31 December. On extraordinary cases the Office of Supervision of the Insurance and Reinsurance Activities may approve, on request, the change of the dates of beginning and ending of the financial year.

ARTICLE 22
Commercial insurance companies have the obligation to submit annually to the Office of Supervision of Insurance and Reinsurance Activity, until 30 June of the following year, the balance sheet and the profit and loss account, as appointed by the general meeting of the shareholders, together with the auditor's report.

They also have the obligation to publish the annual balance sheet in the Official Monitor.

A representative office of foreign insurance companies has the obligation to submit to the Office of Supervision of Insurance and Reinsurance Activity within the term stipulated above, the annual financial situation review which they convey to their mother companies abroad.

Chapter V: Supervision of insurance activity

ARTICLE 23
In order to supervise the legal provisions concerning insurance activity for the prevention of the insolvency of commercial insurance companies and for the

defence of the rights of the insured, the Office of Supervision of the Insurance and Reinsurance Activities is set up within the Finance Ministry.

ARTICLE 24
Insurance companies and insurance and reinsurance companies which conclude motor vehicle insurance will set up the Motor Insurance Bureau which represents the insurance companies in their domestic and international relations, fulfils the tasks and supervises the observance by the companies of their obligations arising from international agreements on third party liability insurance for losses caused by motor accidents.

Chapter VI: Penalties

ARTICLE 25
The infringements by commercial insurance companies of Articles 8, 11, 14, 16 and 22 will be deemed as contravention and sanctioned by a fine of between Lei 10,000 and Lei 150,000.

ARTICLE 26
The infringement by the representative office of foreign commercial insurance companies and by the foreign insurers association of Articles 4 and 22 will be deemed as contravention and sanctioned by a fine of between Lei 10,000 and Lei 150,000.

ARTICLE 27
The actuaries and other specialists who in achieving their assignments concerning the examination of the balance sheets, value placement of any patrimonial element of the commercial insurance companies knowingly draw up false reports will be punished either by a fine (Lei 5,000 to Lei 75,000), unless the committed deeds represent elements of a criminal offence.

ARTICLE 28
Sanctions stipulated by Articles 25-27 will be applied by the ascertaining agent authorised by the Office of Supervision of Insurance and Reinsurance Activities.

Chapter VII: Final, special and transitory provisions

ARTICLE 29
Exempt from taxation, court fees and other taxes are:

- indemnities, insured amounts and any other rights granted by any kind of insurance;
- transfer of placement values and portfolio transfers which occur between insurance companies, insurance and reinsurance companies and reinsurance companies from the assets of the ceding company into those of the concessionary one.

ARTICLE 30

The provisions of this law are to be completed within stipulations of the civil, commercial and criminal laws.

ARTICLE 31

The provisions of this law are not applicable to the mutual insurance co-operatives, mutual associations and mutual help or burial societies.

ARTICLE 32

Commercial insurance companies set up at the date or entering under validity of this law may continue their activity if within six months they make adaptations to the new conditions set by the present law.

ARTICLE 33

This law will come into force 30 days after it is published in the Official Monitor. On the same date, Decree Law 470/1971 and any other stipulations contrary to the provisions of this law become null and void.

Chapter 7

SLOVENIA

Slovenia was Yugoslavia's most western republic, both in location and economic development. It has a GDP per capita of between $6,000 and $7,000 — more than double the average in Yugoslavia as a whole. Slovenia accounts for only 8 per cent of total population in Yugoslavia, but its share in the GDP of the whole country is about 20 per cent. Slovenia was recognised as an independent country in January 1992.

After free elections held in 1990, in which the communist party lost power, all political parties agreed independence was the only workable alternative for the republic. In a plebiscite held in December 1990, nine out of every 10 inhabitants of Slovenia voted for an "independent Slovenia". Even if political differences can be sorted out between the various Yugoslav republics, most Slovenes think they will be better off outside Yugoslavia. After the Yugoslav military intervention in the republic in 1991, there appears little chance of Slovenia staying within the Yugoslav federation.

Reform programme

After declaring its independence, Slovenia's politicians set about putting into place the various laws which would help speed up the transition to a market economy. The main task is the transformation to a market economy. Slovenia's economic policies are:

- reduction of costs per production unit, enabling the economy to compete on the Yugoslav and foreign markets;
- solve the problems in the infrastructure and banking system;
- strong local currency pegged to a stable (hard) currency, probably the Austrian schilling or the European currency unit (Ecu);
- restrictive wage policy to enable employers to stabilise prices and boost competitiveness;

- increase exports and decrease imports, but at the same time eliminate customs barriers;
- maintain Slovenia's market in Yugoslavia through a uniform customs system;
- attract foreign capital through concessions for foreign investors in infrastructure, particularly transport and energy.

Currency

In October 1991, Slovenia introduced its own currency, which was exchanged against the Yugoslav dinar within the state on a one for one basis. The initial currency issue omitted any name for the currency and achieved limited acceptance, as Slovene independence from Yugoslavia had not yet then been achieved. The currency was being used in some border trade, mainly between the state and Italy, by the end of 1991. There are plans in 1992 to issue a currency which will be accepted internationally. All dinars, the Yugoslav currency, were withdrawn from circulation in Slovenia in 1991 and replaced with the new currency.

Stock exchange

Although the capital of the republic, Ljubljana, has opened a stock exchange, no company stocks are being traded and few investors see it as more than a symbolic gesture towards market institutions.

The exchange was officially established on 26 December 1989 by 33 banks from all over Slovenia. Under the Federal Stock Exchange Act (Yugoslavia), which was used as the basis for setting up the exchange, only banks and non-banking financial institutions are allowed to be founders of a stock exchange. The first stock exchange session was held in March 1990, involving 14 brokers trading 11 securities.

Organisation of the stock exchange

Members of the stock exchange are Yugoslav banks and broker companies from both the public and private sectors. To be admitted to the exchange a bank or broker company must meet the following qualifications:

- the company or bank will have as its object of operation the dealing in securities on the stock exchange;
- the persons acting on behalf of the company or bank must have reliability and professional qualifications for dealing;
- the company or bank should have sufficient financial resources;
- a proper settlement of the transactions concluded on the stock exchange must be guaranteed.

The number of trading attorneys may be limited, subject to the business policy of the exchange.

According to the rules and regulations of the stock exchange, the Ljubljana exchange is managed by a board of directors. Other bodies include the admission board, the board of arbitration, the supervision committee and the business conduct committee.

Financing the exchange

The exchange, its administration, office premises and equipment are financed through fees levied on the members of the exchange.

Supervision

Under federal law, the exchange is subject to supervision of the federal securities commission. Since Slovenia declared its independence from Yugoslavia in June 1991, the state is expected to continue to use existing federal legislation until such time as laws specific to Slovenia can be adopted.

Operation

The exchange concludes transactions in securities and equivalent rights. Sessions take place twice a week (Tuesday, Thursday) from 10.30am to 12 noon. Daily operations are expected to begin as soon as possible.

Potential investors place their orders through a member of the exchange. All transactions must be carried out by an authorised broker. When instructing brokers, clients can place 12 different kinds of orders.

Membership cost and settlement

Regular annual membership costs are DM 10,000. Settlement of exchange transactions are carried out within three working days.

Restrictions on foreign participation

According to federal legislation, which still applies to the exchange, membership of the exchange is restricted to Yugoslav subjects. A foreign broker may become a member of the exchange only by setting up a branch or a joint venture company in Yugoslavia.

Draft privatisation law

The entire privatisation procedure was slowed down as the Slovene government is having second thoughts about the privatisation law and some of its main principles. Slovenia's draft privatisation law aims to encourage foreign ownership in large companies. The law on proprietary reform — which transforms enterprises in Slovenia into joint stock companies — was presented to parliament in September 1991. The privatisation law, which had to be rewritten, was expected to be passed by the end of 1991, but with substantial changes to the existing draft.

The privatisation law introduces institutional owners (funds and investment companies) and provides for one free share for each adult citizen of Slovenia. A voucher scheme, absent from earlier drafts of the law, caused controversy in parliament and has attracted much criticism from enterprise managers.

Rights of former owners

The draft law provides protection for the rights of former owners and their heirs. This provision mainly concerns the reimbursement claims, made according to regulations on denationalisation and co-operatives by former owners, their heirs, co-operatives and co-operative associations, churches and religious communities, against companies and their assets undergoing reorganisation.

Proprietary reorganisation of companies

The draft law regulates the proprietary reorganisation of companies with collective capital into companies with known owners and the roles of the Privatisation Agency of Slovenia and the funds of Slovenia in reorganising companies with collective capital. The law does not apply to companies performing economic public services, banks and insurance agencies, companies to be reorganised according to the law on co-operatives and companies undergoing bankruptcy after the bankruptcy procedures are legally initiated.

Large companies with over 500 employees and at least Dinar 1bn of nominal collective capital are to be reorganised as joint stock companies within 60 days after the law comes into effect. There are around 700 middle-sized companies (those with less than 125 employees or over Dinar 200m of collective capital), employing 38 per cent of the work-force and 22.5 per cent of the collective capital of the Slovene economy.

Under the latest draft, around Dinar 184bn of collective capital is to be reorganised in Slovenia. This amounts to 58 per cent of all the capital of the economy. The capital which the privatised companies should transfer to the development fund of the state — around DM 9bn — will then be transferred or distributed to the Slovenian reparation fund (15 per cent of the nominal value of the shares transferred), a fifth of the nominal value to the pension fund, 35 per cent to investment companies (which will further distribute free shares to Slovenian citizens) with the remaining 30 per cent of transferred collective capital, amounting to Dinar 35bn, will be sold by the development fund.

Implementation

According to the draft law, the proprietary reorganisation of companies should be implemented in different ways: by transferring shares to funds and distributing them to investment companies or funds, by publicly auctioning or directly selling companies or by selling all the assets of companies.

These various ways can be achieved in:

- workers' buy-outs where the company sells its employees regular shares at nominal value, corrected according to the index of growth of retail prices in Slovenia until the day of payment to the fund with the purchase money going to the fund;
- direct or public sales of companies, middle-sized or small companies will be sold at public auctions (in exceptional cases, such companies can be sold directly if the Privatisation Agency approves the proposal of the company);
- sales of companies through selling all assets and discontinuing the company, the entire purchase price going to the fund, the liabilities of the company transferred to the fund and the company terminated and deleted from the court register.

Privatisation Fund of Slovenia

The Privatisation Fund of Slovenia is to be empowered to manage the shares and other securities acquired in reorganisation procedures. The fund will manage and control the companies whose shares it has until it transfers the shares to new owners. The transfer of shares to funds is made by the fund through delivering or distributing company shares as follows: 15 per cent of the shares of each company to the Slovenian reparations fund; 15 per cent to the new investment companies; 15 per cent to the pension funds; and 20 per cent remains with the company. The fund also transfers to investment companies a further 35 per cent of the securities acquired in reorganisation procedures, according to instructions to be drafted by the Privatisation Agency. According to the draft law, the fund should not transfer to a particular investment company more than 15 per cent of a particular company.

Investment companies

The law also says the shares of investment companies, with the exception of pension funds, are to be distributed to all adult Slovenian citizens (as of 25 June 1991), with the number of working years taken into consideration.

Privatisation Agency

A Privatisation Agency is to be constituted to carry out expert and technical tasks in the processes of proprietary reorganisation and privatisation of companies and perform other public tasks for which it will be authorised. The agency already exists but is expected to undergo some changes once the privatisation law is passed.

Development fund

A development fund of Slovenia is to be created as a financial organisation to manage and use the shares and other securities acquired in reorganisation procedures. The fund will have the option of selecting and appointing members to the boards of directors of the companies whose shares it will manage and use.

Reparations Fund

The Slovenian Reparations Fund will be a financial organisation, set up in order to settle legally recognised reimbursement claims in denationalisation procedures. The Slovenian Reparations Fund is to acquire 15 per cent of the shares of each company and 10 per cent of the purchase price of small companies.

In cases of liquidation or bankruptcy of companies before proprietary reorganisation their remaining assets after bankruptcy procedures are to be transferred to the fund according to the proportion of collective capital in the permanent capital.

Voucher scheme

The draft of the law sets out a mechanism and criteria for distributing shares to a large segment of the population, while at the same time enabling immediate active influence of these owners on the operation of companies by providing for reparations and pension funds. The function and mechanism of partial distribution has political connotations and aims at including as wide a circle as possible of Slovene citizens in the development of the economy, at first as passive and then as active investors.

First privatisations

The first five companies to be privatised have been selected and the International Finance Corporation, an affiliate of the World Bank, is helping the Privatisation Agency in Slovenia prepare the companies for sale.

The five companies scheduled for privatisation are Svila, Valkarton, Saturnus, Javor and Terme Catez. The first sale was expected in September 1991, but was delayed because of internal conflict in Yugoslavia. The Slovene authorities were hopeful that the sale would go through before the end of 1991 through private placement. Auctions and public sales of shares (similar to those already carried out in Poland) are also planned.

Appendix I

East European insurance regulations (Source: Insurance in Eastern Europe, Salomon Brothers Research Department, May 1991)

Czechoslovakia

Main legislation: 1966 and 1968 insurance laws. New 1991 law still to be passed.

Competition: Two monopolies: Czechoslovak republic and Slovak republic. There should be an end to the geographic monopoly and the admission of new insurance companies, including foreign joint ventures.

Supervision: Ministry of Finance based on German model of control.

Foreign involvement: No shareholdings. Co-operation allowed. In future foreign joint ventures are expected to be allowed, but probably not with majority shareholdings.

Foreign insurance company activity: Generali of Italy has a co-operation agreement with CSP, the Czechoslovakian state insurance company. Zurich Group of Switzerland is opening an office in Czechoslovakia in 1991.

Domestic insurers: Ceska Statni Pojistovna (CSP), handles all compulsory and voluntary insurance in the Czech republic plus international risks, reinsurance (marine, aviation, construction) and export credit through FIRMC; Slovenska Statni Pojistovna (SSP) handles all compulsory and voluntary insurance in the Slovak republic.

Hungary

Main legislation: 1979 act varied by decree, 1986 Reform Law and a new law expected in 1991.

Competition: previously a duopoly (life and household; international and motor). The reform law lifted the duopoly and allowed the creation of new companies and joint stock, mutual and co-operative legal forms. Hungaria Biztosito retains a monopoly on motor liability and export credit insurance. Export credit insurance is to be handled in future by a newly created government agency while motor insurance has now been opened to competition.

Supervision: State Insurance Surveillance reporting to the Finance Ministry.

Foreign involvement: foreign participation in joint ventures is allowed. Majority control is possible subject to Finance Ministry approval. Products have to be approved and manufactured in Hungary.

Foreign insurance company activity: Allianz of Germany has a 49 per cent stake in Hungarian non-life monopoly. Colonia of Germany has a 12 per cent stake in Atlasz, a travel insurer. Generali of Italy has a 20 per cent joint venture stake with Allami. Groupe Assurances Nationale of France has a start-up operation. Wiener Allianz of Austria has a 59 per cent stake in a joint venture with Postabank and the Hungarian Post Office. Erste Allgemeine of Austria has a 20 per cent stake in a joint venture with Allami, the life monopoly insurer. Zurich Group of Switzerland has an unlicensed representative office, but is expected to receive a licence for business in 1991. American Insurance Group of the US has a 52 per cent stake in a new insurer, First Group American/Hungarian Insurance Company and is in partnership with Co-op Savings Bank.

Domestic insurers: Hungaria Biztosito handles commercial property, marine and aviation, export credit, auto, reinsurance and export credit; Allami Biztosito handles life accident, household, pensions and agriculture; Garancia handles life and pensions and household credit insurance; Providencia handles life and pensions and household; Atlasz handles travel insurance; American/Hungarian Insurance Company handles life, pensions and household insurance.

Poland

Main legislation: 1989 law and new law to be passed in 1991.

Competition: allows the creation of new insurance companies and abolished the state majority rule. New companies cannot compete for compulsory insurance business.

Supervision: Finance Ministry.

Foreign involvement: situation unclear. Probably will allow significant minority interest in established insurance companies in future.

Foreign insurance company activity: Colonia of Germany has bought Westa's travel policies. Assurances Generales de France has a 49 per cent stake in a joint venture with Solidarity the trade union selling life and accident insurance. American Insurance Group of the US has a 55 per cent stake in two new joint ventures with Bank Pekao. First American Polish Life and Reinsurance Company, offering life products; and First American Insurance and Reinsurance Company, offering general and personal accident.

Domestic insurers: PZU, all types of life and non-life in domestic market and has a monopoly of mandatory insurance; Warta, a state-owned insurer handling international, non-life insurance and reinsurance; Westa, the private company, handles non-mandatory non-life insurance; Polisa is a private insurer handling non-mandatory and non-life insurance; Varsovia is a private insurer handling non-mandatory and non-life policies. There are also around 10 new companies.

Soviet Union

Main legislation: no real insurance law.

Competition: two effective monopolies (domestic and international). Many new, unregulated companies starting.

Supervision: not clear.

Foreign involvement: 1987 law bans the creation of insurance joint ventures with foreign partners. In October 1990, a decree allowed 100 per cent foreign investment and ownership of property. Separate rules apply in republics but are confusing and no laws yet pertain specifically to insurance companies. It is likely that the newly independent states will need help in establishing international business, particularly with reinsurance. Domestic insurance is likely to remain under majority control of local companies, although foreign investment is likely in many republics.

Foreign insurance company activity: Alianz of Germany has a 95 per cent joint venture holding in Ost-West Allianz with the Soviet state. Technical advice leading to sales later. Colonia of Germany has a co-operation agreement with Rossiya, leading to a 25 per cent stake. Instituto Nazionale Assicurazione of Italy has a co-operation agreement with Gosstrakh, the largest insurance company in the Soviet Union. It intends to form joint life and own-life companies. Unipol of Italy has a co-operation with Gosstrakh on insuring Italian-Soviet joint ventures. Pohjola of Finland has a joint venture with Ingosstrakh to service Finnish joint ventures by joint underwriting. The agreement has been expanded to cover the USSR free trade zones and other developing country markets. The Finnish side is looking for joint ventures in the republics. Trygg-Hansa of Sweden has joint ventures with Ingosstrakh and Eesti Kindlustuse of Estonia.

Domestic insurers: Gosstrakh, domestic life and non-life insurance and industrial insurance; Ingosstrakh, foreign non-life insurance, especially shipping and transport; Rossiya; Dalrossa; Progress, cover for co-operatives; Eesti Kindlustuse (Estonia).

Yugoslavia

Main legislation: 1990 act.

Competition: full competition but effective regional monopolies exist. Joint stock, public, co-operative, captive and joint ventures are allowed.

Supervision: individual regional federal authorities for financial affairs administered by the republican finance ministry.

Foreign involvement: allowed to form joint ventures with between 20 to 49 per cent participation. All insurance must be written in Yugoslavia. Foreign insurance company activity: Generali of Italy has an office in Belgrade. Unipol of Italy has a co-operation agreement with Triglav insuring Italian-Yugoslav joint ventures.

Domestic insurers: Croatia (Croatia); Dunav (Serbia), Triglav (Slovenia), Vojvodina (Vojvodina), Sarajevo (Bosnia-Hercegovcina), Makedonia (Macedonia), Lovcen (Montenegro), Kosovo (Kosovo).

East European insurance product summary

Product category	*USSR*	*Pol*	*Czech*	*Hung*	*Yugo*	*Rom*	*Bul*
Agriculture	COM	COM	COM	OPT	OPT	COM	COM
State enterprise/dept	-	COM	OPT	OPT	OPT	OPT	COM
Co-operatives	OPT	OPT	OPT	OPT	OPT	OPT	-
Private households	COM	OPT	OPT	OPT	OPT	COM	COM
Crops/livestock							
Agriculture	COM	COM	COM	OPT	OPT	COM	COM
State enterprise/dept	-	OPT	-	-	OPT	-	COM
Co-operatives	OPT	OPT	-	-	OPT	-	-
Private households	OPT	OPT	OPT	-	OPT	COM	OPT
Motor							
Own damage	OPT	COM	OPT	OPT	OPT	OPT	COM
Third-party liability	OPT	COM	COM	COM	COM	COM	COM
Passenger	-	-	-	COM	OPT	-	-
Occupational accident							
Agriculture	OPT	OPT	-	OPT	OPT	-	-
State enterprise/dept	OPT	OPT	-	OPT	OPT	-	-
Co-operatives	OPT	OPT	-	OPT	OPT	-	-
General liability							
Agriculture	OPT	COM	OPT	OPT	OPT	-	-
State enterprise/dept	OPT	OPT	OPT	OPT	OPT	-	-
Co-operatives	OPT	OPT	OPT	OPT	OPT	-	-
Private households	OPT	OPT	OPT	OPT	OPT	-	-
Trade							
Transport of goods	OPT	OPT	OPT	OPT	OPT	-	COM
Foreign trade	-	-	-	OPT	OPT	-	-

Product category	*USSR*	*Pol*	*Czech*	*Hung*	*Yugo*	*Rom*	*Bul*
Environmental							
Forest damage	-	-	-	OPT	-	-	-
Nuclear power	-	COM	-	-	COM	-	-
General	-	-	-	OPT	-	-	-
Personal lines							
Social welfare insurance	COM	COM	COM	COM	COM	COM	COM
Supplementary welfare	OPT	OPT	COM	OPT	OPT	OPT	OPT
Term life	OPT	OPT	OPT	OPT	OPT	OPT	OPT
Accident	OPT	OPT	OPT	OPT	OPT	OPT	OPT
Endowment	OPT	OPT	OPT	OPT	OPT	OPT	OPT
Children	OPT	OPT	-	-	OPT	-	-
Travel	OPT	OPT	-	OPT	COM	OPT	-
Professional indemnity	-	-	OPT	OPT	OPT	-	-
Consequential loss	-	-	-	-	OPT	-	-
Surety	-	-	-	-	OPT	-	-
Credit insurance	-	-	OPT	-	-	-	-

COM = Compulsory. OPT = optional. Dashes indicate that such insurance is not normally available.

Source: Insurance in Socialist East Europe, Paul Rodgers. *Insurance in Eastern Europe*, Salomon Brothers Research Department, May 1991.

Appendix II

International Finance Corporation

The International Finance Corporation (IFC) was set up in 1956 as a multilateral development finance institution affiliated with the World Bank. It is an independent legal entity and its mandate is to contribute to the economic growth and development of member countries by promoting growth in private companies. IFC provides financial resources in the form of loans and equity exclusively to the private sector and provides financing and technical assistance.

Privatisation work

It has become involved in privatisation work in several countries, including those in Eastern Europe. For example, in Czechoslovakia IFC is assisting CKD Kompresory, a leading compressor manufacturer in Czechoslovakia, to implement the financial and operational restructuring of the company in preparation for the privatisation. IFC will also develop and implement a privatisation strategy for CKD.

IFC is assisting two textile companies, Elitex Chrastava and Elitex Usti nad Orlici to identify appropriate joint venture partners and negotiate joint venture agreements in preparation for the companies' privatisation. IFC is advising Grand Hotel Puppon on the complete revitalisation and the subsequent privatisation of this historic spa hotel in Karlovy Vary in Czechoslovakia.

IFC has been retained by Sklarny Kavalier, a glassware manufacturer, to review the company's operations and assess the possibility for privatisation. IFC has been retained by Skoda Plzen, the largest industrial group in Czechoslovakia, to review the company's operations and recommend short- and medium-term business strategies. IFC has also been asked to assist the company to review joint venture proposals and advise on the negotiations of appropriate joint venture agreements.

In Poland IFC advised the government on the formulation of a national privatisation programme. IFC was the principal adviser to Swarzedzkie Fabryki Mebli (SFM), a furniture manufacturer, in the design and implementing of a privatisation strategy. SFM was successfully privatised via public offering of its shares in 1991.

In Yugoslavia IFC valued Sava-Semperit, a leading tyre manufacturer in preparation for the possible privatisation of the company. IFC is advising the Privatisation Agency and the Development Fund of Slovenia on the formulation and implementation of a privatisation programme.

In Hungary, IFC is helping in development of capital markets. IFC was instrumental in the creation of The First Hungary Fund, the first investment fund designed to promote the development of the stock market in Hungary. The fund's shares were placed primarily with the US institutional investors. IFC was an adviser and a placement agent for the fund until it sold its stake in the fund in 1991.

IFC extended a line of credit to Budapest Bank to fund export-oriented investments undertaken by co-operatives and private sector enterprises. IFC invested equity in the First American Hungarian Insurance Company, which will focus on life assurance products but will also sell other product lines.

Advisory services

Advisory services are provided by the Corporate Finance Services Department (CFS) in Europe. It was set up in 1990 in response to increased demand for specialised expertise in corporate restructuring and privatisation. The department provides a fee-based advisory service in Czechoslovakia, Poland and Yugoslavia.

Foreign Investment Advisory Service

The reforming Central and East European economies have also sought the advice of the Foreign Investment Advisory Service (FIAS) on a number of issues. The policy environment for foreign direct investment in these countries, more than in others, is closely related to issues such as privatisation, general reform of commercial law, currency convertibility and other issues on which FIAS works closely with the World Bank and the International Monetary Fund. In the financial year 1991, FIAS completed projects in three countries in the region.

In Romania, FIAS carried out a diagnostic study to identify the major impediments to the inward flow of foreign direct investment. The study focused on laws and regulations affecting foreign investment and on the Agency for the Promotion of Foreign Investments and Economic Assistance.

In Hungary, FIAS reviewed three important aspects of the system for attracting and regulating foreign direct investment: the procedures for transforming public enterprises (self-managed or state-managed) into independent entities, and allowing them either to be purchased by foreign investors or to form joint ventures with foreign companies; taxation of foreign direct investment and screening and approval of proposed foreign direct investment.

FIAS's diagnostic review of the domestic environment for foreign direct investment in Czechoslovakia focused on two major aspects: the legal frame work — identification of major problems in the laws, regulations, institutions and procedures; and foreign investment agencies — advice on developing the objectives, functions and structures of the three foreign investment agencies recently established by the federal, Czech and Slovak governments.

Technical Advisory Service

The Technical Advisory Service has undertaken two assignments in Europe: the operational review and restructuring of a textile machinery manufacturer in Czechoslovakia and a market study for a company considering an investment in a Polish cement plant.

The Polish Business Advisory Service (PBAS) was set up in 1991 along the lines of IFC's project development facilities in Africa, the Caribbean and Central America. It will provide technical assistance to Polish entrepreneurs in the preparation of business plans and investment proposals as well as in project implementation. It will also provide operational support. The service will promote the training and use of local business consultants. Funding of about $25m for the first five years of the service's operations will be raised from other multilateral and bilateral sources.

Contact

The IFC's main office is located at 1818 H Street NW, Washington, DC 20433 (USA) (Tel: (202) 477 1234; Fax: (central to World Bank) (202) 477 6391). Offices have been opened in some East European countries. These include: Hungary: Dennis Koromzay (resident representative), 31 Vadasz utca, 1054 Budapest (Tel: (361) 131 3520 or 112 3092; Fax: (361) 131 3741); Czechoslovakia: Vikas Thapar (resident representative), Hotel Ungelt Garni, Apartment 6, Stupartska ul 1, Prague 12 (Tel and Fax: (422) 232 1027); Poland: Anthony Doran (resident representative), LIM Centre, Ninth Floor, Room 14, Aleje Jerozolimskie 65/79, 00 950 Warsaw (Tel: (4822) 300 758 or 300 949; Fax; (4822) 300 759).

European Community Phare programme

Phare is the acronym for the European Community (EC) programme of financial and technical assistance for the reforming countries of Eastern Europe. It stands for Poland and Hungary: assistance for the restructuring of their economies. The programme originally applied only to Poland and Hungary. In July 1990 it was extended to Bulgaria, Czechoslovakia, eastern Germany and

Yugoslavia. Projects in the former East Germany agreed in September 1990 before unification were eligible for Phare funding, but after that date no funds were available. Around Ecu 3bn has been allocated from the EC's structural funds to help reform in eastern Germany (now known as the five new laender (states)). In January 1991, Romania was given access to the programme and later in the same year, the Soviet Union was admitted.

Funding

The assistance is funded by EC member states out of the EC budget and is co-ordinated by the commission. Funding is targeted on priorities identified by the recipient country. Phare will provide almost $2bn over 1991-92 in the region.

Following the Paris summit of 1989 of the group of seven (G-7) most industrialised countries (this includes the US, Canada, Japan, France, Germany, Britain and Italy), a programme of assistance was agreed for Central and Eastern Europe. The initiative was adopted by the 24 members of the OECD (Group of 24) and the EC commission was given the task of co-ordinating all Western aid to Poland and Hungary. Later aid was extended to cover all the countries in the region.

A first meeting of the Group of 24 (held in August 1989), agreed that priorities should be set up for assistance to these countries and an action plan be drawn up. This provided the basis for the Phare programme for Poland and Hungary.

The fundamental objective of the EC Phare programme is to support the process of transformation from a centralised system to a market economy. The EC has decided to concentrate on key sectors of the reform process in order to prevent dilution of effort and to ensure the maximum efficiency and effectiveness of its contributions to multilateral assistance.

Priority areas

There are four priority areas for Phare funding: agriculture; industry and investment; the environment; and training, mainly as it helps the economic reform and structural adjustment processes. There are four main areas targeted for funds:

- restructuring of public enterprises, including legal and regulatory aspects;
- modernisation of financial services including the commercial operation of the banking system, development of capital and securities markets, insurance, accounting and tax systems as well as other related sectors;
- promotion of the private sector, particularly small- and medium-sized enterprises (including training);
- development of the labour market and social sectors.

Budget

Over $335m was provided for the Phare's first year of operation (1990). The

1991 budget was Ecu 785 (around $880m) and for 1992 it is expected to reach Ecu 1bn (approximately $1.12bn). To the end of 1992, the overall Phare budget of $2bn is expected to be broken down as follows:

- 75-80 per cent for national programmes including a multidisciplinary provision for small projects;
- 10-15 per cent for regional activity;
- 5-10 per cent for humanitarian aid;
- 5 per cent as a mini-budget and general reserve.

Allocations for each country, taking into account their absorption capacity and objective factors such as population, GDP and debt burden, each country is to receive the following:

- Bulgaria: between 10 and 20 per cent (Ecu 135m-270m);
- Czechoslovakia: between 15 and 25 per cent (Ecu 200m-330m);
- Hungary: between 15 and 25 per cent (Ecu 200m-330m);
- Poland: between 20 and 30 per cent (Ecu 270m-410m);
- Romania: between 15 and 25 per cent (Ecu 200m-330m);
- Yugoslavia: between 15 and 25 per cent (Ecu 200m-330m).

Programmes

The overall programme of support under Phare is initiated by a programme mission which is sent by the EC commission to the country. An indicative programme of objectives and priorities is then agreed between the EC and the country involved. This is then broken down into a series of projects and programmes followed by a financing proposal. General priorities for assistance to help economic stabilisation have been identified by the EC as improved access to Western markets, food supply, training, the environment, investment and economic restructuring. These provide the basis for all the individual priority areas for each country:

- Bulgaria: agriculture and agri-foodstuffs industry; the environment; investment (transport and telecommunications); training (management, financial services, scientific and technical); restructuring (chemical and light industry); tourism; improved access to markets.
- Czechoslovakia: industrial restructuring; the environment (pollution control, industrial waste, nuclear safety); energy; training and youth exchange; investment (transport and telecommunications); scientific and technical co-operation; and improved access to markets.
- Hungary: enterprise restructuring and privatisation; agriculture and agricultural processing (market information and infrastructure, restructuring of the collective sector); labour market restructuring including the development of youth and adult training; trade infrastructure and promotion (including development of trade support agencies, customs

computerisation projects); higher education and research; the environment (national environmental strategy, public environmental management): and energy (energy policy advisory unit to assist in co-ordination and exploiting research and in developing medium-term strategy for production, distribution, pricing and consumption).

- Poland: restructuring of enterprises, demonopolisation and privatisation; modernisation of financial sector (tax reform, restructuring of banking system, development of capital market institutions); unemployment and labour; private sector development (especially small- and medium-sized enterprises); agriculture (state farms restructuring, rural banks and co-operatives, countryside unemployment, development of land market mechanism); education (language training, vocational education, reform of higher education); civic society (public administration reform, development of local government, civic dialogue); environmental protection; healthcare system; and energy, transport and communications.
- Romania: agriculture and food supply (research, production technology, joint ventures); the environment; investment (transport, tourism, smaller enterprises); training (management, banking, tourism, communications, agri-foodstuffs industry); and improved access to markets.
- Yugoslavia: agriculture; the environment (pollution of the Danube and Save basins and of the Adriatic coast); investment; restructuring of the banking sector and the industrial sector; training (banking, management, taxation systems); constructural adjustment, including social aspects; and improved access to markets.

Administration

Phare is administered by the directorate general for external relations (DG1) in the European commission. The Phare section of DG1 works closely with other services of the commission specialising in, for example, agriculture, the environment, banking, small- and medium-sized enterprises and training.

Contacts and addresses

Phare Operational Service, Directorate General I, European Commission, Rue de la Loi 84, B-1049 Brussels.

Unit Two deals with finance amongst other areas. Peter Van den Heuvel is in charge of finance, tax, accounting and related questions (Tel: 235 3378). Robert McDonald is in charge of Tempus relations, horizontal planning programme follow-up and privatisation (Tel: 235 6124).

Contacts in the countries of Eastern Europe are:

- Hungary: Delegation of the Commission of the EC: Jean Trestour, Phare adviser, Berc utca 23, H-1016 Budapest (Tel: 166 4487 or 4587; Fax: 166 4221; Telex: 225984).
- Poland: Delegation of the Commission of the EC: Economic advisers are

Andrew Rasbash and Dino Sinigallia, Aleja Ujazdowski 14, Warsaw 00-567 (Tel: 216 401 or 625 0770; Fax: 307 232 or 625 0430).

- Yugoslavia: Delegation of the Commission of the EC: Economic and commercial questions to Aldo Cricchio, Kablarsku 29, Senjak 11040, Belgrade (Tel: 648 666; Fax: 651 458; Telex: 11949).

Co-ordination of the Phare programme:

- Bulgaria: Minister of Foreign Trade, 12 Sofilska Komuna Street, Sofia (Tel: 880 391; Fax: 803 968); Dr Mariana Todorova, vice-minister for foreign assistance co-ordination; Serafim Sofroniev (Tel: 803 525 or 882 011; Fax: 874 262 or 802 236).
- Czechoslovakia: Economics Minister, Nam Kpt Jarose 1000, 17032 Prague 7 (Tel: 389 1111 or 2797 or 2299; Fax: 375 641 or 375 948); Zdenek Drabek, president of the bureau for co-ordination of foreign assistance and Petr Samek, director.
- Hungary: Foreign Trade Minister, Honved utca 13-15, H-1055 Budapest (Tel: 153 0000; Fax: 153 2794; Mr I Gyurkovics, director Phare secretariat.
- Poland: Jacek Sariusz-Wolski, under secretary of state, Council of Ministers, Al Ujasdowskie 1/3, PL-00-950 Warsaw (Tel: 280 315 or 288 630; Fax: 294 888).
- Romania: Romanian Development Agency, Bdul Magheru 7, Bucharest (Tel: 156 686 or 154 698; Telex: 11027).
- Yugoslavia: Federal secretary for development, SIV 3, Omiadinska Brigada 1, 11000 Belgrade (Tel: 148 227; Fax: 222 2909); Z Knezevic, director, federal secretariat for development, technical assistance bureau.

Recipient institutions for Phare funds for privatisation programmes

- Hungary: State Property Agency, 1399 Budapest, P O Box 708 (tel: 111 0200; Fax: 111 6037); External expert: Tamas Karo (financial administrator).
- Poland: International Foundation for Capital Market Development and Ownership Changes in Poland, Centre for Privatisation, ul Mysia 5, Warsaw 00 950 (Tel: 283 261 or 292 010; Fax: 292 010 or 213 361); Managing director: Henryk Sterniczuk; External expert, Mike Barrington (financial administrator).

European Bank for Reconstruction and Development

The European Bank for Reconstruction and Development (EBRD) began operations in 1991. The idea for the bank was put forward by President François Mitterrand of France in October 1989 and in May 1990, the commission of the European Community (EC), 40 countries and the European Investment Bank signed its founding documents. The bank is in London, where operations began in April 1991.

Purpose

The purpose of EBRD, according to its founding agreement, is to 'foster the transition towards open market-oriented economies and to promote private and entrepreneurial initiative' in the countries of Central and Eastern Europe (Bulgaria, Czechoslovakia, Hungary, Poland, Romania, the Soviet Union and Yugoslavia). The EBRD endeavours to help the economies of these countries integrate into the international economy.

One of EBRD's aims is to provide technical assistance and training for Eastern Europe. The bank plans to co-ordinate and participate in the financing of, technical assistance, the transfer of technology and training in accounting, management, banking, distribution and services, from both private and public sources.

The bank will support the evolution of a business environment which will support the private sector. EBRD will focus on policies and measures affecting the operations of the private sector and on advising governments on the steps necessary for the development of an appropriate business environment and an associated policy framework. It will assist in implementing structural and sectoral economic reforms, including demonopolisation, decentralisation and privatisation.

Financing

EBRD will finance the upgrading of infrastructure to support the functioning of modern, competitive market economies and help structure and manage public projects that allow revenue from them to become the basis for private sector financing.

Mobilising savings for productive investment is a problem facing the East European members and the bank will be helping the region develop an efficient banking system and capital markets as well as assisting in restructuring of state-owned industry and in the privatisation process. EBRD plans to operate with investment banks in structuring projects for prospective investors and participate in equity and debt financing.

EBRD will pay particular attention to economic sectors where strong productivity gains can be achieved within a short time by private enterprises. It intends to support agricultural credit systems and services to give private farmers access to technology and equipment necessary to improve productivity.

Special attention will be given to regional trade and projects within the region and between Eastern Europe and the rest of Europe. Transport, telecommunications and energy are among the priority areas, along with cross-border implications for the environment. The bank will devote substantial resources to developing expertise in environmental rehabilitation and to promoting environmentally sound and sustainable projects.

Subscribed capital

The initial subscribed capital of the EBRD was Ecu 10bn of which 30 per cent was paid in five equal annual instalments, beginning in 1991. The member countries of the EC, together with the European Investment Bank, hold the majority of the capital. The US is the largest individual shareholder, with 10 per cent of subscribed capital followed by France, Germany, Italy, Japan and Britain. Each holds 8.5 per cent of the shares.

Central and East European countries have a total of 11.9 per cent of the shares, including 6 per cent held by the USSR. Membership is open to European countries and non-European countries which are members of the International Monetary Fund (IMF).

Borrowing

EBRD will borrow in various currencies on world capital markets.

The bank will merge the operating principles and practices of development and merchant banking. It will lend for specific projects and investment programmes and co-finance with multilateral institutions, commercial banks and other lenders. Joint ventures will be used as one method of mobilising domestic and foreign capital as well as experienced management. It will also invest in the equity capital of private and state-owned enterprises and facilitate access to domestic international capital by underwriting securities offerings and providing guarantees, financial advice and other forms of assistance.

Loan and equity investment

At least 60 per cent or more of the bank's total loan and equity investments will be in the private sector, to financial intermediaries for on-lending to the private sector or in state-owned enterprises to facilitate their transition to private ownership and control. Not more than 40 per cent of the bank's loan and equity investments in the aggregate and in each country may be provided to the state sector, including local administration. State-sector loans or investments will generally be for infrastructure or environmental projects necessary for economic development and transition to a market economy.

Up to 30 per cent of subscribed capital may be used for equity participations. The bank will neither seek to obtain a controlling interest in enterprises nor assume direct responsibility for managing enterprises.

The bank will operate on the basis of sound banking principles and financial policies, seeking to generate adequate income to maintain prudent financial ratios. It will also maintain proper risk diversification in its portfolio of investments.

Concessionary funding will not be provided from its ordinary capital resources. The bank will provide both equity and debt financing on commercial terms that are based on a long-term perspective. Outstanding loans, equity investments and guarantees must not exceed unimpaired ordinary subscribed capital, reserves and surpluses. EBRD also has the capacity to establish special funds for concessionary funding consistent with its mandate and may set up co-operation funds for technical assistance, training and project development.

The bank is divided into several departments including: operations (development and merchant banking); finance; personnel and administration; project evaluation; secretary general; chief economists; general counsels; communications and press and internal audit.

Development banking

Development banking develops the bank's strategy in each country, interfaces with the countries in discussions of its role and priorities, develops programmes for the enhancement of publicly-owned infrastructure, creates and executes financing and advisory projects to develop physical infrastructure and further the overall reform of financial infrastructure, and provides technical assistance and training in supporting projects and clients.

Merchant banking

The merchant banking section finances and advises all enterprises which are run in an autonomous and commercial fashion (public or private), participates in restructuring and privatisation of state-owned companies, focuses on the development and the creation of individual financial intermediaries and on the provision of finance to small businesses through local financial institutions.

Finance

The finance department is responsible for the bank's borrowing and placing of funds, corporate planning and budgeting, accounting, financial reporting, information technology and risk management.

Contact

European Bank for Reconstruction and Development, 122 Leadenhall Street, London EC3V 4QL (Tel: (071) 338 6372; Fax: (071) 338 6690).

Central East European Privatisation Network (CEEPN)

In June 1991 representatives of six East European countries established a Central East European Privatisation Network (CEEPN) at a meeting in Budapest. The meeting was organised by the United Nations Development Programme (UNDP) and hosted by the Hungarian Finance Ministry. The founding members of CEEPN are Bulgaria, Czechoslovakia, Hungary, Poland, Romania and Yugoslavia. Other countries have the possibility to join.

The main objective of CEEPN is to support privatisation agencies, ministries and other government institutions involved in the privatisation process in the region by providing ways for sharing experience, know-how, documentation and skills in privatisation.

The programmes of the network will focus on the technical aspects of the implementation of the privatisation process common to all member countries. Initially the network will organise workshops on relevant subjects and annual review conferences. It intends to publish articles and booklets on specific subjects relevant to privatisation. Later, training seminars, the development of regional privatisation databases and an information centre and publication of a newsletter are envisaged.

The network will also provide a framework for international and bilateral development agencies supporting these countries' privatisation processes through technical and financial assistance.

CEEPN is a co-operative, self-governing association of countries and privatisation agencies in the region governed by a steering committee on which each member has a representative. This committee meets at least twice a year to decide on strategic issues related to the structure and operation of CEEPN and to approve the work programme. Decisions are taken by a majority vote.

The chairman of the steering committee is elected for a one-year term. The day-to-day work of the network is undertaken by a secretariat.

CEEPN Secretariat (Ms Andreja Bohm), Titova 104, 61000 Ljubljana, Slovenia (Tel: (3861) 346 361; Fax: (3861) 346 389).

Appendix III

List of major reform measures in Bulgaria: January-May 1991

Accounting law
Passed 3 January 1991
Became effective 1 April 1991
Brings Bulgarian accounting procedures in line with European Community standards

Streamlining turnover tax
Implemented January 1991
Reduced the previous 43 tax rates to three rates and broadened the base

Liberalisation of interest rates
Passed 18 January 1991
Eliminated restrictions on new lending rates and transferred the authority to set rates from the Council of Ministers to the Bulgarian National Bank
On 1 February 1991, interest rates were raised to 45 per cent; by June the rate had risen to 52 per cent

Law on ownership and use of agricultural lands
Passed 22 February 1991
Law will privatise agricultural lands

Reduction of profit taxes
Implemented February 1991
Reduced the tax for state enterprises from 65 per cent to 50 per cent and reduced the tax for private enterprises to 40 per cent

Adoption of a unified, partially internally convertible currency
Implemented in February 1991
Eliminated three-tiered exchange rate regime and adopted a unified floating

exchange rate system based on an inter-bank market
Restrictions on most current account transactions eliminated
Capital account transactions require the approval of the Bulgarian National Bank

Budget deficit reduction plan
Approved February 1991
Plan proposes to cut budget deficit from 13 per cent of GDP to 3.5 per cent of GDP in 1991. According to the International Monetary Fund, these cuts would be equivalent to a balance budget after debt rescheduling

Liberalisation of housing controls
Implemented 1 April 1991
Many of the controls over the price and disposition of existing housing units owned by individuals were eliminated. (Eighty-five per cent of the housing in Bulgaria is privately owned.)

Protection of competition act
Passed 26 April 1991
First anti-trust law adopted in Bulgaria and the first step towards large-scale privatisation. Law designed to demonopolise Bulgaria's economy. The government and local councils have six months in which to demonopolise the companies and organisations that they have set up

Paris Club rescheduling of Bulgaria's official debt
Agreement reached 17 April 1991
Paris Club has agreed to reschedule the $1.2bn worth of official credits which were extended to the Bulgarian Government by Western governments

Elimination of state monopoly on oil products
Passed 3 May 1991
Ends the state monopoly on the import and trade in oil and oil products. First step in the Bulgarian Government's plan to privatise half the petrol stations in the country

Lifting the ban on the sale of state property
Implemented 4 May 1991
Lifts the ban on disposing of state and municipal property which was imposed in August 1990 and intended to prevent abuses such as the selling-off of property at bargain prices. Paves the way for privatisation of industry

Company act
Passed 16 May 1991
This is a commercial code based on Bulgaria's pre-communist business legislation and supplemented with the principles of commercial laws geared towards the expected European Community integration in 1992. It defines the status of economic units within the country, their functions and interrelations. It also provides the legal basis for the privatisation of state industries

Foreign investment act
Passed 17 May 1991

Liberalises the existing investment regime. Foreigners may invest in all sectors of the economy. Special permission now is only required in the defence and banking industries or for the acquisition of rights in immovable property. Allows for the repatriation in hard currency of profits earned in both domestic and hard currency.

Czechoslovak banks (as of January 1991)

Commercial and savings banks

Agrobanka Hradec Kralove, Nerudova 37 Hradec Kralove 501 01 (Tel: 049 38011; Telex: 194222; Fax: 049 34192)
Director: Frantisek Posptsil
Shareholders: Agrobanka Prague, Cukrovary (sugar plants, refineries), Hradec Kralove, milk processing co-operatives, state-owned farms, joint ventures
Legal form: stock company
The bank focuses primarily on enterprises from all branches of farming, food processing and organisations involved in other related activities. It grants short-term credits. The bank does not carry out foreign trade operations but can mediate these services for clients through financial institutions.

Agrobanka is to set up a network of branches in rural areas. The bank created additional branches and agencies in 1991 in Chrudim, Rychnov nad Kneznou and Jicin and is to continue the process. Agencies are to be set up in villages and on the premises of large companies.

Agrobanka Mlada Boleslav, Belska 151, Mlada Boleslav (Tel: 0326 21764 or 25395; Fax: 0326 23769)
General Manager: Jan Sulc
Shareholders: Agrobanka Prague, agricultural and food processing companies and agricultural co-operatives
Legal form: stock company
The bank is active with clients from the agricultural and food processing area. It provides all banking and financial services with the exception of foreign exchange, consultancy, advisory and mediation services.

Agrobanka Olomouc, Blanicka 1, 772 26 Olomouc (Tel: 068 29512-17; Fax: 068 28285)
General manager: Jaroslav Snasel
Shareholders: Agrobanka Prague, agricultural and consumer co-operatives and food processing companies
Legal form: stock company
This is a universal bank belonging to the Agrobanka network with activities located in northern Moravia. It provides full banking services, particularly focusing on clients in agricultural and food processing companies and the rural population. In credit its focus is on food producers, services for farmers and the development of small business and individual farms.

A network of branches and agencies is provided in concentrated areas of agricultural and food processing companies at Zabreh, Sumperk, Bruntal, Jesenik and others.

The bank can grant guarantees required by Ceskoslovenska Obchodni Bank for international business and is to expand its activities in foreign trade banking services, investment in capital and financial advisory and mediating services. International banking is mediated by Agrobanka Prague and Ceskoslovenska Obchodni Bank Prague.

Agrobanka Plzen, Nerudova 35, Pilsner (Plzen) 306 29 (Tel: 019 221 252; Fax: 220 949
General manager: Ivana Kocourkova
Shareholders: agricultural, food processing and industrial companies and Agrobanka Prague
Legal form: stock company
The bank provides a full range of banking and financial services including foreign currency exchange, advisory and consultancy services primarily rendered to agricultural and food processing companies.

The bank is building a network of branches and agencies. Branches in 1991 were at Sokolov, Karlovy Vary (Carlsbad), Klatovy and Domazlice.

The bank intends to focus on financial consultancy and advisory services, specialised assistance for projects and insurance activities as well as in the evaluation and mediation of sales of real estate. It will co-operate with Agrobanka Prague and other regional Agrobanks. Capital is to be increased and activities enlarged.

Agrobanka Prague (Agro Bank), Rumunska 1, 120 00 Prague (Tel: 295 398; Fax: 263 415 and 265 587)
General manager: Jan Kral
Shareholders: 748 shareholders composed of domestic companies in the agricultural and food processing area, Koospol, Ceskoslovenska Obchodni Bank, Ceska Statni Sporitelna and nearly 100 individuals
Number of branches: 11
Agrobanka has a network of small deposit agencies supported by a head office in Prague which functions as the strategic and methodical centre. The bank has regional banks at Mlada Boleslav, Hradec Kralove, Olomouc, Prostejov, Plzen (Pilsen) and Usti nad Labem. They are independent stock companies located close to concentrations of agricultural and food production. There are additional branches in Prague, Brno, Pardubice, Nymburk, Ceska Skalice, Ceske Budejovice, Liberec, Svitavy, Jindrichuv Hradec, Novy Jicin and Pribram.

Branches provide all banking services, including deposit collection, credits in local and foreign currencies, exchange services, securities operations in foreign currencies and information services, consultancy, expert analysis and mediating services. Other services offered include customer accounts that may be turned into credits, introduction of marketable deposit certificates with fixed maturity and bond issues as well as credit cards for non-cash payments, the introduction of automatic money transfers and renting safe deposit boxes.

The bank offers small business owners credits including mortgage and bills of exchange.

Branches at Tabor, Strakonice, Tachov, Cheb, Zdar nad Sazavou, Rakovnik, Zatec, Zlin and Banska Bystrica. The bank is to participate in operations related to privatisation.

The bank is providing customers with large commitments with short-term bridging credits for highly effective and non-risk development projects for four to five years, long-term credits to support centrally organised development projects subsidised by the state for another five years.

Agrobanka Hana, Prostejov, ul Ujezd 12, Prostejov 796 40, Post Box 1, Prostejov 1 (Tel: 0508 4035)
General Manger: Josef Sedlacek
Shareholders: Agrochemicky podnik, spolecny podnik Prostejov, Agrobanka Prague, 30 other shareholders, co-operative farms and agricultural and food processing companies
Legal form: stock company
This is a universal bank established when the existing Agrobanka Prague was expanded. Its aim is to support institutions and other legal bodies, especially in the agricultural and food industries. The bank will join the system of commercial banks and develop its activities. The bank provides full banking services as well as advisory, consultancy and mediation services. Branches are in Prostejov, Kromeriz and Vyskov. Agencies are to be established in the relatively large centres of the region — Konice, Urcice, Bedihost, Plumlov, Nemcice, Kvasice, Hulin, Ivanovice, Rousinov. Agencies will collect deposits, provide teller services, information and consultancy services and mediate loans to individuals.

Bank Bohemia, Husinecka 111a, 130 00 Prague 3 (Tel: 691 2002; Telex: 276614; Fax: 276 614)
Director: Arnost Klesla
Shareholders: trade unions, Skoda Prague, joint stock companies
Legal form: joint stock company
This is a universal bank focusing on retail banking and small-scale companies. Its activities support all forms of enterprise. The bank intends to set up branches in Prague and Bratislava and other large cities such as Brno, Ceske Budejovice, Zilina, Hradec Kralove and others.

The bank hopes to raise its capital to $10m with the involvement of capital from Western Europe.

Czechoslovak Commercial Bank Inc (Ceskoslovenska obchodni banka, as), Na Prikope 14, 11520 Prague 1 (Tel: 2132, 224 444; Telex: 122201; Fax: 229 034)
President: Rostislav Petras
Shareholders: Statni Banka Ceskoslovenska (50.5 per cent); other Czechoslovak banks (8.1 per cent); Czechoslovak foreign trade companies (21.4 per cent); employees (4.8 per cent)
Number of branches: 11

Number of representatives abroad: 6 (Frankfurt am Main, Paris and Zurich) The bank is a universal commercial bank specialising in international banking. The main activity of the bank is to keep accounts in local and foreign currencies for corporations and individuals, term deposits in local and foreign currencies, granting of loans in local and foreign currencies, foreign exchange operations, international and domestic payments.

In 1991 the bank introduced an integrated business and information system.

Ekoagrobanka Usti nad Labem, Kralova vysina 3132/7, Usti nad Labem 400 01 (Tel: 26019)
General manager: Miroslav Adamek
Shareholders: agricultural and food processing companies. The main shareholders are Severoceske tukove zavody and Agrobanka Prague
Legal form: joint stock company
The bank is a universal bank focused on agricultural and food processing, ecology and retail banking for customers outside large urban areas. In future the bank is to provide foreign exchange operations. It intends to provide primarily deposit and credit services, equity share in ecological projects. It is to set up a network of branches and agencies. The bank focuses on supporting agricultural and food processing companies, small businesses and the emerging private sector. It will provide credit for projects related to small-scale privatisation. Future activities include participation in the secondary securities market and development of financial services for small business owners, corporations and individuals.

Investicni bank, Na Prikope 28, Prague 1 (Tel: 235 3547; Telex: 122459; Fax: 235 6189)
General manager: Miroslav Tucek
Legal form: state financial institution
Number of branches 13
Number of agencies: 111
The bank, founded by the Finance Ministry, formed part of the assets and liabilities of the former State Bank. Co-operative housing and large industrial project credits were allocated to this bank. The most important operation of the bank is the funding and granting of credits to large investment projects in Czechoslovakia and abroad and preparation for privatisation of large state-owned enterprises.

The bank maintains government and private securities issued in the past including the pre-war period. Specific activities in business, consultancy and mediation are concentrated in newly established subsidiaries and joint ventures. Its primary customer group is state economic institutions, joint stock companies, co-operatives and a growing number of small businesses.

Komercni Bank Prague (Commercial Bank Prague), Na Prikope 28, 110 03 Prague 1 (Tel: 235 9737; Telex: 121093; Fax: 235 6158, 236 7007)
General manager: Richard Salzmann
Number of branches: 83

Number of agencies: 85
Legal form: state financial institution
The bank was set up when the State Bank separated out its commercial operations. It is a bank with a universal commercial charter providing all the usual financial services in active and passive business. The first phase of structural development is focused on achieving a stable and proportional market share in the credit market. It will increase deposits, new banking services and investment contracts. The development of international banking and foreign exchange trade will be emphasised. The bank has several joint venture stock companies. The largest project of this type is a joint venture Czechoslovak-French bank, Société Géneral-Komercni Banka, a joint venture Czechoslovak-Austrian leading company and financial services company, All In. The bank has equity interest in other companies related to the work of the bank.

Pragobanka, Jungmannova 32, 110 00 Prague 1 (Tel: 220 128; Fax: 220 128)
General manager: Jiri Bek
Shareholders: main shareholders include Pragoexport, Ceska Statni sporitelna, ZPA Cakovice, Exico Prague, Tesla Hradec Kralove
Legal form: joint stock company
The bank has focused on credit and deposit activity in local currency. Only the bank's head office operates. No branches or agencies have been set up and are unlikely to be set up in the near future. The bank is considering expanding its activity throughout the country and will concentrate on credits in domestic and international banking. The bank is preparing a plan for exchange offices, consultancy and mediation services related to the opening of the securities market.

Slovenska polnohospodarska Bank, Mileticova 21, 824 82 Bratislava (Tel: 076 1485; Fax: 617110)
General manager: Ludovit Posa
Shareholders: total number 211 composed of agricultural and food processing corporations, agricultural services companies, Slovenska statna pojistovna
Legal form: joint stock company
The bank is a universal one providing a full range of banking and financial operations with the exception of foreign exchange. The aim of the bank is to support agricultural enterprises by providing other services, such as consultancy and leasing. The bank will remain primarily a rural area bank with its main customer group amongst agricultural companies, co-operatives, corporations, small businesses and individuals. From 1 February 1991 branches were set up in Bratislava, Nove Zamky, Martin, Lucenec, Presov and Nitra. More branches are to be set up in Trnava, Prievidza, Zvolen, Liptovsky Mikulas, Spisska Nova Ves, Poprad, Kosice, Dunajska Streda.

Vseobecna uverova banka, nam SNP 19, 818 56 Bratislava (Tel: 07 319 1111; Telex: 6693346-7; Fax: 07 51483)
General manager: Josef Mudrik
Legal form: state financial institution

Number of branches: 39
Number of agencies: 2
The bank is the second largest commercial bank in the country and the largest bank in the Slovak republic. There are 39 branches and 22 agencies in all regions of Slovakia and Bratislava. It is a universal bank primarily focused on the granting of credits, deposits in local and foreign currencies, payments and clearing, teller and exchange office activities, guarantees for credits granted by other banks and advisory and consultancy services. International banking and clearing were secured from 1 January 1991. It aims to provide specialised consultancy services, and has set up a consultancy joint stock company with the Dutch bank NMB Post Bank Grope of Amsterdam. In future business will focus on the growth of an active deposit policy in primary deposits, introduction of credit cards and services related to sales, safekeeping and maintenance of securities. Leasing services are also to be provided. The bank in its international operations concentrates on dealing and investment banking.

Zivnostenska banka, Na Prikope 20, 113 80 Prague 1 (Tel: 224 346, 263 341; Telex: 122313; Fax: 263 381)
General manager: Jiri Kunert
Legal form: state financial institution
Number of domestic branches: 1
Number of foreign branches: 1 (London)
The bank is a state financial institution with its primary activity in international payments for retail customers. Apart from traditional banking services for individuals, the bank also offers to invest deposits in foreign currency accounts. The main focus in the past was international payments for individual customers and travel agencies. The London branch provides business funding, deposit, foreign exchange operations and bank credits.

Ceska Statni Sporitelna (Czech State Savings Bank Prague), Vaclavske namesti 42, 110 00 Prague 1 (Tel: 2116, 225 237; Telex: 121010; Fax: 267 023)
General manager: Miloslav Kohoutek
Legal form: state financial institution
Number of district offices: 72
Number of local branches 735
Number of agencies: 1,875
The bank is undergoing a change to a universal commercial bank (savings). Apart from its original activity of savings for individuals it has developed other wholesale services. The bank belongs to the largest financial institution in the Czech republic. Customers are individuals, small businesses and small-scale corporations. The bank collects deposits, keeps current accounts for corporate clients and accounts in foreign currencies. Services include foreign currency exchange, renting safe deposit boxes, and sales of government lottery tickets.

In the longer term the bank wants to assume the function of a community bank, supporting the gradual reconstruction of municipal and communal property. It is to enlarge its services and operations in foreign exchange. In 1991 it formed a joint venture with the Austrian bank Zentralsparkasse und Kommerzialbank Wein.

Slovenska Statna Sporitelna (Slovak State Savings Bank Bratislava), Namestie SNP 19, Bratislava 816 07 (Tel: 07 50655, 52300; Telex: 93300; Fax: 52087)
General manager: Alojz Ondra
Legal form: state financial institution
Number of branches: 323
Number of agencies: 453

The bank collects deposits from individuals and corporations, grants credits to legal bodies and individuals based on its own funds and deposits, provides domestic payments, clearing, exchange office and securities operations and provides foreign currency and deposit services. Its shareholders are Tatrbanka, Contrade Metal, GUT, Hotel B Poprad, Satel, Kssico and SSB-Anti. In future it plans to enlarge its services in foreign payments and clearing as well as set up a community bank in co-operation with municipal authorities.

State Bank of Czechoslovakia (Statni banka Ceskoslovenska), Na Prikope 28, 110 03 Prague 1 (Tel: 235 3830 or 2112; Telex: 121555; Fax: 235 4141)
Chairman: Josef Tosovsky
Vice-chairmen: Miroslav Kerous, Jaromir Zahradnik
Contact: Vlastislav Navratil, director (Tel: 235 6769)
Number of branch offices: 12 plus headquarters

Joint venture banks in Czechoslovakia

Bankovni dum Skala, Opletalova 4, Prague 1 (Tel: 265 741-9, 265 751-9; Fax: 311 5391)
Director: Miroslav Roskot
Legal form: joint venture, joint stock company
Shareholders: V Skala, W Seufferle, F Mackovitz, Mr Mandik
Skala is a joint stock company with a large foreign share. It conducts its activities in paid contractual co-operation with Agrobanka by using its banking capacities for all payments and clearing operations.

The bank will focus on the development of private enterprises, mainly by financing housing projects and taking a financial stake in selected investment projects. It provides banking services in the area of deposit collection and granting credits. It does not process payments related to international banking although it will grant credits guaranteed exclusively by real estate.

EKO Bank, Kromeriz, Vejvanovskeho 384, 767 01 Kromeriz (Tel: 0634 21788; Fax: 0634 21788)
General manager: Rudolf Chury
Legal form: joint stock company
Shareholders: Mr Slavicek (Germany), citizens of Czechoslovakia
The bank is a universal one with its exchange office activities initially limited to tourism.

The main aim of the bank is to raise foreign capital share in the developing Czechoslovak market by giving credits to foreign companies investing in the country. It will support Czechoslovak enterprise by deposits primarily from foreign companies and through a money market. It also provides consultancy, advisory and mediation services including real estate sales.

The bank plans to enlarge its activities by establishing branches throughout the country.

Postovni Bank, Plzenska 139, PO Box 31, Posta 56, 150 06 Prague 5 (head office for the Czech republic) (Tel: 549 549, 549 251; Fax: 544 949); head office for the Slovak republic is at Tr L Novomeskeho 34, PO Box 149, 814 99 Bratislava 1 (Tel: 322 561; Fax: 322 605)
This is a post office bank operating as a universal bank. The primary aim is to establish conditions and an institutional environment for postal payments for individuals and corporations. Through a network of 5,200 post offices, modern financial and banking services will be brought closer to the public.

Société Générale-Komercni Bank, Na Prikope 3-5, Prague 1 (Tel: 269 668-672, 269 674-679; Telex: 122729, 123370)
General manager: Jean Luis Berger
Legal form: joint stock company
The activities of the bank are personal deposit services in local and foreign currencies, granting operational and investment credits to individuals and legal bodies in local and foreign currencies, payments, teller and exchange office operations, currency conversions including arbitrage.

In future the bank is to establish branches in Bratislava and perhaps other cities.

Tatra Bank, Vajanskeho Nabr 5, 811 02 Bratislava (Tel: 331 351; Fax: 334 656)
General manager: Milan Vrsovsky
Legal form: joint stock company
Largest shareholders: Raiffeisen Zentralbank Osterreich (Vienna), Credit Suisse First Boston (London), Vseobecna uverova banka Bratislava, Slovenska statni sporitelna Bratislava, Slovenska statni pojisiovna Bratislava, Slovensky svaz spotrebnich druzstev, Slovensky svaz syobnich druzstev and approximately 1,200 domestic and foreign individuals and legal bodies.
Tatra is a universal bank which plans to build a branch network, particularly in Slovakia. The bank renders a full range of services including foreign exchange primarily to medium- and small-scale companies.

Representative offices of foreign banks in Czechoslovakia (as of February 1991)

Algemene Bank Nederland, Amsterdam

Banque Nationale de Paris, Na Mustku 9 (CKD House), Prague 1 (Tel: 235

9044, 235 9158; Fax: 235 9094)
Representatives: Mr P Ehretsmann and Mr Dvorak

Banque de Union Européenne, Vodickova 17, Prague 1 (Tel: 235 1114; Fax: 236 8010)
Representatives: A S Lenard, Mr Spalek

Barclays Bank, London
Representative: J B S Connel

Bayerische Hypotheken u Wechselbank, Munich (Tel: 9244-0)

Bayerische Vereinsbank, Prague

Berliner Bank, Narodni trida 10, Prague 1 (Tel: 203 983)
Representative: Mr Nemec

Citibank NA, E Benese 15, Prague 6 (Hotel Diplomat) (Tel: 331 4336, 331 4338; Fax: 331 4369)
Representatives: Dr Kaltenbrunne, Ms Bicanova

Commerzbank, Frankfurt (Tel: 1362-0)
Representative: J v d Borne

Creditanstalt-Bankverein, Londynska 54, Prague 2 (Tel: 254 371) and at Cintorinska 5, Bratislava (Tel: 07/55289)
Representatives: V Zahalka (Prague), P Korvin (Bratislava)

Crédit Commercial de France, Siroka 9, Prague 1 (Tel: 231 8744)
Representative: Mr Kohout

Crédit Lyonnais Nam Curieovych 43/5, Prague 1 (Hotel Intercontinental) Tel: 280 0403; Fax: 280 0414)
Representative: Jean Medard

Deutsche Bank AG, Narodni trida 10, Prague 1 (Tel: 262 105, 203 939, 203 961)
Representative: Mr Kudena

Dialogbank, Narodni tr 10, Prague 1 (Tel: 296 967)
Representative: Mr Varaus

Dresdner Bank, Panska 12, Prague 1 (Hotel Palace) (Tel: 236 9616, 216 1093)
Representatives: G Kowalke, H Kasik

Financière Crédit Suisse First Boston, V Jame 1, Prague 1 (Tel: 235 5837)
Representative: Mr Z Bakala

Girozentrale u Bank d Oster. Sparkassen, Ovocny trh 15, Prague 1 (Tel: 267 588)
Representatives: J Vrba and Mr Raska

Karl Schmidt Bankgeschaft Hof, BRD, Plzen

Kulturbank Rt Budapest, Matejkova 1089, Prague 10 (Tel: 82 25 15)
Contact: Mr Tolgyesi

Landerbank, Stuparska 646, Prague 1 (Hotel Ungelt) (Tel: 232 1093)
Representative: P Linhart

Ljubljanska Bank, Lazarska 5, Prague 1 (Tel: 291 107)
Representatives: Mr Loncnar, Ms Mlejnkova

NMB Postbank Groep NV Amsterdam, Drienova 27, Bratislava (Tel: 234 830; Fax: 235 261)
Representative: Ms M Holla

Osterreichische Volksbanken AG (Radnicka 11, Brno (Tel: 24735; Fax: 24735)
Representative: Mr P Zajac
In Bratislava, at nam F Zupky
Representative: Mr Carnogursky

Prager Handelsbank, Frankfurt

Raiffeisen Zentralbank, Senovazne nam 3, Prague 1 (Tel: 266 260, 266 148)
Representatives: M Ulicny, Dr Kolmanova

Skandinavian Banking Partners, Parizska 25, Prague 1 (Tel: 231 4698, 231 4673; Fax: 231 4656)
Representatives: K Jokinen, Ms Sidoova

Société Générale, Vodickova 34/1, Prague 1 (Tel: 236 8258, 236 8260)
Representative: Matus Pull

Zentralsparkasse u Kommerzial Bank, Revolucni 15, Prague 1 (Tel: 231 2040; Fax: 231 2360)
Representative: Mr Gedeon

Foreign banks in Czechoslovakia

Citibank, Edwarda Benese 178, 160 67 Prague 6 (Tel: 331 4338; Fax: 331 4369)
General manager; Karl Swoboda
Legal form: joint stock company
Shareholders: Citibank Group New York (100 per cent)
The bank provides a full range of banking and financial services including foreign exchange for domestic and foreign corporations, joint ventures, government agencies and other banks, including financial institutions and insurance companies as well as individuals.

The bank is putting emphasis on relations with enterprises, government agencies and state bank, providing them with financial services in local and foreign currencies. It will render exchange office services and collect deposits, participate in funding business, grant short-term credits and provide funding for operational capital.

In future the bank will provide leasing, project funding, consultancy services, including joint venture operations, acquisitions and services related to the establishment of new enterprises. It will participate in the local capital market and be a general investor including investment fund creation and operation. The bank intends to give employees additional training in investment analysis.

Creditanstalt, Siroka 5, 110 00 Prague 1 (Tel: 213 1217; Fax: 232 5130)
Executive managers: Jan Valek and Gert Rienmuller
Legal form: joint stock company
Shareholders: Creditanstalt-Bankverein Vienna
This is a universal bank providing factoring, leasing and consultancy operations and operations related to credit cards. The aim of the bank is to introduce modern banking techniques.

InterBank, Washingtonova 25, 110 00 Prague 1 (Tel: 222 532, 236 2565-74, 236 73700-73; Fax: 228 388)
General manager: Karol Tolgyesi
Legal form: joint stock company
Shareholders: Julturbank Budapest (50 per cent) and Portus (Cham) (50 per cent)
The bank is to open a branch in Bratislava. The bank provides specialised banking business and financial services for domestic and foreign legal bodies and individuals. It will specialise in the assistance of Czechoslovak corporations during privatisation. The bank has the right to collect deposits and grant credits in foreign currencies and carry out foreign payments.

Czechoslovak banking association

Banking Association of Czechoslovakia, Klimova 844, Prague 9 (Tel: 684 5692; Telex: 121093; Fax: 235 6158, 236 7007)
President: Jiri Kunert
The association is a group of Czechoslovak commercial and savings banks and insurance companies based on common interests. Its purpose is to protect and co-ordinate the common interests of its members. The aim of the association is to remove regulatory, administrative and economic barriers to enterprise development in the finance and insurance industries. It intends to speed up enterprise development of commercial banks, savings banks and insurance companies and introduce new banking products and services. The association will assist in the development of training for employees of the members and in making international contacts in the area of finance. The association will also assist in the development of training for employees of the members and in making international contacts. Membership in the association is voluntary.

Members of the agreement on trading in securities in Hungary

Agrobank, Tanacs korut 6, Budapest V (Tel: 118 8933; Fax: 117 5650)

State Insurance Company, Ullo i ut 1, 1091 Budapest IX (Tel: 117 8566; Fax: 111 3058)
General Banking and Trust, Szamuely utca 32, 1093 Budapest IX (Tel: 118 8688; Fax: 118 8695)
General Venture Finance Bank, Stollar Bela utca 3/a, 1055 Budapest V (Tel: 132 6590; Fax: 131 3181)
Budapest Bank, Deak Ferenc utca 5, 1052 Budapest V (Tel: 118 1200; Fax: 118 6308)
CA-BB Brokers, Nagysandor J utca 10, 1051 Budapest V (Tel: 111 2229; Fax: 111 2229)
Citibank Budapest, Vaci utca 19-21, 1052 Budapest V (Tel: 138 2666; Fax: 118 9694)
Co-Nexus Corporation, Roham utca 1, 1013 Budpaest I (Tel: 175 0375; Fax: 156 9493)
Duna Investment Bank, Bathory utca 12, 1054 Budapest V (Tel: 153 1000; Fax: 117 5587)
First American-Hungarian Securities Corp, Parisi utca 1, 1052 Budapest V (Tel: 118 8082; Fax: 118 7092)
First German Securities in Hungary, Feherhajo utca 8-10, 1052 Budapest V
Bank for Building Industry Innovation, Sziv utca 53, 1063 Budapest VI (Tel: 112 9010; Fax: 132 0567)
Hungaria Insurance, Bank ban utca 17/b, 1115 Budapest XI (Tel: 166 9550; Fax: 166 8643)
Innofinance, Vorosmarty ter 2, 1051 Budapest V (Tel: 138 3366; Fax: 117 7800)
Interbank, Szabadsag ter 14, 1054 Budapest V (Tel: 132 0170; Fax: 153 4850)
Investbank, Kepiro utca 9, 1053 Budapest V (Tel: 117 5333; Fax: 118 4400)
Bank for Industrial Development, Rosenberg hp utca 23, 1054 Budapest V (Tel: 132 0320; Fax: 112 9552)
Bank for the Development of Industrial Co-operatives, Gerloczy utca 5, 1052 Budapest V (Tel: 117 6811; Fax: 117 1921)
Culture Bank, Pozsonyi u 77-79, 1133 Budapest (Tel: 140 3940)
Hungarian Credit Bank, Szabadsag ter 5-6, 1051 Budapest V (Tel: 153 2600; Fax: 131 5981)
Hungarian Foreign Trade Bank, Szent Istvan ter 11, 1051 Budapest V (Tel: 132 9360; Fax: 132 2568)
National Bank of Hungary, Szabadsag ter 8-9, 1054 Budapest V (Tel: 132 3320; Fax: 132 3913)
Bank of Hungarian Savings Co-operations, Szabadsag ter 14, 1054 Budapest V (Tel: 153 4222; Fax: 111 4158)
Merkantil Bank, Jozsef A utca 24, 1054 Budapest V (Tel: 118 2688; Fax: 117 2331)
Mezobank, Bajcsy Zs ut 65, 1054 Budapest V (Tel: 112 3241; Fax: 153 2253)
Commercial and Credit Bank, Arany J utca 24, 1051 Budapest V (Tel: 112 5200; Fax: 111 3845)
National Savings Bank, Munnich F utca 16, 1051 Budapest V (Tel: 153 1444; Fax: 111 6887)

Postal Savings Bank, Jozsef nador ter 1, 1051 Budapest V (Tel: 118 0855; Fax: 117 1369)

Securities listed on the Budapest stock exchange as of June 1991

Fotext (photographic services)
Ibusz (travel, tourism and services)
Sztrada-Skala (miscellaneous trading)
Konzum (industrial trading) and Styl (garment manufacturing)

Securities traded on the Budapest stock exchange as of June 1991

Elso Magyar Szovetkezeti Sorgyar (brewing)
Dunaholding (investments)
Muszi (farm management, consulting and computer services)
Skala-Co-op (wholesale and retail trading)
Nitroil
Novotrade (diversified computer services, trading and publishing)
Bonbon Hemingway (confectionery)
Budaflax (textiles)

Shares contained in the securities list of the Budapest stock exchange involved in transactions carried out in 1990

Agrobank, Altalano Vallalkozasi Bank, Magyar Kulkereskedelmi Bank, Budapest Bank, Orszagos Kereskedelmi es Hitelbank, Konzumbank, Magyar Hitelbank and Trade-Co-op

Members of the Budapest stock exchange as of 31 May 1991

Agrobank
Altalanos Vallakozasi Bank
Anker Ertekpapirugynokseg
Arany Broker Ertekpapir Ugynokseg
AB Moneta Befekteo es Tanacsado
Budapest Ertekpapir es Befekteto
CA-BB Ertekpapir Ugynokseg
Citibank Budapest
Co-Nexus
Confides es tarsai Hungaria Brokerhause
Crédit Suisse First Boston Budapest
Daiwa-MKB
Dunabank
Elso Angol-Magyar Broker
Elso Magyarorszagi Nemet Ertekpapirkereskedelmi
Egszi Borze
Eszak-Magyarorszagi ICP

Gazdasag
Generalbroker
Girozentrale Befektetesi
Hungaro Broker
Hungaro-securities
Ingatlanbank
Innofinance
Inter-Europa Bank
Investbank
Investrade
Ipari Fejlesztesi Bank
Ipari Szovetkezeti Fejlesztesi Bank
Konzumbank
Kozep-Europai Hitelbank
Kozep-Europai Ertekforgalmi
Kulturvest Befektetesi
Landerbank Broker Budapest
Lupis Brokerhaz
Magyar Hitelbank
Magyar Nemzeti Bank
Merkantil Bank
Mezobank, MID-Broker
New York Broker Budapest
Nordline
Orszagos Kereskedelmi es Hitelbank
OTP Ertekpapir Ugynokseg
Postabank es Takarekpenztar
Szenzor-Takarek Broker
Ybl Epitoipari Innovacios Bank

Twenty companies listed in Hungary's first privatisation programme

Centrum Department Stores: a retail trade company with department stores in Budapest and throughout the country
Advisers: Barclays de Zoete Wedd, Coopers & Lybrand (British and Hungarian)

Danubius Hotel and Spa: the company specialises in health tourism and a wide range of activities in tourist trade, it has several hotels in Budapest and the countryside
Advisers: Nomura, J Capel, Postabank, Panell Kerr Forster (Japanese, British and Hungarian)

Forest Machinery Producing Company: a medium-sized company based in Szentendre producing small series of forestry and farm machinery, public vehicles and special purpose vehicles

Adviser: Co-Nexus (Hungarian)

Gamm Works: a Budapest-based company producing medical instruments, computer and telecommunications equipment and geophysical instruments
Adviser: Penzugkutato (Hungarian)

Hollohazi Porcelain Works: a company producing fine porcelain wares, household and catering products and decorative ornamental artifacts
Advisers: BMO Nesbitt Thomson, CEDC AKT Munche (Canadian, Hungarian, German)

Hungarhotels: a Budapest-based company active in the hotel and catering industry
Advisers: Swiss Bank Corp, Cazenove (Swiss, British)

Hungexpo: trade fair and advertising company which organises exhibitions and fairs in Hungary and abroad. Shares are quoted on the Budapest and Vienna stock exchanges.
Advisers: Credit Commercial de France (French)

Ibusz: company activities include tourism and foreign currency exchange; shares are quoted on the Budapest and Vienna stock exchanges
Advisers: N M Rothschild, Intereuropa Bank (British, Hungarian)

Idex Foreign Trading, Engineering and General Contracting (Idex): a company active in foreign trade of industrial products
Advisers: HYDEA, Agriconsulting, Euromobiliare, Cohfin (Italian, Hungarian)

Interglob: a company based at Bekecsaba and Gyoma, printing books and producing paper packaging materials
Advisers: CCF, Paris, Magyar Hitelbank (French, Hungarian)

Kner Printing: the company, based at Bekescsaba and Gyoma, prints books and produces paper packaging materials.
Advisers: CCF, Paris, Magyar Hitelbank (French, Hungarian)

Kunep: a construction company also engaged in domestic trade and industrial activities
Advisers: Ernst & Young (British, Hungarian)

MEH Scrap Processing Trust: the company's main activities include recycling, collecting and use of all kinds of waste materials
Advisers: Edmond de Rothschild Bank, Paris (French)

Pannonia Hotel and Catering: the oldest hotel chain in Hungary with several hotels and restaurants in Budapest and throughout the country
Advisers: J P Morgan, Magyar Kulkereskedelmi Bank (US, Hungarian)

Pannoplast: a Budapest-based company producing plastic household goods and industrial items
Advisers: Crédit Suisse First Boston (CSFB) (US, Hungarian)

Pietra Building Ceramic: a Budapest-based company producing bricks, ceramic tiles, covering plates for buildings and products for the timber industry
Advisers: Wricor Group (US, Austrian, Hungarian)

Gedeon Richter Chemicals: activities include production of pharmaceuticals, plant protective agents, cosmetic and household chemical products and research and development activities
Advisers: Nomura, Orszagos Kereskedelmi es Hitelbank (Japanese, Hungarian)

Salgotarjan Plat Glass Factory: the company produces and processes plate glass
Advisers: Daiwa, Magyar Kulkereskedelmi Bank (Japanese, Hungarian)

Tritex Trading Joint Stock (Tritex): based in Pecs, it is a wholesale company for garments
Advisers: Osterreichische Landerbank Capital Markets (Austrian)

Volantefu: the company has a nationwide network and its activity covers freight forwarding and other related services in road transport in Hungary and abroad
Advisers: KPMG, Orszagos Kereskedelmi es Hitelbank (British, Hungarian)

Major Hungarian banks

Hungarian Credit Bank was established in 1987. It is Hungary's largest commercial bank. The State Property Agency owns 49 per cent of the equity while state-owned enterprises hold most of the rest of the equity, although small investors are a vocal group. The bank was formed out of several departments of the central bank and started with a portfolio concentrating on heavy and light industry, construction, transport and telecommunications. It has expanded its customer base into agriculture and trade. Main office is Szabadsag ter 5-6, 1054 Budapest (Tel: 132 7100; Fax: 131 5981; Telex: 202505). The international office is at Pozsonyi ut 77-79, Budapest (Tel: 140 3940; Fax: 160 2960; Telex: 202884.

InterEuropa Bank (IEB) was set up in 1981 and granted a banking licence in 1985, receiving a full commercial banking licence in 1989. San Paolo Bank purchased a 22.5 per cent shareholding in June 1989 and the bank then took its current name. Other shareholders include Hungary's leading exporters and manufacturers. IEB is one of the smaller local banks but is growing rapidly. The bank is at Szabadsag ter 15, 1054 Budapest (PO Box 65, 1264 Budapest) (Tel: 132 1070; Fax: 153 4850; Telex 227879).

Commercial and Credit Bank (K & H Bank) is the third largest commercial bank in Hungary with a 21.7 per cent share of market assets. It was set up in January 1987 and the state owns 35 per cent of the equity with the national social security organisation owning another 10 per cent. The bank was one of three second-tier banks formed from the commercial activities of the National Bank at the beginning of 1987. The bank's original commercial activities came from the agricultural and food industry departments of the National Bank. K & H

Bank is located at Arany Janos U 24, Budapest V, H-1821 (Tel: 153 2052; Fax: 111 1845; Telex: 223200).

Central European International Bank (CIB) was established in 1979. CIB is a dollar-based offshore bank and started in operations in 1980 with the National Bank of Hungary owning 34 per cent of the equity and several leading international banks holding the remainder. The bank's main line of business is pre-export trade finance and it is also active in leasing, factoring, forfaiting and medium-term facilities to Hungarian companies. The bank is not permitted to undertake Hungarian onshore transactions. It formed a domestic banking subsidiary in 1988 and a trading company in 1989. The domestic banking arm makes up 29 per cent of group assets. The bank is at V Vaci utca 16, H-1364 Budapest, PO Box 170 (Tel: 118 8377; Fax: 118 9415; Telex: 224759).

Kulturbank was established in 1990. It is 95 per cent owned by Portus, a Swiss-registered company. The bank started as a 50/50 joint venture between the Hungarian Culture Ministry and IMI Securities (London). Portus bought out the ministry soon after the bank was established. The bank received its licence for international operations in June 1991. The bank is at Rakoczi ut 1-3, Budapest H-1088 (Tel: 252 2713 or 2885 or 2954; Fax: 251 5231; Telex: 222173).

Unicbank was established in December 1987. It is one of the smaller commercial banks in the Hungarian market. Foreign shareholders are Raiffeisen Zentralbank Osterreich with a 30 per cent stake and International Finance Corporation (an affiliate of the World Bank) with 15 per cent. Central Bank of Exchange and Credit - a subsidiary of the National Bank of Hungary - holds 20 per cent with the National Savings Bank holding 11 per cent and four central co-operative associations 6 per cent each. Unicbank has a full foreign exchange licence and concentrates on medium-sized companies and the private sector. The bank is at Vaci Utca 19-21, H-1052 Budapest (Tel: 118 2088; Fax: 138 2336; Telex: 223172).

National Savings and Commercial Bank (NSB) was set up in 1949 and is Hungary's largest bank with a 44 per cent share of the market's deposits and the largest branch network, using Hungary's 3,200 post offices as outlets. It is a state-owned bank transformed into a joint stock company at the beginning of 1991. It is to be partially privatised but the state is expected to maintain a majority shareholding. The bank is at Nador u 16, PO Box 501, Budapest H-1876 (Tel: 153 1444; Fax: 112 6858; Telex: 224280 or 4432).

Hungarian Foreign Trade Bank (MKB) was established in 1990 and is the third largest commercial bank in Hungary. It is minority-owned by the state and operates with a full foreign exchange licence. The bank launched Hungarian foreign business and local ventures in the early 1980s, becoming a full-service commercial bank in 1987 with the establishment of the two-tier banking system in Hungary. Regular commercial foreign trade transactions started in 1990 when the Central Bank decentralised responsibility for foreign trade operations. The bank is at Szent Istvan ter 11, Budapest V, H-1821 (Tel: 132 9360 or 153 4211; Fax: 132 2568, Telex. 226941 or 225106).

Citibank Budapest (CB) was established in December 1985 and began operations in January 1986. The bank was the first onshore joint venture bank in Eastern Europe and is 80 per cent controlled by Citicorp, and a subsidiary of the National Bank of Hungary holds the other 20 per cent. CB is a wholesale bank that specialises in short-term loans to companies that are a source of export transactions. The bank is at Vaci utca 19-21, H-1052 Budapest V (Tel: 138 2666; Fax: 118 9694; Telex: 227822).

National Bank of Hungary (NBH) was set up in 1924. Before 1987 it used to be the sole source of commercial credits to the productive sectors of the economy. The National Savings Bank handled transactions with the household sector but funnelled surplus deposits to the NBH for on-lending to the productive sector. The Government split the functions the the NBH monobank at the beginning of 1987 and it became the central bank and two second tier banks, NHB and K & H. Some NBH branches also joined Budapest Bank. In 1990 it authorised 14 banks to handle foreign trade transactions as part of the process by which the bank withdrew from foreign trade transactions. It continues to issue foreign currency yield bonds and raise foreign currency yield loans.

Budapest Bank (BB) was set up in January 1987 and is a full commercial bank. It was formed by the merger of the largest country directorate of the National Bank of Hungary and 12 other National Bank branches, the Budapest Credit Bank and the credit wing of the State Development Bank. BB is now 42 per cent owned by the state with the remainder held by corporate and institutional investors. It specialises in handling securities issues and trading on the Budapest stock exchange. Budapest Bank (BB) is at Deak Ferenc utca 5, Budapest V, H-1852 (Tel: 118 1200; Fax: 118 4712; Telex: 223013) and the international office is at Alpari Gyula u 5, Budapest V (Tel: 117 1179; Fax: 117 1622; Telex: 222571 or 202799).

General Banking and Trust (GBY) was established in 1922 and is one of Hungary's oldest financial institutions. After 1939 it concentrated on property dealing. It was granted a full commercial banking licence with the restructuring of the banking system in 1987. This widened the bank's range of activities to include domestic currency commercial banking. The Finance Ministry and Central European Development Corporation (Canada) each own half the bank's equity. The bank is at Szamuely utca 30-32, PO Box 1991, H-1093 Budapest (Tel: 118 8323 or 8523 or 8723; Fax: 118 8659; Telex: 223578) and the international office is at Szamuely utca 38, H-1093 Budapest (Tel: 118 9506 or 117 1255; Fax: 118 9429; Telex: 226548.

Post Bank and Savings Bank Corporation (Postabank) was established in June 1988. It is the second bank to concentrate on the household savings sector. It is the sixth largest local bank and is 41.4 per cent owned by the Finance Minister and the Post Office with two Austrian institutions purchasing a 16 per cent share in March 1990. Its main marketing outlet is the Post Office. The bank is at Jozsef nador ter 1, 1920 Budapest (Tel: 118 0855; Fax: 117 1369; Telex: 223294).

Source: BREE Consulting Services, Cyprus.

Useful contacts and addresses for Hungary

Hungarian-American Enterprise Fund, Suite 703, 1620 Eye Street NW, Washington, DC 20006 (Tel: (202) 467 5444; Fax: (202) 467 5469)
Contact: Alexander Tomlinson, president

Hungarian-American Enterprise Fund, East-West Building (sixth floor), Rakoczi ut 1-3, 1088 Budapest, Hungary (Tel: 251 7175, 7230; Fax: 251 7086)
Contact: Charles Huebner, managing director
The fund is a privately-managed fund established by the US Government through the 1989 support for East European democracy (SEED) Act. The primary purpose of the fund is to promote the development of the Hungarian private sector by investing in joint ventures between US and Hungarian companies and other methods.

National Bank of Hungary, Szabdsag ter 8-9, 1850 Budapest (Tel: 153 3044; Telex: 227267; Fax: 153 1058)

InvestCenter-TradeInform, Dorottya utca 4, 1051 Budapest (Tel: 118 8220, 118 6064; Telex: 225191; Fax: 118 3732)
General manager: Bariela Falus
The centre is administered by the Hungarian Foreign Trade Ministry. It can set up appointments for foreign companies with appropriate Hungarian companies and government agencies as well as assist foreign companies in all aspects of making investments in Hungary.

Hungarian Chamber of Commerce Business Contact Service, Kossuth Lajos ter 6-8, 1055 Budapest (Tel: 153 3333, 153 3853; Fax: 153 1285)

Foreign Trade Ministry, Honved U 13-15, 1880 Budapest (Tel: 153 0000; Fax: 153 2794, 131 4186)

Investment and Trade Promotion Agency, Foreign Trade Ministry, Honved U 13-15, 1880 Budapest (Tel: 153 0000; Telex: 225578; Fax: 153 2794)
Joint venture department: Janos Balassa

Licensing Department Agency, Foreign Trade Ministry, Honved U 13-15, 1880 Budapest (Tel: 111 8433; Telex: 202802; Fax: 153 2794)
Director of licensing: Janos Csendes

Finance Ministry, Department of International Financial Affairs, Jozsef nador ter 2/4, 1051 Budapest (Tel: 118 5670, 118 2066; Telex: 225942; Fax: 118 2570
Department head: Csaba Repassy

Ministry of Industry and Domestic Trade, PO Box 96, 85 Martirok utja, 1525 Budapest (Tel: 156 5191; Telex: 225376; Fax: 175 3295)

State Property Agency, Vigado utca 6, 1051 Budapest; Postal address: PF 708, 1399 Budapest) (Tel: 118 5044; Fax: 118 7155)
Director: Lajos Csepi

Deputy director: Karoly Szabo

State Property Agency Information Office, Harsfa utca 21, 1074 Budapest (Tel: 142 7734; Telex: 226564; Fax: 142 7337)

Association of Industrial Co-operatives (OKISZ), Thokoly ut 58-60, 1146 Budapest (Tel: 141 4752; Telex: 227576; Fax: 141 5521)

Association of Entrepreneurs (VOSZ), Szuret ut 15, 1118 Budapest (Tel: 185 3377; Telex: 223436; Fax: 182 0316)

Foundation for Small Enterprise Economic Development (SEED), Andor utca 60, 1119 Budapest (Tel: 181 0590; Fax: 181 2959)

Central Corporation of Banking Companies, Szamuely u 38, 1093 Budapest (Tel: 117 1255; Fax: 118 8149)

State Taxation Office (APEH), Haman Kato ut 3-5, 1096 Budapest

Office of Foreigners' Affairs (KEOKH), Andrassy ut 12, 1061 Budapest (Tel: 118 0800)

Hungarian Chamber of Commerce Arbitration Court, Kossuth Lajos ter 6-8, 1055 Budapest (Tel: 153 2425)

Polish banks with foreign exchange licences and foreign banks in Poland

The National Bank of Poland issued a list of 14 banks in March 1991 which may distribute currency loans and make foreign trade payments. The banks include:

Bank Handlowy w Warszawie
Polska Kasa Oszczednosci
Bank Rozwoju Eksportu
Bank Gospodarki Zywnosciowe
Bank Inicjatyw Gospodarczych
Bank Gdanski, Gdansk
Bank Slaski, Katowice
Bank Depozytowo-Kredytowy, Lublin
Popwszechna Kasa Oszczednosci
Kredty Bank
Panstwony Bank Kredytowny, Warsaw
Pomorski Bank Kredytowy, Szczecin
Powszechny Bank Gospodarczy, Lodz
Wielkopolski Bank Kredytowy, Poznan

The following foreign banks have set up representative offices in Warsaw:

Société Générale
Centro Internationale Handelsbank
Pekao Trading Corp

Deutsche Bank
Dresdner Bank
Mitteleuropaeische Handelsbank
Scandinavian Banking Partners
Citibank
Banque Nationale de Paris
Banca Commerciale Italiana
Crédit Industriel et Commercial de Paris-Banque de l'Union Européenne.

List of insurers authorised by the Finance Ministry to provide insurance in Poland (as of 31 December 1990)

National Insurance Company (PZU), ul Traugutta 5A, Warsaw (Tel: 20 03 11; Fax: 26 97 43)
President: Krzysztof Jarmuszczak (Tel: 26 91 15; 694 3456)
Scope of activity: contractual and regulated (compulsory) insurance, some automobile insurance

Association of Insurance and Reinsurance Warta SA, ul Traugutta 5A, Warsaw (Tel: 20 03 11; Fax: 27 33 12; Telex: 813549)
President: Janusz Staniszewski (Tel: 27 26 25; 694 5103)
Scope of activity: contractural and regulated (compulsory) insurance, automobile insurance

Co-operative Insurance Company Westa, ul Piotrkowska 17, Lodz (Tel: 42 34 00 07; Fax: 42 33 62 37)
President: Maria Sybilak
Scope of activity: contractual and personal insurance, automobile insurance

Co-operative Insurance-Reinsurance Association Polisa, ul Zurawia 47, Warsaw (Tel: 28 72 01 ext 258; Fax: 21 42 53)
President: Marek Binieda (Tel: 21 48 60)
Date of authorisation: 9 November 1988 (amended 3 March 1989, 26 October 1989, 15 March 1990)
Scope of activity: contractual property and personal insurance, automobile insurance

Association of Tourist Insurance ATU SA, ul Mlynarska 16, Warsaw (Tel: 32 39 18; 32 09 59; 32 39 19; Telex: 816353; Fax: 32 08 32)
President: Waclaw Zygmunt (Tel: 32 39 18)
Date of authorisation: 13 November 1989
Scope of activity: contractual property and personal insurance, automobile insurance

Association of Automobile Insurance Ltd, ul Ossolinskich 6, Warsaw (Tel: 266 49 17)
President: Zenon Zalega
Date of authorisation: 31 January 1990

Scope of activity: contractual property and personal insurance, automobile insurance

Insurance Association Compensa SA, ul Traugutta 5A, Warsaw (Tel: 694 3236)
President: Zofia Pawlak (Tel: 694 3215)
Date of authorisation: 12 February 1990
Scope of activity: contractual property and personal insurance

Insurance and Reinsurance Company Polonia SA, ul Piotrkowska 17, Lodz (Tel: 42 32 00 87)
President: Wojciech Kopec
Date of authorisation: 12 February 1990
Scope of activity: contractual property and personal insurance

Financial Industrial Corporation Pirobud Ltd, ul Czerwonej Armii 69, Lubon k Poznan (Tel: 61 13 07 43)
Office: ul Glogowska 41, Poznan (Tel: 61 66 52 47, 66 61 10; Fax: 61 41 42 32)
President: Jerzy Pielin
Date of authorisation: 22 February 1990
Scope of activity: contractual property and personal insurance

Insurance Association Samopomoc, ul Kopernika 30, Warsaw (Tel: 26 03 19)
Date of authorisation: 28 February 1990
Scope of activity: contractual property and personal insurance

BM Insurance Ltd, ul Mickiewicza 45, Gliwice (Tel: 32 31 37 08)
President: Wojciech Bertisch
Date of authorisation: 28 March 1990
Scope of activity: life insurance

Insurance Company Hestja SA, ul Warszawsaka 183/185, Poznan
President: Ryszard Piechaczyk
Date of authorisation: 16 July 1990
Scope of activity: contractual property and personal insurance, except life insurance and credit insurance

First Polish-American Life Insurance and Reinsurance Association SA, ul Stawki 6, Warsaw
President: Thomas Mintoft-Czyz
Date of authorisation: 30 November 1990
Scope of activity: Section I, groups 1, 2, 3 based on attachment to the law of 28 July 1990 about insurance activity, Dz U 59, item 344

First Polish-American Insurance and Reinsurance Association SA, ul Stawki 6, Warsaw
President: Thomas Mintoft-Czyz
Date of authorisation: 30 November 1990
Scope of activity: Section II, groups: 1-18 based on attachment to the law of 28 July 1990 about insurance activity, Dz U 59, item 344

Sopot Insurance Association Hestia Insurance SA, ul Reja 13/15, Warsaw
Date of authorisation: 29 December 1990
Scope of activity: Section II, groups, 1, 3, 5, 6, 7, 9, 10, 11, 12, 13, 14, 16 based on attachment to the law of 28 July 1990 about insurance activity, Dz U 59, item 344

Promeranian Insurance Association SA, ul Krocowej Jadwigi 18, Bydgoszcz
Date of authorisation: 29 December 1990
Scope of activity: Section II, groups: 1, 2, 3, 4, 7, 8, 9, 10, 13, 14, 15, 16 based on attachment to the law of 28 July 1990 about insurance activity, Dz U 59, item 344

Useful contacts in Poland

Finance Minister, ul Swietokrzyska 12, 00 916 Warsaw (Tel: 200 311; Telex: 815529)

Industry Ministry, ul Wspolna 4, 00 926 Warsaw (Tel: 210 351; Telex: 814 267 or 814 261)

Ministry of Ownership Transformation (Privatisation Ministry), ul Mysia 5, 00 950 Warsaw (Tel: 283 261; Telex: 816521; Fax: 292 010)

Central Statistical Office, Al Niepodleglosci 208, 00 925 Warsaw (Tel: 253 241)

National Bank of Poland, ul Swietokrzyska 11/21, 00 950 Warsaw (Tel: 200 321; Telex: 814 681)

Information

Finance Ministry, Banking and Financial Institutions Department, ul Swietokrzyska 12, 00-916 Warsaw (Tel: 268 987 or 694 3388; Fax: 691 3950; Telex: 815592)

National Bank of Poland, Foreign Department, ul Swietokrzyska 11/21, 00-950 Warsaw (Tel: 265 611; Fax: 265 645; Telex: 814681)

The Ministry of Ownership Changes (the Privatisation Ministry) is located at ul Mysia 5, 00-513 Warsaw (Tel: (4822) 28 32 61; Fax: (4822) 21 33 61; Telex: 816521).

Information on the privatisation process can also be obtained from the International Foundation for Capital Market Development and Ownership Changes in Poland (Tel and Fax: (4822) 29 20 10) as well as from the Finance Ministry (Swietokrzyska 12, 00-916 Warsaw, Tel: (4822) 20 03 11; Telex 815592), and various branch ministries and other organisations.

Office of Banking System and Financial Institutions, ul Swietokrzyska 12, 00-916 Warsaw

Banks in Romania

Romanian Bank for Foreign Trade SA, 22-24 Calea Victoriai, Bucharest
Telex: 11235 ebank r
Fax: 00.400 141598
Tel: 149190 147378
Chief Executive: Dan Pascariu

Commercial Bank of Romania, 14 Bulevardul Republicii, Bucharest
Tel: 141190 142166
Chief Executive: Ion Ghica

Mindbank, 46-48 Calea Plevnei, Bucharest
Telex: 10585 ucecoom r
Tel: 130788
Chief Executive: Ion Prundus

Commercial Bank 'Ion Tiriac', 12 Doamnei Streeet, Bucharest
Tel: 142833
Chief Executive: C Dun

Agriculture Bank, 3 Smirdan Street, Bucharest
Telex: 11709
Tel: 44260
Chief Executive: N Barbulescu

Romanian Bank for Development, 4 Doamnei Street, Bucharest
Tel: 158909; 164456
Chief Executive: M Crisan

Frankfurt-Bukarest Bank, 22-24 Calea Victoriai, Bucharest
Telex: 10976 10972 frabu bank r
Fax: 00.400 158094
Tel: 131030 130040
Chief Executive: O Neun

Misr Romanian Bank, Hotel Bukuresti, 4 Prelengirea Cosmonautiler, Bucharest
Telex: 11387 mrb b
Fax: 00.400 153682
Tel: 153688
Chief Executive: D Lungu

Manufacturers Hanover Trust, 16 Bulevardul Republicii, Bucharest
Telex: 11572 mht
Fax: 136892
Tel: 158415 158416

Société Générale, 22 Bulevardul Nicolas Balcesco, Bucharest
Telex: 10651 sogab

Fax: 148647
Tel: 151730

Bankcoop, 20 Hoxa Street, Bucharest
Telex: 10070
Tel: 592705
Chief Executive: A Dinulescu

National Bank of Romania, 25 Lipscani Street, Bucharest
Telex: 11136
Fax: 145910
Governor: M Isarescu

Twenty companies listed in Romania's first privatisation programme

	Activity	*Employment*	*Turnover★*
Apullum, Alba Iulia	porcelain	2,565	2.3
Apsa SA, Baia Mare	vehicle parts	1,744	1.7
Armatura, Clujhydro	equipment	2,292	1.78
Bucur, Bucharest	foodstuffs	1,636	23.8
CTT, Bucharest	tourism	2,208	3.2
Electrofar, Bucharest	light fixtures	1,162	1.06
Electromontaj, Bucharest	electrical equipment	6,080	5.9
Energoconstructii, Bucharest	construction materials	7,801	6.1
Energomontaj, Bucharest	electrical equipment	9,270	7.26
Famos, Odorhei	furniture	2,371	1.21
Flaro, Sibiu	textile equipment	2,959	2.13
Litoral, Constanta	tourism	691	0.88
Milcov, Focsani	knitwear	1,100	0.73
ONT Carpati, Bucharest	tourism	290	3.3
Pantera, Jimbolia	footwear	810	0.5
Simat, Sighisoara	textiles	710	0.8
Somplast, Bistrita	plastics	939	1.4
Ursus, Cluj	beer	479	0.8
Valco, Baia Mare	spirits	162	0.48
Vranco, Focsani	garments	4,288	2.5

★Turnover is in millions of US dollars for the first six months of 1991.

Ljubljana stock exchange

Selected securities listed as of June 1991

Corporate bonds and debentures: Yulon, textile; Juteks, textile; Lasko, brewery; Lesnia, wood processing and furniture; Meblo, wood processing and furniture; Gorenje, electric machines and household appliances; Lek I, pharmaceuticals; Lek II, pharmaceuticals; Metalna, heavy constructions; PTT Lj, post, telephone and telegraph; Rogska, health resort

Municipal and government bonds: City of Ljubljana (municipal bond, fixed 10 per cent); Republic of Slovenia I (government bond, fixed 8 per cent); Republic of Slovenia II (government bond, fixed 9.5 per cent)

Stocks: Grad, consulting; Ilirija Banka ZG, banking; Mladinska Knjiga, edition

Slovene banks with foreign exchange rights: Abanka Ljubljana; Kreditna Banka, Maribor; Ljubljanska Banka, Ljubljana; Landerbank, Ljubljana; Nova Banka, Ljubljana; Probanka, Maribor; Hipobanka, Brezice

Ljubljana Stock Exchange members as of September 1991: Abanka, Agencija za Prenovo Podjetij; Alpe Adria Foreign; Banka Slovenije; Banka VIPA; Capita; Centre za Gosp Svetovanje; Dadas; Factor; Gorenje Finance; Grad; Gramex; ITEO; Interfin; Iskra Telekom; Kompas International; Kovinotehna Celje; LB Banka Domzale; LB Banka Velenje; LB Banka Zasavje; LB Dolenjska Banka; LB Gorenjska Banka Kranj; LB Kom Banka Nova Gorica; LB Koroska Banka; LB Kreditna Banka Maribor; LB Pomurska Banka; LB Posavska Banka Krsko; LB Spl Banka Celje; LB Spl Banka Koper; Lesnina Interles; Ljubljanska Banka; M & M; Nika; Nova Banka; Petrol Trgovina; Poslovni Sistem Mercator; Razvojni Centre IRRI; Relax; Rudis; SKB; SKB PE Novo Mesto; Sklad r Slovenije za Razvoj; Slov Zadr Kmetijska Banka; Tima Ib SFO Maribor; UBK Banka

Ljubljana Stock Exchange, Kardeljev trg 1, 61000 Ljubljana (Tel: 302 109; Fax: 301 950; Telex: 31606)

SOURCES

The following publications and organisations provided background material for this book:

'Accelerating Privatisation in Eastern Europe', Jeffrey Sachs, 25-26 April 1991, Washington DC, World Bank Annual Conference on Development Economics 1991

BBC Summary of World Broadcasts

BREE Consulting Services, Cyprus

British Department of Trade and Industry

'Business in New Poland: Foreign Investor's Guide to Poland', Warsaw 1990, prepared in March 1990 by Ernst & Young working with the Foreign Investment Agency of Poland and UNIDO's Warsaw office.

Cole Corette & Abrutyn, London: Highlights of recent USSR legal developments (August 12 1991)

Commersant Newspaper

'Discovering Investment Opportunities in Eastern Europe: A Framework'. Salomon Brothers (Dirk W Damrau, John F H Purcell, Andrew B Jonas, Gerhard A Baumgard), July 1990

'Financial Institutions and Finance Markets in Bulgaria', Mileti Mladenov, Deputy-governor, Bulgarian National Bank, paper at Sofia conference, September 1991

Financial Times

First International Conference of Restructuring and Privatisation of the East European Economies, Zagreb, 25-26 October 1990

Information from Slovenia, Press Centre, Ljubjana, Yugoslavia

'Insurance in Eastern Europe: Massive Potential Will Attract Patient American and European Insurers'. Salomon Brothers Research Department (A Michael Frinquelli, Margaret M Alexandre, Robin Mitra and Steven I Davis), May 1991

International Economy, April/May 1990, 'How to Set up a Stock Exchange', Teresa Barger, Senior Investment Officer, Capital Markets Department, International Finance Corporation

International Finance Corporation, Statement of qualifications for privatisation assignments

'Issues in the Introduction of Market Forces in Eastern European Socialist Economies', Manuel Hinds, March 1990

Moscow Narodny Bank Press Bulletin

MTI EcoNews (Hungarian economic and business news service)

OKO Trading

PlanEcon Business Report

PlanEcon Inc, Papers from conference, London, April 1991

Pole Position: a newsletter on privatisation in Poland, the Foundation for Privatisation in Poland

Privatisation in Eastern Europe: current implementation issues (with a collection of privatisation laws), International Centre for Public Enterprises in Developing Countries and the Economic Development Institute of the World Bank, edited by Andreja Bohm and Vladimir G Dreacic

'Privatisation in Post-communist Societies', Branko Milanovic, *Communist Economies and Economic Transformation*, Vol. 3, Number 1, 1991

Radio Free Europe

Romanian newsletter

The Economist

'The Future of Acquisitions in the New Eastern Europe' by John Lindquist and William Browder, Bost Consulting Group, London, January/February 1990, Mergers and Acquisitions Europe

'The Role of Foreign Investment in the East European Privatisation Process; Hungary, Poland and Czechoslovakia', Dirk Kamrau, vice-president, Salomon Brothers. Discussion paper for the Woodrow Wilson International Centre Conference, Sofia, Bulgaria, September 1991.

'The Securities Market in the Soviet Union' (31 July 1990), Paul H Aron, Daiwa Securities America Inc

'The Transformation of Economies in Centre and Eastern Europe: Issues, Progress and Prospects' by Alan Gelb and Cheryl Gray, Policy, Research and External Affairs, The World Bank, June 1991

Wall Street Journal (Europe)